The British Car Industry
Our Part In Its Downfall

The British Car Industry
Our Part In Its Downfall

James Ruppert

PUBLICATIONS

First published in 2008 by Foresight Publications, part of Action Automotive Limited.

More information at www.jamesruppert.co.uk

A CIP catalogue record for this book is available from the British Library

ISBN 978-0-9559529-0-6

Printed and bound in Great Britain

Contents

James Ruppert is an *Independent on Sunday* motoring correspondent and columnist for Britain's oldest car magazine, *Autocar*. Author of and internationally recognised guru for *Bangernomics*, a manifesto for commonsense motoring, James has written loads of books and been on countless TV and radio programmes droning on about cars. At any one time he owns at least two motor vehicles and one motorcycle (Land Rover Series 3, Austin Mini Cooper and BSA Bantam) that have been hand crafted in Britain, by proud Britains working in the now distant past for British owned companies.

1 The End – May 2005

In the garage: Well there was Volkswagen Golf and when that went, just some old tools, a lawn mower, bits of wood and other things that have outlived their usefulness.

I'm glad I wasn't there the day my Dad lost his car. To be honest, he didn't actually lose it in the sense that he parked his 1989 Volkswagen Golf GL automatic in a multi-story and then forget which floor. It was actually taken away from him, but in a nice way, or at least the nicest possible way under the circumstances.

My sister Marion and I had already agreed that Dad's driving days were pretty much over, so it seemed the right thing to do. Even Dad had voluntarily stopped driving to the hospital every day to sit by our mother's bed. Never mind about the questionable sanitary conditions inside; outside, in the car park, it was a jungle. Broken concrete, gravel and inclines that resembled mid-1980s Beirut. The hospital trust even had the cheek to charge those who managed by some fluke to find an empty, car-sized section of waste ground to park on. And those who abandoned their cars elsewhere as they helped their loved-ones limp to A&E were simply clamped, fined and most probably used for medical experiments against their will. So it was the sheer hassle and expense of it all that drove my dad back on to the buses.

In the current carbon footprint and climate change, er, climate, there are many eco-fascists who might see encouraging people out of their cars by draconian parking measures as a good thing. Except that for a frail old man in his late seventies, it was a less than ideal way of travelling safely and healthily. But the thought of our dad picking up the keys again out of sheer frustration was a risk we couldn't take as a family. He wasn't well enough to drive, so we would do our best to run him to the hospital or get the local mini-cabbers involved. First, though, we, or rather my sister who lived nearer, had to take the car into protective custody, which wasn't easy. According to Marion, our Dad just seemed so sad and lost as he succumbed to the inevitable. Standing on the front step of his house he watched his son-in-law and grandson jump-start the Golf and bring an end to his independence. After more than 50 years behind the wheel, Dad had come to the end of his road.

So what has all this got to do with the British car industry? Absolutely everything. Reginald Dennis Ruppert, like so many others, learned to drive and started motoring in the 1950s. Not for fun, but out of necessity. Not only that he was a car-driving company representative, before it was abbreviated to just "rep". This was also a slightly sepia-tinged age before the motorways arrived, which meant he covered thousands of miles each year on the inadequate A and B roads of Britain in equally inadequate vehicles. That may explain his subsequent choice of vehicles and why he eventually did the unthinkable and bought foreign. Now this was back in the early 1970s, when it was still a slightly suspect thing to do. Even so, he continued to buy British when the vehicles were criminally awful. He often chose good and sometimes great cars that were sadly indifferently built and terrible value for money. It was no surprise when the rest of middle England followed his example and adopted the Volkswagen Golf as their transport of choice for the next few decades.

It seemed to me that my Dad's experiences, attitudes and purchases mirrored what was going on in the country when it came to making and selling cars. From the optimistic 50s to the plentiful 60s, depressing 70s and pretty awful 80s, a slight upward blip in the early 90s followed by the terminal 00s. Dad witnessed the slow death of the British car industry at first hand, not just as a consumer, but as someone who attended the Earls Court Motor Shows in a professional capacity, building exhibition stands. Armed with his exhibitor's pass, Dad brushed aside all those ex-army commissionaires without a murmur. That allowed me to see behind the scenes and sit in the driving seat of exotic vehicles that remained forever roped off to other, no less deserving, but less well connected children.

Even motor sport, which remains a reassuringly successful branch of the British motor industry, did not escape Dad's involvement in the very early 1960s. Well, when I say motor sport, this involved a very famous racing driver, a toy racing track, Scalextric, a London department store, the promotion of some long-forgotten product and some naughty school kids. "While we were setting up the track the children swiped the controls and were racing plastic Coopers and Ferraris around the huge circuit," Dad told me. "They were really good, and I let them get on with it, but then I had to make a fuss and shoo them away because we had the world champion turning up: Jack Brabham. I made a big show of handing him the control. He duly pressed it, and zoom, his Cooper flew off at the first corner into the crowd, and the children couldn't stop laughing. After that Brabham couldn't keep it on the track, and I think he was terribly embarrassed and a bit annoyed with himself really."

At one point, Dad owned a magazine distribution business that circulated the hugely influential Car magazine, which by coincidence I would be a columnist for many years later.

So I wondered just how we got here and what exactly had happened to the British car industry, which had seemed so strong, sexy and innovative. Because when Dad stopped driving it was only just possible to buy a family hatchback made in Britain by a British-owned company. Within a year, though, that situation had changed forever with the bankruptcy of MG Rover. After the demise of the biggest British-owned car manufacturer there were no family cars available. Sports cars yes. Cars without any doors, no problem. Fantastically expensive, hand-built gentleman's carriages, of course. There was also an even smaller special-interest group of blokes based in industrial units who would sell the bits and pieces to other blokes with sheds so that they could make a kit car out of their MoT-failed Ford Sierras. Which is admirable in a way, and a tribute to British ingenuity, grit and willingness to use a socket set and welding kit. The reality is that most consumers, not car enthusiasts, or bigots, simply want a well-made, quality product from a proper factory, ideally based in the UK, employing highly-skilled workers and earning money for the country. Now I know cars are still built in Britain, which is good. But we should at least own the means of production, rather than being grateful for the work. I mean, Rolls-Royce owned by BMW and Bentley owned by VW – how the hell did we let that happen?

Is it our fault? Or the government's? Is the EU to blame? Or globalisation? Or those pesky old unions? Or Britain's inability to manage almost any going concern? Maybe it was the simple fact that an engineer in Britain commands far less respect than a decent nanny these days. I wasn't entirely sure, but I thought it was worth checking back to see where it all went wrong, and I knew that Dad could help me. But don't worry: this won't be a mawkish, sentimental story with cars in it. Dad would hate that. His purchases and experiences will pop up at appropriate points. Reginald Dennis Ruppert – Reg to his seven brothers and sister, Denny to his friends and to confuse the issue Danny to business associates – will stop me from making this a dreary tome full of facts, quotes from industry figures and all those things that help pad out a book. The British Car Industry, Our Part In Its Downfall, is a fairly chronological story, taking us from 1945, when the British car industry seemingly had every possible opportunity to lead the world, until the bitter end in 2005, when mass manufacturing of British cars ended forever.

Underpinning it all are the cars that Dad bought. There were not that many, and where possible, Dad bought British. He was incredibly proud of this country and even flew on Concorde for one business trip. Not because it was quicker, or because he could charge it to his clients as a legitimate expense, but because it represented British engineering at its very best. I know the French were involved, it cost a fortune, never turned a profit, or any of that, but Dad never complained once about the waste of tax payers' money on something as brilliant as Concorde. He did have an issue, though, with a state-owned car manufacturer (British Leyland) making vehicles that he bought and which subsequently failed in spectacular fashion.

Note 1

Although I refer to the British car industry throughout this book, technically the industry was almost exclusively based in England. More to the point, it would be even more accurate to describe it as the Midlands motor industry. However, I thought that might hurt sales in Hillman Imped Scotland, Wales (with its only indigenous manufacturer, Gilbern) and Northern, De Lorean Ireland. And anyway, the British motor industry sounds a lot better, even though I did consider calling it the British motor dynasty to further confuse matters. It certainly seemed that, on occasions, our industry was run by autocratic, slightly unstable men, often with peerages and knighthoods. But I thought better of it. And as for the "Our part in Its downfall" bit – well if you like Spike Milligan as much as me and my Dad do, you'll know it's a nod to his brilliant war memoir.

Note 2

I sincerely promise not to baffle you with technical terms that could send you to sleep and just look bemusing on the page. Should I feel it strictly necessary to use such language, I shall try my best to explain it fully. Also there won't be loads and loads of figures, flow charts and Venn diagrams. I'll use big figures to make a point, because in 1984, British Leyland exported one – count it – ONE car to America. Otherwise, I won't be flinging that many figures at you because this is not a test and mostly there is nothing more boring than market segment percentages and car production stats unless you are in the marketing, brand management game. However, there are some end-of-decade stats, which are interesting, with births marriages and deaths lists to let you know the various comings, goings and coming-togethers among the Brit manufacturers and the foreign new arrivals. Oh yes, and not every single kit car maker or micro manufacturer is included as there just wouldn't be enough room.

There won't be a blow-by-blow account of union/management meetings, a list of every vehicle produced in Britain, or interviews with all the important industry movers and shakers. But I can point you in the right direction when it comes to all that stuff. My job here is hopefully to entertain, occasionally inform and overall reach broad generalisations with the help of Dad as a device to cut out some of the boring bits.

Obviously I could save you all the bother of reading any further by reducing it down to these simple reasons why we don't make British cars any more: because we built mediocre cars badly, good cars indifferently and, worst of all, offered cars that no one else in the world was really interested in. But there is a bit more to it than that, and lots of stories along the way, which is why I know you will keep on reading.

Thanks to
Steve Cropley, Richard Bremner and Gavin Green for letting me write for *Car* magazine back in 1987. Steve Cropley again and Chas Hallet, for letting me spout nonsense in *Autocar* magazine since 2006.

Matt Tumbridge at *Used Car Expert* for reading the draft manuscript and making important suggestions.

Tom Evans at MSN for valuable feedback before publication.

David Newnham for knocking the text into shape.

Society of Motor Manufacturers and Traders, who may find the contents of this book upsetting, but who supplied me with the best-sellers stats.

All the press offices who could remember when their cars arrived in this country.

My wonderful wife Dee for letting me get on with the business of writing.

Olivia for asking the cleverest questions about what I was actually doing.

My sister Marion for selling me my first car, being an integral part of this story and reminding me about things I had long forgotten.

Brother-in-law Stephen King (no not that one) who found most of the period pictures.

Most of all, the late and much missed Charles and Florence Ruppert, the best Uncle and Auntie a boy could ever have.

Further Reading and surfing
Kidnap of the Flying Lady – Richard Feast
Cars of the Rootes Group – Graham Robson
Cars of BMC – Graham Robson
The Breakdown of Austin Rover – Williams, Williams & Haslam
Wheels of Misfortune – Jonathan Wood
End of the Road – Chris Brady and Andrew Lorenz
Car Magazines over the last few decades
Autocar and *Motor* Magazine over the last century or two. *Practical Classics*, *Your Classic* and *Classic Cars* magazines since the 1980s.
You should also surf to Keith Adams' brilliant website where you will learn far more about BMC and British Leyland and Austin Morris and Rover and all the other assumed names that were used by the industry at www.austin-rover.co.uk

Picture Credits

Website
Pictures and film of Ruppert family cars on my website www.jamesruppert.co.uk

Dedication
Reginald Dennis Ruppert
Priscilla Sarah Ruppert

Published by
Foresight Publications, part of Action Automotive Limited.

Cover Picture
Probably taken by my sister Marion in 1963. Dad is cleaning his car and that's me with the wonky haircut. The car is a Vauxhall Wyvern, built in Britain by an American-owned company, General Motors.

Rear Picture
Taken by a bunch of Rupperts through the decades. Mum, Auntie Flo and Uncle Charles on and in the Land Rover, Mum and Dad in 1970 next to the Hillman Minx. The troublesome Daimler Soveriegn, Fleet shot of Audi 100LS, Triumph Dolly, 1963 Mini and 1977 Mini Clubman. And Dad's last car a VW Golf.

2 Lethal Belgian Brickweave and the German Patient 1945–47

In the garage: Nothing – in fact there isn't even a garage, but here is a picture of a period one for you to enjoy. Meanwhile my Uncle Charles, Dad's brother, gets a Humber Super Snipe, which is a sort of 1930s people carrier.

It's the end of Second World War and Dad is stationed in Norwich serving with the Royal Engineers. Within a few weeks he has become a corporal, then a sergeant, and goes on to run the personnel selection operation for his regiment. This is wartime HR, but with a bit more edge, effectively deciding who dug trenches and built bridges and who told them to dig and build. My dad would set tests and ask questions, and the one bit of insight he did offer me was, "if anyone admitted to playing drums I immediately marked them down as mentally unstable. No hesitation, I made sure they went to see the trick cyclist (psychiatrist) as soon as possible."

Not surprisingly, I kept my admiration for Cream drummer Ginger Baker, Led Zeppelin sticks genius John Bonham and jazz tub thumper Buddy Rich well suppressed throughout my youth. During his youth, my Dad kept the Royal Engineers on the mental straight and narrow and didn't give cars a first or even second thought. Private vehicles did not have any relevance to anyone from a large working class Roman Catholic family in the East End of London, when there were perfectly good buses, trains and pushbikes around.

Pre-war cars were a middle and upper-class thing, but that didn't stop our industry becoming the biggest in Europe. At the outbreak of the Second World War we had six major manufacturers: Austin, Ford, Morris, Rootes, Standard and Vauxhall. It is worth pointing out that Ford was American owned, whilst Vauxhall had been taken over by General Motors, so it is nothing new to have foreign-owned companies building cars in this country. As for Rootes, you may not have heard of the Rootes Roadster, Runnabout or Rocker, because as brilliant as those names sound, they never actually existed. The Rootes brothers' (Billy and Reggie) strategy was to bring together smaller marques and make them profitable by sharing parts. So under the Rootes umbrella were Hillman, Humber, Sunbeam and Talbot. In fact grouping together once popular but struggling marques would come to characterise the desperation of the British motor industry in later years.

Plenty of long forgotten marques didn't make it through the war, and were probably fortunate not to be glued together under the Rootes or British Motor Corporation (BMC) banner and die an even slower and more painful death. For instance, ALTA was a typical one-man marque. In a small workshop off the Kingston By-pass, Geoffrey Taylor built, in tiny numbers, what he thought was the perfect sports car. He built 13 of his 9HP model, which obviously wasn't particularly lucky for him. But it had a lovely long bonnet with a swept-back radiator. Although it could be had with a supercharger that made it go a bit faster, Taylor rightly decided to fit a bigger engine, in one instance double the size, and again supercharge the whole thing. In a package that weighed little more than a few sacks of spuds, the 2-litre model could crack 120mph. In the late 1930s, that was the speed of light, if not a little bit faster. Taylor made a few of those before the war got in the way. Then, after the conflict was over, he decided to concentrate on building racing cars and engines. Despite giving up on road cars though, Taylor defined what it is to be a British engineer: toiling away in a shed or small industrial unit to build unique vehicles in handfuls, and losing a fortune in the process. They still do it today, which is reassuring, as it is the only guarantee we have that car making on any scale will continue in the UK.

Motorcycle manufacturer Brough Superior, so called because they believed that their bikes were superior to everyone else's, also had a crack at cars. Like other companies, they believed that marrying up huge American engines to English-made frames and coachwork was a short cut to success. It wasn't, and only 75 of these sporty and expensive cars were made before the war broke out. So not that superior then. Meanwhile, BSA, which stood for Birmingham Small Arms, were equally well known for their motorbikes as for their guns. And although not many remember it, they also made a substantial number of cars. From tiny three-wheelers to sports cars and saloons, more than 10,000 left the Midlands before the war, because they were great value and easy to drive. However, upmarket Daimler, which owned the marque, decided against making any downmarket three- or four-wheelers after 1945.

So as well as large and sporting cars, Britain excelled at producing reassuringly odd small cars. The Cleco was a genuine attempt at introducing an electric car to a rightly sceptical buying public. Encouraged by the relative success of their light vans, Cleco Electric Industries of Leicester misguidedly built a car. Actually, it was half a dozen cars before interest waned. It may have been capable of 90 miles at just 14mph, but £375 was the cost of three proper petrol-engined cars like the Morris 8. It also didn't help that the Cleco Coupe looked ridiculous, resembling a pedal car that had mated with a micro caravan. Rather more successful, but no less odd, was the Rytecraft Scootacar. Now this really did look like a pedal car, except there was a small engine powering the rear wheels. It had just the one pedal: press down to press on and release to engage the brake. As any idiot could drive it, these saw service as delivery vans and fairground dodgem cars. And for rich kids, it was a car they didn't even need to pedal.

With its automotive minnows and its big six fish, the British car industry was clearly a colourful place in 1939, and unmatched anywhere else. France had its grande trios of Renault, Citroën and Peugeot. In Germany there was a grosser fier comprising Opel, Auto Union, Mercedes-Benz and Ford. Over in Italy there was really just the uno company, Fiat. Although Britain were still ahead, it was Opel who were the single largest manufacturer in Europe. However, what went on over on the continent didn't really seem to concern our self-satisfied six, who didn't need the complication of an engine driving the front wheels like a Citroën, or a diesel engine like Mercedes had (although a British engineering company, Ricardo, had designed a successful diesel for Citroën). Exports to Europe were fairly marginal. And after five years of conflict, had anything really changed?

Well, the government had. In came Labour and Mr Clement Attlee. Dad was a card-carrying member of the party, which in later years he blamed on his local priest, Father Jones. "He'd give us leaflets that we would hand out in the streets – he said it was the godly thing to do!" Dad even bumped into old Clem and his pipe at a local Labour Party dance in Stepney. This was the party of change that would make Britain a land fit for the returning heroes like my Uncle Joe, who'd fought through Africa, Italy and into Germany.

For the British car industry, the very thought of a government with a socialist agenda was only slightly scary, while the new government felt that this industry should start to pull its weight. With that in mind, they appointed the most unsocialist sounding socialist (although Anthony Wedgwood Benn gives him a close run) to be the President of the Board of Trade. A former lawyer and chemist, Sir Stafford Cripps held views so extreme that he had even been booted out of the Labour Party in 1939. That didn't stop him being appointed as ambassador to Moscow in the coalition government (presumably because they reckoned he would feel at home there) before moving on to be Minister for Aircraft Production which, thank goodness, he was pretty good at, hence his post-war transfer to Trade.

While there were those within the Labour Party who openly advocated nationalisation, Cripps reckoned that he could persuade the industry to change the way it did business. He chose the annual dinner of the Society of Motor Manufacturers and Traders (SMMT) in November 1945 to do this. "We must provide a cheap, tough, good looking car of decent size – not the sort of car we have hitherto produced for smooth roads and short journeys in this country," he announced. "And we must produce them in sufficient quantities to get the benefits of mass production."

Cripps was obviously thinking of the pre-war model ranges, where seemingly identical cars were slightly scaled up and down to satisfy a niche within a niche. For instance, you could buy an Austin 20HP Long, Austin 20HP Short and Austin 20HP Whitehall, and finally before the model was discontinued, a plain old Austin 20HP. Yes, it was as confusing as it is today. There were a lot of broadly similar models aimed at just about everyone who might be vaguely interested in a car. Cripps was making the point that sometimes, less can be so much more. He added, "We cannot succeed in getting the volume of exports we must have if we disperse our efforts over numberless types and makes." The bottom line was that he wanted a minimum of 50 per cent of output to be exported. Among the cigars and dinner jackets there were more than murmurs of discontent. At least three Captains of the Motor Industry said "poppycock!" quite loudly, and at least one said "tripe!"

The response from Cripps was priceless: "I have often wondered whether you thought that Great Britain was here to support the motor industry, or the industry was here to support Great Britain. I gather from your cries that you think it is the former." Those remarks would come back to haunt the industry in the 70s, 80s, 90s and, er, the noughties. For the moment though, the industry followed Cripps' plea for simplicity and an export-focused production by carrying on much as before. As a result, by 1947, Austin was offering the largest range of cars in Europe, with plenty of pre-war models like the 8HP, 10HP and 12/16HP from 1940, plus the new A40 Dorset and Devon. Indeed, plenty of other manufacturers were continuing to offer old models and some new ones. So did anyone actually listen to Cripps?

Well, before we answer that one, we need to consider a little local difficulty they were having over in the occupied territory in 1945. It all started in the 1930s, when Adolf Hitler proposed that a "People's Car" should be built. Doctor Ferdinand Porsche came up with the Type 60, a hotchpotch of 1930s technology that effectively borrowed the streamlined styling and engineering technology from Czech-built Tatras (which themselves looked like giant mutant beetles). Porsche's design also looked like a beetle because, apparently, Hitler has told him it should. It was badged as the KdF Wagen, which stood for Kraft durch Freude, the motto of the German Labour Front which literally translates as Strength through Joy. This zippy, advertising-friendly name was suggested by a Mr A Hitler of Berlin.

In 1938, a production plant – the Volkswagenwerke, or "people's car factory", was built on a soggy plain at Wolfsburg and modelled on Ford's own factory at Rouge River in Detroit. Hitler admired the Ford organisation and certainly Henry Ford leaned a little bit to the right himself. Indeed, Ford sent Hitler a cheque for $50,000 on his birthday, when possibly a card would have been sufficient. Unlike Ford, Hitler didn't rely on private enterprise to fund his factory as this was going to be very fascist undertaking using money confiscated from the trade unions and the labour of Italian construction workers on loan from nearby dictator Mussolini. The new car, which would cost 999 Reichsmarks, was to be financed by a savings plan – a sort of Green Shield Stamps scheme – but rather more red, and it turned out to be something of a scam. However, 270,000 had subscribed by 1939, and despite collecting the red stamps which featured the white outline of the KdF, faithfully sticking them into savings books and paying five reichsmarks a week to the German Labour Front, none of the "people" actually got to own a car.

If the World War hindered civilian car production, it nonetheless inspired Porsche to design numerous military versions. Best known were the Schwimmwagen, which was an amphibious four-wheel-drive vehicle, and the Kübelwagen, which was very similar to a Jeep. The latter served with distinction under extreme conditions in all theatres of war, was praised by the Desert Fox himself, Field Marshall Rommel, and even proved adept at traversing snow on the ill-fated Eastern Front. Nazi Party product endorsements were the last thing it needed as the Volkswagen factory began to use forced labour from concentration camps and Russian prisoners of war to make, among other things, the fuselage and wings of the V-1 flying bomb that would wreak havoc and destruction on the south of England. However, the allies had been impressed enough with the vehicle's performance that the Americans published a manual called "The German Jeep". It contained instructions on how to maintain and drive it once captured. They clearly believed that it could be re-educated into being a much nicer vehicle.

In all, 80,000 military versions of the Beetle were built, which proved just how versatile and sound the original design was. These qualities inevitably contributed to the car's longevity and adaptability, as the basic theme was stretched to breaking point over the next 30 years. In 1945, however, there was not much future for the KdF Wagen to look forward to. A ruined factory and the fact that not a single KdF Wagen had ever been built was not good. Luckily, a combination of the British and the Beetle saved the day.

What the army found when they arrived was a half-built city called KdF-Stadt which they promptly renamed Wolfsburg after a nearby castle. Initially they did not like the name Volkswagen, so they called the factory the Wolfsburg Motor Works. Dad's regiment, the Royal Electrical and Mechanical Engineers, were dispatched to see whether vehicle production could be recommended. They managed to unearth a single surviving KdF Wagen, which at the very least proved to be useful as a demonstration vehicle for the military authorities. It needed to be repaired and repainted, a nice dark green rather than the compulsory grey-blue of the very limited edition Hitler model.

Major Ivan Hirst was put in charge, and managed to galvanise the small workforce into action. Initially, they simply repaired any vehicles that had managed to make it through the war. After that, Major Hirst managed to get the workforce to assemble some Kubelwagens from surviving parts. However, as the body presses for the KdF still existed, it was possible to begin proper production in late 1945. By the end of the year, Major Hirst and his team had managed to satisfy the urgent need for light transport, turning out 1,785 vehicles for the British Army and the German post office. Major Hirst had achieved the impossible, and as output topped 10,000 in 1946, he skilfully foiled attempts to dismantle the factory in lieu of war reparations and ship it all to Australia. Henry Ford had rejected the plant on the grounds that it was too near the Commies. Even the French didn't want it, preferring instead to take its designer, Doctor Porsche, back to help kick-start their motor industry. So surely the Brits would take it on? Especially as one of ours was in charge and seemed to be doing an excellent job, too?

Unfortunately, we can attribute the survival of Volkswagen to the misjudgement of another Englishman, Sir William (Billy) Rootes. When visiting the factory as the head of the Rootes Commission, he was unimpressed and recommended demolition, or "it will collapse of its own inertia within two years". The Commission also stated that "the vehicle does not meet the fundamental technical requirements of a motor car. As regards performance and design it is quite unattractive to the average car buyer. It is too ugly and noisy." They concluded that "to build the car commercially would be a completely uneconomic enterprise." Rootes apparently addressed Hirst with the words, "if you think you're going to build cars in this place, young man, you're a bloody fool."

But Hirst was an officer and a gentleman and wouldn't be spoken to like that. It was his duty to prove Rootes very wrong. It certainly helped that the Military Government of the Allied Zone needed 20,000 cars ASAP. They backed this up with a deposit of 20 million marks, which enabled Hirst to start finding raw materials, getting German prisoners of war transferred to the production line and the Type One, as they were now calling it, rolling off the production lines. However, the factory was constantly under threat, not least because the Russians would have quite fancied taking it down and then carting it off in an easterly direction. Indeed, in 1946 the allied authorities threatened that, if production was not increased to 1,000 vehicles a month, the factory would be broken up.

Now hindsight is a wonderful thing, and in the ruined surroundings of a defeated country, the Beetle (as it was not yet called) could not have looked an attractive proposition. Nevertheless, Cripps' words come to mind again: "We must produce a cheap, tough, good-looking car of decent size... and we must produce them in sufficient quantities to get the benefits of mass production." He could almost have been planning the Volkswagen Golf 30 years hence, but his remarks perfectly fitted the fledgling Beetle and the one-model policy.

Meanwhile, Captain Hirst not only supervised production as it climbed rapidly, he also made some vital decisions. One was the retention of the pre-war V-over-W emblem and with it the adoption of the Volkswagen name. After all, Wolfsburg Motor Works would never have caught on, or nor would "I've got a WMW". Secondly, he appointed a former Opel executive Heinrich Nordhoff as the first civilian boss. He didn't seem like the ideal person to take on the role, not least because he didn't like the car and is quoted as saying, "It has more faults than a dog has fleas." Charming, but he was right for the job. Then, in 1949, two significant events occurred: the first Beetle was shipped to America, and control was handed over to the Germans. A year later, the 100,000th Beetle had been built.

Volkswagen and the Beetle was an opportunity not so much missed as utterly squandered. The clear leadership and resourcefulness of Hirst and his team were quite remarkable. On one occasion, when they ran out of carburettor bodies, they sourced parts from a camera factory and adapted them to fit. Hirst should have been given a top job with one of the six big players on his return. Obviously he wasn't, but he was a decent man who to Volkswagen's credit, was never forgotten by the company he saved.

So how were we getting on in Britain? Mostly, we were not building a Beetle, or anything like it. The one-model policy that the government was so keen to encourage was being ignored by most of the major manufacturers, with two exceptions. Rover had the Land Rover that we all know and love, while Standard built the utterly unloved Vanguard.

Standard already made the Ferguson tractor as proof that a simple, tough and practical vehicle was all you needed to make it in manufacturing after the war. At one point, the company was even building more tractors than cars. So Britain, without any real competition, had become the number one exporter of cars, and they seemed to go to the same places as they had before the war: Australia, Belgium, New Zealand, India, South Africa and Switzerland. America was trying really hard to keep up with home demand, while the other European countries were rebuilding themselves after the war. It was clearly an open goal and Britain could not only score, but also dominate exports for years to come. The trouble was that Brit cars never travelled very well. Part of the problem was that many were of pre-war design and, according to a Canadian commentator, "the product of the British motor industry, with its narrow tracks, small luggage space and reputed inability to stand up to bad roads, has been criticised to the point of monotony." Even worse, we had cars that couldn't even cope with Belgium.

Let's take a slightly closer look at the Standard Vanguard, which was bravely billed as "Made in Britain – designed for the World." Firstly, it looked American, which wasn't surprising given that the stylist Walter Belgrove had camped outside the American embassy with his sketch pad drawing cars as they drew up outside. Try that today and you would be interrogated by the CIA.

Anyway, the bodywork with no separate boot was similar in some ways to the Beetle, but it was bigger and had two more doors. However, it was an all-new model, and in 1948 it replaced the entire Standard range. Its body was attached to a separate chassis, which had all the important oily bits like the engine, gearbox and prop-shaft that took the power to the rear wheels. The gearbox was a three-speed job and it had something called synchromesh on the first gear, which meant that there were no more nasty grinding noises when drivers engaged that gear. There was a reasonably economical 2-litre engine, too, and it cost £544. Between 1948 and 1952, 185,000 found buyers. So it must have been brilliant then? Er, no.

Standard was staffed by engineers and designers who for the most part hadn't been outside of Britain. The prototype Vanguards had only been taken as far as Wales. There, the steep hills and farm tracks were the nearest they could get to replicating overseas terrain. Given the state of Europe and the limited time available, it was understandable that they didn't stray too far. Maybe, though, they should have popped across the Channel to Belgium to drive up and down on that weird paving that used to be so common. Who would have thought that a brick-weave surface could have done so much harm? Certainly not Standard, who despatched their Service Manager for Scotland, Freddie Toop (on the basis that he was one of the few employees with a passport) to find out.

What he discovered was that the suspension, and indeed the whole structure of the Vanguard, was being shaken to bits. There were cracks in the metal, which had occurred after just a few thousand miles. The suspension parts called shock absorbers had absorbed all the shocks they possibly could and then broken. As a stopgap, the Belgians put extra fluid in the absorbers, which only succeeded in making them solid. So when the Vanguard hit a bump, it would fracture the bolts holding it to the chassis half of the car, and they would eventually punch their way through the front wings. It must have been a spectacular if a frankly terrifying experience. Clearly the Vanguard wasn't suited to any where more challenging than rural Wales. It stayed in production until 1963 in various restyled and reworked ways with a better and bigger engine, but obviously it was all too late and sales in the UK, never mind anywhere else in the rutted, paved or potholed world, were marginal.

Another car company seemed to have a better grasp on the one-model – or at least the simplified-model – policy. Maurice Wilks, technical director at Rover, had been an apprentice at General Motors before the war, and understood the value of having common parts shared among several models. However, in 1945 his most pressing problem was how to use the huge amount of factory space in Solihull during peacetime. For a while, the company toyed with the idea of a small car, but rightly reckoned that there was limited export potential. The vehicle they did come up with to fill that space was born not in the engineering department, or by asking what customers thought, or getting a bunch of people into a laboratory and asking them to vote for design A, B, or C, which seems to happen a lot these days. Nope, the vehicle was born on a farm – a farm that belonged to Wilks on the Isle of Anglesey. On his 250 acres, Wilks had something called a Ford half-track, which had the tracks from a tank at the rear and normal steerable wheels at the front. On a battlefield, this was quite useful, but on a small farm, it was clumsy. To replace it, he bought an army-surplus Jeep. It was the four-wheel drive system that Wilks found so useful, but less clever was the patchy reliability, that meant he regularly had to send it to the Rover factory in Solihull for repairs. His brother Spencer, who also worked at the company, asked what he would get when the Jeep finally expired. Maurice said he would get another because there wasn't anything else.

Here, then, was a new idea for a vehicle, which Maurice named the Land Rover. His brief to the Rover engineers was simple enough: "...to design a vehicle rather similar to a Jeep, but even more useful to the farmer... to be able to be used as a tractor at times... to be able to do everything." So here was the blueprint for the multi-purpose vehicle that is still with us today. First, though, they took the Jeep's chassis, powered it with a Rover Ten engine and used the rear axle and suspension parts from other Rover cars. As steel was in short supply, they opted to use more costly aluminium, which was easier to work with by hand. When 50 prototypes had been built, the President of the Board of Trade, Sir Stafford Cripps, popped into the works for a closer look. He agreed that this was a brilliant new concept that used a lot of non-rationed materials would not just be a boon to farmers, but also for exports. Not only that, but when Cripps was promoted to Chancellor of the Exchequer, he exempted the Land Rover from purchase tax. Indeed when my dad bought one more than 30 years later, it was the fact that it was exempt from VAT, the successor to purchase tax, which was part of the attraction.

Launched at the Amsterdam Motor Show of 1948 and costing £450, this tough, no-nonsense, Belgian- pave-conquering vehicle was wanted by everyone. By 1954, 100,000 had been built and some 70 per cent of output after that went overseas. Incredibly, the Land Rover was only meant to be a stopgap, keeping the factory busy until they could get their new range of cars ready. Instead they had stumbled upon the recipe for a vehicle that appealed to the world.

At home, the company had also been listening to Cripps, and adopted a one-model policy with the Rover 75 in 1949. Owners, journalists and pedestrians alike nicknamed it "Auntie" because it was big, reliable and comfortable. There was nothing complicated about it, just wood and leather inside, plus a large amount of sound deadening and an engine that could take it to 80 miles an hour. There was little evidence that any were ever taken to such supersonic speeds, but it was great value at £1,106. This meant that retired colonels and the middle classes who could not afford a Bentley at four times the price, or thought a Jaguar too vulgar, could happily snuggle up in a 75. Never a huge seller, it was nonetheless consistently popular, getting bigger engines and semi-automatic transmissions until it was laid to rest in 1964 after 130,342 had been built.

The 75 was not a car my Dad or anyone in the family could have afforded. Dad wouldn't actually need a car because he was still in the army, and rather than be demobbed, he even opted to stay in for an extra year. His brother, my Uncle Charles, though, was back on civvie street after learning to drive lorries in the army. The urge to go where he wanted when he wanted was overwhelming. In 1947, Dad married Priscilla Cary. Priscilla's sister, Florence, married Dad's brother, Charles. So honeymoons were in order. Catching a train to Blackpool would have been far too easy, so Uncle Charles had to get a car. And that wasn't at all easy to do in the 1940s.

A new car was out of the question, not least because steel was in short supply and the priority was to sell them for export. To stop the speculators from buying new cars and then selling them for more than they paid, the government made purchasers sign a covenant to guarantee that they would not sell for one year. This was later increased to two years. Consequently, used cars were at a premium, too, since anything on four wheels that still worked could easily be resold. It was a good time to be a car dealer if you could get the cars, but the more difficult task was getting the strictly rationed petrol to put in them. That also meant that some of the larger engined pre-war cars could struggle to sell. Uncle Charles, though, was keen to buy.

He got to hear about some Humber Snipes. These were large saloons that weighed one and half tons and were powered by a big six-cylinder engine. Made from 1936 to 1940, most of the later models ended up as staff cars for the higher ranks in the army. But somehow, my Uncle bought one for £25, and even more remarkably found fresh petrol to put in the tank.

It was a good job he did, because a wonderful time was had by all on the north Norfolk coast, around Hemsby and Yarmouth. I know they had a wonderful time because I have the pictures to prove it. Young, optimistic and having a laugh, that's exactly what the reborn British car industry should have been doing. Looking to the future while having the time of their lives in the present...

That didn't happen, just like Major Ivan Hirst didn't end up as the head of Austin, Rover or Standard. The industry never even paid close attention to just how VW were becoming front-runners in Germany's post-war miracle. They could have learnt quite a lot about how to market cars better both at home and particularly abroad.

Shockingly, these roles would be reversed some 50 years later. Instead of Volkswagen, we would have an ailing British car company, not quite as shattered and shell-shocked as Wolsfburg had been, although its future would seem just as marginal. And coming to the rescue, in the Major Hirst role, would be the head of BMW, Bernd Pischetsrieder. We will hear more about him at the end of this book, but for the moment, all you need to know is that the seemingly unpronounceable and unspellable, name (for an Englishman anyway) actually means, "he who gathers wood for the bishop". His decision to buy the company cost him his job, but the price paid by the so-called "English Patient", Rover (who says the Germans don't have a sense of humour?) would be much more serious.

Births
1946 Healey
1946 Invicta
1946 Lloyd

In the Car Park
In this Chapter you will have come across some of the following vehicles and personalities ...

From left to right there's a Standard Vanguard on the docks and waiting to be exported and boost British balance of payments. Next to it is a prototype Standard Vanguard with Standard Boss Sir John Black at the wheel whilst testing in Wales, shame he didn't get as far as Belgium.

The Austin Devon left was quietly successful in export markets. The Land Rover did the best of all and in the background of the picture if you use a microscope there is a Shire horse, which it effectively replaced.

Top right is an advert to buy a KdF Wagen with saving stamps. Left under the turret of that tank training vehicle is a Beetle. Bottom right, in peacetime Major Ivan Hirst drives the thousandth Beetle off the production line. Finally bottom left the original Rover 75, which wasn't just nicknamed 'Auntie', but also 'Cyclops' because of the headlamp mounted in the middle of the grille.

3 Issywassi's Bloody Name and some Minor Disappointments 1947–1950

 In the garage: Still no garage, but there was soon to be a prefab. In the meantime here's a prefrabricated home for a motor vehicle.

1947 overall was quite a year really. Apart from multiple marriages in the Ruppert family, there were also a lot of important cars that were seen for the first time. We've already met the Beetle, the Vanguard and the Land Rover, but there were plenty more to come that would be just as significant, like the Morris Minor.

Incredibly, the Minor, which went on to become the first British car to sell a million, almost didn't get made. From Lord Nuffield, the company's chairman, down, there was indifference and often downright hostility to what was a very advanced and clever small car. Consequently it took a clever, stubborn, though shy designer to create the Minor, a Mr Alexander Arnold Constantine Issigonis.

He was born in the Greek city of Smyrna (Izmir) in 1906, and his cosmopolitan background was a result of his father's being a naturalised Briton of Greek descent while his mother was German. That German connection would come back to haunt the British car industry as BMW, which bought Rover in 1994, was headed by Bernd Pischetsrieder, who was Issigonis's great nephew. Issigonis's father ran a marine engineering company and his son was fascinated by machinery and was gifted enough to express his ideas in illustrations, much like Leonardo da Vinci, in fact. The Greek motor industry's loss was Britain's gain when the family was evacuated to these shores by the Royal Navy in 1922. Sadly, Issigonis senior died in Malta, and Alexander and his mother had no option but to come to Britain. After enrolling at the Battersea Polytechnic to study automotive engineering, Issigonis graduated in 1928. He went on to become a draughtsman for a London design office before the Rootes group gave him a break. In 1933 he went to Coventry and designed suspension systems for Humber and Hillman cars and furthered his suspension credentials at Morris Motors in Cowley from 1936. So far, it's a conventional enough motor industry career.

During the war, Issigonis worked on a number of projects for the War Department, including an off-road vehicle which could have turned into something Land Roverish. But a new, small Morris for civilians when the war was over became the priority. Codenamed Mosquito, the radical design incorporated a large number of important innovations. Rather than being built in two parts, as was usual, with a lower half, called the chassis, bolted to the body, the Mosquito was all one. What's more, the suspension was independent at the front, which meant a smoother ride, and the steering was by rack and pinion, which meant it was much more responsive. Putting the engine as far ahead of the front wheels as he could meant that the weight distribution was better. To cap it all, the wheels were tiny for the time, at just 14 inches – a good four inches less than the norm.

What Issigonis had designed was a sports car, albeit a very slow one with an old engine from a Morris 8, rather than the new one, to keep costs down. So whereas most 1930s cars would fall over when cornering and then shake your spine to bits over the ruts, here was a car that handled sweetly and rode smoothly, even if it looked a bit odd. More on that later.

It was unusual at the time for just one man to be responsible for all aspects of a car, designing everything from the suspension to the door handles. Issigonis, though, was ably assisted by two draughtsmen, Jack Daniels and Reg Job, who had to turn his pencil sketches into engineering reality. If only Leonardo had had those two blokes on his side then the helicopter would have been available several hundred years earlier. Issigonis said he was very influenced by American designs, although to the best of anyone's knowledge, he never sat outside an embassy furtively scribbling. That is probably why he came up with something that looked more mid-Atlantic, so it was far more twee and to UK scale. With it's rounded bonnet and wings becoming part of the bodywork, it managed to upset some important people at Morris. In particular, the most important person of all – the boss, Lord Nuffield. He bumped into a prototype sometime in 1947 and was apparently shocked at the lack of a separate radiator in the tradition of just about every British car until then. He ranted at everyone, except Issigonis, that it resembled a "poached egg".

Refusing to drive it or even be pictured with it, the old fella would be forced to eat his words. Indeed Issigonis only met his boss twice "and the second time was 11 years later when we'd made a million Morris Minors. Then he had the grace to thank me," he later remembered. Nuffield, though, always had a problem remembering Issigonis, and was often heard to say, "Issywassi's bloody name" when trying to recall his best designer.

Maybe it did look a little bit poached to Issigonis, which explains why at the last minute he cut the prototype in half and added an extra four inches to the width. You can see the join, as the bonnet has a 4-inch ridge in it. Not only that, but production was already so far advanced that the front bumpers had been produced so they had to be cut and a spacing plate was bolted on to join the two halves together. The company also decided to launch two super-sized versions – what could only unofficially be described as Major Minors – in the shape of the Oxford (which my dad would buy a few years later) and the Six. While these models looked less than happy and struggled to find buyers, the Minor had no trouble selling its million. A star of the 1948 London Motor Show, here was Britain's most popular car – unarguably the best small car in the world, and certainly better than the Beetle. So why didn't it sell as many?

Seeing as the Minor had pseudo-American styling, many might have thought it would have been welcomed there and everywhere else for that matter. It seems, though, that not only was Nuffield wary of the Minor, so were the rest of the management team. It was just too unusual, and in the prevailing export-at-all-costs climate, Morris preferred to concentrate their marketing efforts on those Major Minors, the Oxford and the Six. Even so, it was the Minor which dominated exports, and in the first four years of production, up to 90 per cent went abroad. But after satisfying the traditional Commonwealth markets like Australia and South Africa, all efforts were concentrated on the home market from the early 1950s. In the largest export market of all, North America, although they loved their skyscraper-high fins, blinding chrome and huge engines, there was an increasing demand for handy-sized European cars – ones that were easy to manoeuvre and cheap to buy and run. A perfect environment then for the Minor... oh yes, and the Beetle. Actually, in the Minor's best year, 1959, some 14,991 found new homes on the other side of the Atlantic. But the German immigrant did rather better, with 120,442 Beetles staging their own mini-invasion.

Given that Britain and America were on the same side in the war, how come a car named and inspired by Hitler prove to be so popular? The odds were certainly stacked against VW, who not only had to deal with a lot of anti-German sentiment but also the fact that the Beetle was a brand new model with no pedigree. What it did have in its favour, however, was reliability. The Morris Minor certainly wasn't unreliable – not in Britain anyway. But on a continent where there were earthquakes, sandstorms, hurricanes, killer bee swarms and potholes the size of the Grand Canyon, any weakness is bound to show up quickly. Indeed, a whole batch of Minors had been sent to sub-zero Sweden without heaters, which is an indication of how wrong Morris could get it.

Once again, it was a case of failing to understand and prepare for adverse conditions – the very thing that had already scuppered the Standard Vanguard's chances of becoming an export miracle. By comparison with Minor, the Beetle was virtually indestructible, and it helped that the engine was simple and cooled by air, and that it drove the wheels that were directly underneath it. In short, there was much less in the way of complex plumbing and moving parts to go wrong. Even more crucial to their success was the fact that VW concentrated on getting their support network right by making sure that dealers were eager, well stocked with spares and highly efficient. Morris didn't. American owners often referred to "Lucas, Prince of Darkness" as Lucas, the British company that made the lights and other electrics, were not entirely to be relied upon. At least the Americans saw the funny side.

The Beetle did so well not just because Major Hirst had installed such a strong belief in the workforce, but because he also installed the perfect boss. Heinrich Nordoff was the perfect dictatorial boss for those difficult times. He didn't just establish Volkswagen in America – he took the company global, building assembly plants in Brazil, Australia, Belgium, Ireland, Mexico, New Zealand, the Philippines and South Africa. That's how the Beetle became a worldwide phenomenon and the Minor became something driven by Miss Marple. Nordoff's decision to stick with Hirst's one-model policy paid off, and explains his favourite motto: "Change only to improve". He did introduce some variations on the basic Beetle theme, which included a sports car the Karmann Ghia coupe and cabriolet, a light commercial van (Type 2), and even one of the earliest people carriers (the Kombi). There were alternative Minors of course – a van, a two- and four- door, plus a convertible and a mock Tudor estate car with timber as part of the rear bodywork, so there was versatility, and some humour, in the design. Not only that, but it drove very sweetly.

By contrast the Beetle wasn't that great on the road, which might have been a drawback for many models, but became a lovable quirk that owners were happy to put up with, provided they didn't break down. The Beetle was improved over the years, but blink and you could easily miss the subtle update, like the pull heating control that was replaced by a rotary knob in 1953, or the leatherette headlining from 1963. By the time the last example left the production line, there had been 78,000 separate modifications. Yet fundamental shortcomings like restricted interior space, lacklustre performance and dicey handling, were never properly addressed. It would be possible to argue for a very long time which was the better car, but the ultimate decider has to be the final scores at the end of their respective production runs. The Beetle was made from 1946 to 1979 in Germany, although production continued elsewhere (Mexico until 2003) and the 20,000,000th was made in Mexico in May 1981. Ford got a bit miffed, though, and disputed these figures as it left their 15,000,000 Model T trailing. One thing is certain, though. It sold loads more than Morris Minor. The British Motor Industry Heritage Trust reckon that between 1948, when production began, and 1971, when the last one rolled off the line, 1,619,658 were made. Apparently, though, a customer specifically requested that a car be built from spare parts, and it was duly delivered in October 1974. So maybe the final figure should be 1,619,659.

So the Minor was no Beetle when it came to worldwide sales, which makes Britain's reluctance to run Volkswagen all the more galling. But then British mismanagement could have cocked the Beetle up on a worldwide scale. And if we turned down Volkswagen, what German engineering gems did we pick up as so-called war reparations? Well if I told you we got a BMW, that may surprise you. But even more surprising is the fact that one of the companies who took fullest advantage of BMW's technology is, at the time of typing this anyway, still

British and still in business.

With the war over, the Bristol Aeroplane Company was at a loose end, but with plenty of engineering capacity and skilled workers. Then suddenly, in 1947, it entered the car business with a brand new model, which surprised everyone, not least because it bore an uncanny resemblance to pre-war BMWs. That's because, from the distinctive kidney grille at the front to the flowing bodywork that followed on behind and the excellent engine underneath, it could all be traced back to Germany.

Apparently, the head of Bristol, Sir George White, came to an agreement with HJ Aldington, who ran AFN. And AFN not only made the Frazer Nash sports cars but also imported BMWs. In 1945, Aldington spent a lot of time at what was left of BMW's headquarters in Munich. He returned with a 328 BMW, which was a highly-advanced racing car and just one of six to be built. He reckoned that this could be the basis for a new Frazer Nash. It was a design that had been widely admired, and Jaguar's own XK120 was directly inspired by it. Bristol Cars were keen for Aldington to go back, which he did. This time, though, he did not return with a car, but with something potentially more valuable – namely blueprints and other information about the whole pre-war range of BMWs. Bristol now had something to copy.

The Bristol 400, which was unveiled in 1947, had its undercarriage (there's an aircraft term for you, instead of chassis) based on the BMW 326. Attached to that was a powerful engine from the 328 model. It was all encased in a bodywork that drew heavily on the 327 Coupe, and even included the distinctive kidney grille. At least the badge above the grille was different. Originally it should have read Frazer Nash-Bristol, but the bosses of both companies had fallen out, so it was just plain old Bristol. Such thoroughbred ingredients and the fact that it was built to extremely high aircraft standards meant the Bristol was not a cheap car. In a world that needed basic transportation, here was an intercontinental grand tourer costing a quite alarming £1,853. Just 69 of the 700 production run went overseas. That was 1950, and since then, Bristol Cars have carried on in their own wonderfully arrogant and uncompromising way, making small numbers of very expensive hand-built cars for their discerning buyers who demand under-statement rather than excess.

It would be easy to look at Bristol as an opportunity lost. Surely if they had made a bit more effort and been a bit less superior about the business of building perfect cars, they could have turned themselves into the British BMW? Nobody knows, and it is pointless to speculate. In the first place, the path to success from worn-torn Germany, where the major part of the factory was occupied by the Russian army, wasn't an easy one.

After being forced to make pots and pans and anything else to stay in business BMW, had to go back to the drawing board. Reviving their old models didn't stop them flirting with bankruptcy for the next 15 years. BMW were even reduced to building Bubble cars under licence from Italy, which ultimately inspired Issigonis to do better and design the Mini, which people ended up buying anyway. Indeed, BMW, originally an aircraft company like Bristol, had made their first car, which was a tiny Austin Seven, in the 1920s, illustrating what a small, close-knit and interrelated business it is. So perhaps BMW were more ambitious than Bristol, but it still took them until the early 60s to build the model that would be the foundation of their uber success. The rest is history, and the world seems to belong to BMW, who continue to build charismatic cars profitably all around the world. Meanwhile Bristol, who don't reveal sales figures, continue in their own unique way.

At least one explanation as to why the European and Japanese motor industries became so productive and so much better than the British, is that their factories were bombed into oblivion. With nothing but a large hole in the ground and wreckage everywhere, the only way was to start again with a brand new factory. Utilising all the aid available, especially from America, who figured that if they had strong economies, they would be less likely to turn into Commies. What chance did the plucky Brits stand? Yes, the country was penniless, tired, and keen to get working again, but conditions were far from primitive. The truth is the motor industry in particular had some lovely new factories to move into and utilise.

"Shadow" factories had been built nearby the existing ones to make aircraft and other parts. Before the war, the government had seen to it that these were built. Indeed, before the war was officially over, both Standard and Rover leased their shadow plants. Not long after, Rootes took over its nearby factory in Stoke on Trent, and Daimler did the same with two plants. In fact everyone who had one would ultimately take them over, and that included Austin in 1950. The major problem was that manufacturers who wanted to build their own factories needed a piece of paper called an Industrial Development Certificate. You only got one of these planning permission chits if the factory was sited in a depressed area. This forced companies to consider areas of high unemployment in Scotland, South Wales, West Cumberland and Tyneside, which sounded sensible in principle, but was a disaster in practice.

This is the sort of thing that governments are good at – interfering and manipulating when they should leave well alone. Industries are in various regions for pretty good reasons. The clay soil around Stoke established the pottery industry, the high salt deposits in Cheshire led directly to chemicals being the primary industry, and it was the nearby sticky rock mountains with Great Yarmouth written all the way through them that helped the coastal town become a popular holiday resort. Not really. But attempting to spread the car industry around the country was a well-meaning but seriously flawed idea that would come back to haunt the car makers and the government.

Don't worry, because although not taking full advantage of BMW's engineering excellence can be seen as an opportunity missed, at least British industry managed to get a lift on the back of the one other significant vehicle to come our way from Germany – and it had just the two wheels.

Now I know this isn't a book about the British Bike Industry. The best book on that subject has already been written, and it is "Whatever happened to the British Motorcycle Industry", by Bert Hopton. You do need to love bikes to get through it, but it was written by a bloke who was a proper engineer and held senior positions in all the major bike companies. The story he tells is a very sad one that would make even the hardest biker cry, but it is the restrained stiff upper lip tone that he uses that most impresses. Like the car industry, bikes went to the scrap yard and like the car business, no one saw it, or rather the Japanese, coming. Hopton doesn't even swear or rant. He was too much of a gentleman for that. But I digress, a bit. You see, I've got a 1957 BSA Bantam that belonged to my dearly missed late brother-in-law, Jimmy Smart. At heart, he was a mod, with an impeccable taste in great music and a definitive collection of Who records and late 60s rock. On the road, though, he was a rocker. No fey Vespa or Lambretta scooters that buzzed around with a million rear view mirrors, but a proper Brit Bike. However, getting mobile as teenager in the 60s meant only one thing – buying a BSA Bantam. Jimmy and his dad Bill created a mutant one with the frame of a D1 and the larger engine of a D3, which won't mean much unless you are a studded leather anorak. However, for an apprentice printer, it was good enough for getting to work and back.

Jimmy's Bantam has still got the last tax disc it sported in May 1972, when constant tinkering and oil leaks saw it retired from the road to begin a static life under tarpaulin. A few years later, though, I pushed it with Jimmy the two miles from his house to ours. There, over the next few years, I failed to make it start. I took it to pieces and resprayed parts in my bedroom. Mum overlooked the obvious speckled paint outlines on the carpet as all great mums would. Several house moves later, and after losing some mechanical bits when I put them in the dubious care of a local greasy bikers' shop, I finally reassembled it, so the bike looks pretty. Unfortunately, there is a hole in the frame where the engine should be, so it still hasn't started. I must sort that out.

The point is that the BSA Bantam wasn't so much a Bantam as a DKW, effectively a small German motorcycle. It all came down to war reparations. Although nothing was announced officially, BSA got access to the blueprints for a small, simple engine. Certainly Britain needed a cheap, lightweight motorcycle design to help get it mobile again. So the Bantam had a DKW RT125 engine. Encouragingly, though, BSA did not slavishly copy the whole bike. First, they rearranged the components so that the kickstart and gear lever were now on the right, where they should have been all along, of course. BSA also did the decent thing and converted all the measurements from metric to imperial, so proper inches and pints were the order of the day. Significantly, BSA also designed their own frame and parts, so this became a thoroughly Brit bike. By contrast, the Americans, who also took the DKW blueprints, produced a photocopy. It was called a Hummer in the USA – after a motorcycle dealer, not a stupidly large, ugly, military 4 x 4 that has become strangely popular. It was made by Harley Davidson, although a Hells Angel probably wouldn't be seen dead on one. Or rather would soon be dead as a result of his beer gut, which would most likely over balance the small frame and spread him all over the Pacific Coast Highway, or something very like that.

For BSA, the Bantam was a spectacular success as some 500,000 were sold over 23 years. Indeed, anyone who is really, really old will remember that the Post Office bought thousands of them, painted them red and sent small boys out on them to deliver telegrams. But getting back to my original diversion, the DKW RT125 engine had been built at the Zschopau factory (now there's a mouthful) in Saxony, which later became the base of MZ motorcycles, when the initials were reversed. Now Jimmy bought the East German (long before the Berlin Wall came down) MZ 250 in 1973, simply because the Bantam no longer existed and he needed a cheap, reliable pair of wheels to get to work on. Obviously you couldn't buy a decent British bike anymore.

Little did Jimmy, or anyone else for that matter, realise that the British motorcycle industries' demise was not going to be an isolated case. Actually, buying a British-built car wasn't going to be a problem for quite a few years, although even when Jimmy bought his foreign bike, actually buying a British-built car that was decently designed and reliable had started to become a problem. But for the moment – and this is still 1950 – there didn't seem too much to worry about.

Births
1947 Bristol
1948 Bond
1949 Buckler
1949 Connaught
1949 Dellow

Marriage
1947 Lagonda to Aston Martin

In the Car Park

In this Chapter you will have come across some of the following vehicles and personalities...

Top left the original Minor MM which was designed by Alec Issigonis on the right.

Below them is a later Minor usually driven by maiden aunts, district nurses, the clergy and other respectable pillars of society. There was also the mock Tudor

half-timbered estate. At the bottom are the big Chiefs of British car building. Bottom left is Lord Nuffield and Leonard Lord working together at Morris in the 1930s. Lord (on the right) left to go to Austin and then take over Morris with the creation of BMC. On the right are the Rootes Brothers with sensible accountant type Reginald on the left and the rather more maverick Sir William (Billy) on the right both pondering which ailing car company they could buy for fun and profit.

On this page top left is a Bristol 400 which looks suspiciously like the BMW 327 on the right, down to the distinctive kidney grille and the engine under the bonnet. The motorcycle is a BSA Bantam which was also based on a German design by a company called DKW, although BSA engineers changed quite a lot to adapt it for British conditions.

4 Two Lords, one BMW and some Sports Cars in America. 1950–1954

In the garage: Still no garage, but at least there is somewhere to park a car when it eventually arrives. Indeed, in place of a garage Dad could have bought a folding garage like this one, which was called a Clear-Fit. According to the advertisement it could be operated by a small child, like my sister.

Into the 1950s, and mum and dad were settling down into what was generally known as their Prefab. Not something that they would want to be reminded of in later years on the grounds of pride, but really there wasn't much alternative at the time. A prefabricated home erected where real homes used to be before the Luftwaffe passed overhead. With their little garden areas, it was a huge change from the London terraces. Most significantly, there was also somewhere to park a car. And that's exactly what Mum and Dad's neighbours did. It was a pre-war Morris 8, which had doors and wheels and, in the great British tradition – maybe they started it – would be routinely washed every week. What amused my car-less Mum and Dad hugely was the statement regularly uttered by their upwardly mobile neighbour when it arrived. "Do you know what, Mrs Ruppert? We can now go out and about when we want, stop where we want and do whatever we like. The world's our oyster."

In the five years that Mum and Dad lived there, it never moved once. Maybe the idea of a car was exciting, but when they finally got it, they were just a bit clueless, or frightened of what actually lay beyond the end of the road. The world wasn't even their whelk. A bit like the British car industry which, according to me so far in this book, doesn't look too healthy and is just a little bit stupid. I might have given the impression that we couldn't export so much as a kiddie's pedal car, but I was wrong. The truth is that, back in the 1930s, Britain never exported more than 24 per cent of vehicle output in any one year. However, by the late 1940s, that figure had risen to the giddy heights of 80 per cent. In 1950, Britain was the world's second biggest producer of cars, some way behind America. And Britain had also become the leading exporter of cars, for a while. In fact we sold three times more in overseas markets than the Americans. Indeed we were selling most of those cars to the Americans.

Luckily for us, the Americans had never understood or attempted to make a sports car. All they were concerned with was mass-producing profitable cars for families and business. This meant that the whole concept of open-topped sports cars, hand-crafted from wood and metal, never existed for them. That left MG as the largest sports car manufacturer in Europe. So when MG craftily renamed their pre-war TB car the TC so that no one would notice that it was woefully ancient and out of date, it worked. The Americans fell for it in a huge way and couldn't get enough of this quirky two-seater that had no discernable suspension, a joke of hood and little else in the way of comfort. None of that mattered, because being a British car, it could go round corners and was much more responsive than the slow-witted things that Americans endured. Most of all, though, it looked so different from their slab-sided dinosaurs. Even though the TC also came from an almost prehistoric motoring age, the wire wheels, shiny grille and low-slung body with sweeping mudguards saved it.

Consequently you might imagine that hundreds of thousands were sold, rather than just 2001. But it was to be the inspiration for other manufacturers and the start of a British sports car invasion that would last for the next 30 years. The stunning success of the TC alerted other manufacturers that there was a massive market for their quirky little cars. MG had a head start, of course, and while the TC could trace its origins back to 1935 and the design philosophy behind it to the 1920s, the follow-up TD in 1950 had to be more modern, and it was. Even so, it was still built in the fiercely traditional manner of the British craftsman with steel skin panels on a coach-built wooden frame, still with separate wings over the wheels and separate chrome headlights and grille. MG, though, had got their act together sales-wise, and 80 per cent of TDs built found buyers in the States.

Already Jaguar had the XK120, which was to prove so influential, successful and profitable. But it began life as just a stopgap. After the war, Jaguar... well let's hold on a minute there, because originally, the company had been called SS cars. That stood for Swallow Sidecars, because that's what they made – sidecars for motorcycles, like Gromit (out of Wallace &) sits in. Unfortunately, those two previously innocent letters had been tainted by their association with the Nazi party and Hitler's personal bodyguard, the Schutzstaffel. Just as the Strength through Joy car became the Volkswagen Type 1 and then the rather more cuddly Beetle, SS Cars made a smooth transition into becoming Jaguar Cars. That's because, back in 1936, a new range of SS Cars needed a model name, and the owner of SS, William Lyons, asked his advertising agency to list a load of animal names and, in his own words, "pounced on Jaguar". It wasn't just that it sounded good, but Lyons remembered that one of his friends in the first world war had worked on an aircraft engine that was called a Jaguar. So having registered the big cat back in the 1930s, it was no problem to adopt the new and highly appropriate name.

That's how Jaguar became Jaguar, and they were eager to launch a saloon car with their new and very powerful XK engine, but the body tooling was delayed. So purely for marketing and promotional purposes, the company hurriedly designed a sports car in 1948. It looked a bit like the pre-war BMW 328, which wasn't too surprising as, when an example was brought to the UK, Jaguar was one of several manufacturers who took a very close look at this advanced car. However, Lyons was an accomplished stylist, and instead of just copying what he saw, he drew much more flowing and coherent bodylines that implied it was bloody quick. As mentioned in the last chapter, Bristol turned the pre-war BMW range into their highly bespoke 400 that they sold to a few people in Britain. Lyons was lot more ambitious and managed to sell many thousands to America and it was crucial in establishing his company in the States. In 1948, though, he wasn't looking beyond the very short term when the Super Sports (we're back to SS again) was launched at the motor show.

The response was overwhelming, and Jaguar got enough orders to justify full-scale production (at just £998 that was hardly surprising). Getting back into SS hot water led to a name change to XK, after the engine, followed by 120, which indicated the top speed. The success of the XK120 actually changed Jaguar's whole policy. Pre-war, they had just concerned themselves with making cars exclusively for the UK market. But Lyons had noticed that there was a big, car-hungry world out there, so decided that exporting Jaguars was going to be very good for his business.

The success of the MG TD and Jaguar XK120 was not lost on their competitors, and in particular, Sir John Black, who ran Standard, noticed that there was room for a sports car somewhere in the middle of those two. He reckoned that the quickest way to fill the gap was to buy Morgan. This family-run Wiltshire company had quietly been doing its own thing since 1909 when HFS Morgan built a three-wheeled runabout. Standard, though, had supplied engines to Morgan since 1939, so reckoned they could persuade the Morgan family to take not exactly early, but fairly late retirement. Luckily for the British car industry, the Morgan clan declined, otherwise they probably would have perished, forgotten and forlorn amid the wreckage of all the other great British car marques in the 1970s or 1980s. Fortunately for Black, he had bought the bankrupt Triumph company in 1945, which became part of the Standard group.

He put his engineers to work, and they quickly came up with the TR, which stood for Triumph Roadster. Badged as the TR1, this was shown off at the 1952 Motor Show. However, they had come up with it a bit too quickly, taking a huge shortcut by basing it on a pre-war design. That meant the TR1 wasn't fast, particularly good looking or, crucially for a sports car, accomplished at going around corners. Black sent them back to their drawing boards and they quickly returned with a thoroughly redesigned model. It used an engine from the almost unexportable Vanguard saloon, and used chunkier, more macho styling. Not surprisingly, it was called the TR2, but far more surprisingly, it did 100mph, which was remarkably quick at the time.

A huge part of its appeal, though, was the bargain asking price of just £555.

Instantly the MGs seemed slow and expensive and not nearly as economical. Then the TR2 won the RAC Rally around Britain and its legendary status was assured. The car was popular in America, and the TR3 even more so, establishing the whole Triumph marque over there. And more TR models followed: the TR4, TR5, TR6 and TR7, in case you wondered…

Americans, though, didn't buy everything from Blighty that just happened to have the roof missing. Riley had lost their Coventry factory to bombing, which gave them the opportunity to start afresh with their sporty cars. They were yet another British manufacturer who had taken a good old look at the BMW 328 and come up with their own version of it. Riley also looked abroad and modelled their suspension and steering on advanced Citroën innovations. However, they stuck resolutely to traditional building methods, which meant expensive hand-built bodywork and wooden structures. With an eye on the American market, the RMC roadster, an open topped sports car from 1948, was an odd beast. Instead of sitting two up front, it had room for three, just like a van. A huge 20-gallon fuel tank meant that buyers could go so much further without filling up, which seemed perfect for the wide-open spaces of North America. However, just 510 buyers took the gamble, and found that sitting three abreast was a bit crowded. The fact that some tacky bits of chrome were stuck on to the bodywork to appeal specifically to American tastes didn't work either. If finding customers in strange and exotic locations like America was a problem for Riley, finding customers closer to home was also proving difficult.

Riley's range of pricey-to-build cars were struggling, and as part of Morris, which was founded and run by Lord Nuffield, it was not the only marque in trouble. Wolseley had reintroduced its extensive pre-war range of well-equipped, middle-class cars in 1945. They offered lots of choice, but the scant resources meant limited numbers were made. Moving factories in 1949 from the Midlands to Cowley in Oxford, the home of Morris, hardly made any difference. What must have pleased Lord Nuffield, though, was that Wolseley were keen to stick their distinctive radiator grille on to the poached egg Morris Minor shape he so despised. This created the rather more acceptable – well, to Nuffield anyway – Wolseley 6/80. Here was a Minor than had been pumped up, but much, much uglier, and the only bright spot was the famous illuminated Wolseley badge. As the advertising ran at the time, it was "the only car with it's name in lights". Big deal.

Despite these problems, and having to cope with running 16 diverse factories with few parts shared between any of the models, the whole Nuffield organisation was Britain's most profitable car maker. Correction: Britain's second most profitable car maker, as that title belonged almost in perpetuity to the efficient and cost-conscious American-owned Ford. Morris could trace their strong performance to one model, the Minor – reason enough, you'd have thought, for keeping Alec Issigonis on the payroll at all costs, even if Nuffield personally hated the car. But Issigonis had seen what was coming and left before the inevitable merger.

So while Issigonis went off to another car manufacturer, Alvis, to work on a large-engined car that was the antithesis of the Minor, the two giants of the British car industry eyed each other up nervously. In 1950, Leonard Lord, who ran Austin, telephoned Lord Nuffield to wish him happy birthday, which was nice, but really he was sounding him out about getting together. It was nice because the so-called Lords of Cowley (that's Nuffield) and Longbridge (Lord) had plenty of previous. Indeed, they hadn't spoken to each other since 1936 when Lord walked out on Morris and vowed that he would take the company (Morris) apart, "brick by bloody brick". Not surprisingly, Nuffield wasn't interested in getting together, and Lord's response was to go off and develop a new model to rival the Minor.

That's the sort of petty, school playground level of squabbling that would dog the British car industry ever after. When the companies were finally brought together, there would be jealously, rivalry, little fiefdoms and vicious infighting when they really should have been facing up to the threat from their rivals.

However, Nuffield must have thought about it for a year, because in 1951, they reached an agreement to create the British Motor Corporation, BMC.

Now it looked like a merger, as the management positions were handed out evenly among the Morris and Austin directors, but in essence, this was a full-scale takeover by Austin. Compared to Morris, Austin was the dowdy but reliable purveyor of inoffensive and ever so slightly old fashioned motor vehicles. However, when they actually came up with something all new in 1948, it proved to be a strong and impressive seller. The model designation was A40, but the twee, southern counties names of Dorset for the two-door and Devon for the four-door were much more friendly. They were export hits, too, going down well, in Australia and over the pond in America. Stretching the format, though, wasn't a good idea. Just as Riley had misjudged the American market with their three-seater RMC Roadster, Austin got the A90 Atlantic convertible spectacularly wrong. They sold just 350 of them, 160 less than the Riley. The A90 certainly looked the part on paper as, sensationally for a British-built car, it was available with unimaginable luxuries that included electric windows, an electric hood, adjustable steering wheel, a heater and even a radio. In the metal it looked the part too, with fashionable styling, full-width bodywork – i.e. no running boards or mudguards – and a Cyclops centre headlamp. At night it must have looked like a motorcycle display team was coming at you. The Atlantic also shifted because the big engine delivered a hairy top speed of over 90mph.

Unfortunately, the Americans were not impressed, either by the name Atlantic or much else, which even included almost giving them away by slashing $1,000 off the price. Austin, though, never learned their lesson and had already embarked on a project to make an A40 Sports version of their popular saloon so that they could rival MG. They linked up with sports car builder Jensen to make the bodyshells. Sadly, the result looked just a little bit dull, and the specially-made body was heavy, so it was also slow. The two most important factors in making a successful sports car had been comprehensively fluffed. Never mind though, because along with Riley, Wolseley and Morris, the acquisitive Leonard Lord and Austin had now also picked up the ultimate sporting marque: MG. And this at the very time when Lord was just about to create yet another sports brand, Austin Healey.

So what was Leonard Lord thinking? Ideally, Austin and Morris should have merged straight after the war, but instead they had both spent fortunes duplicating each other's range of cars. And now Lord was at it again. Maybe he was following the example set by the Rootes brothers. Now there was a company run not by manufacturers, but savvy car dealers who bought failing brands, reorganised them and seemed to make decent profits. The roots, if you will forgive the pun, of the Rootes car business were not the manufacturing heartland that is the Midlands but the home county of Kent. With financial backing from their father, brothers Billy and Reggie Rootes set about becoming the largest vehicle distributors in the country by acquiring chains of garages. Billy was the abrasive, visionary salesman (even though he did pass on the Beetle) and Reggie the more reserved, double-entry book-keeping end of the partnership.

In the 1920s and 30s, colourful Billy was a regular visitor to the United States– so much so that colleagues noticed a distinct mid-Atlantic twang to his accent. What Billy noticed was the unstoppable success of General Motors and their range of distinctive marques, from Chevrolet and Buick to Oldsmobile and Cadillac, which appealed to very different car buyers. This allowed the company to tweak a model by adding or subtracting important elements such as the engine size, specification or styling and aim it at a buyer's pocket. So it was Chevrolets for the workers and Cadillacs for the filthy rich and Buicks and Oldsmobiles for those in the middle. By contrast, Ford had just the one option – cars for the people, with limited and lower profit appeal. The answer for Billy Rootes was to start buying companies in the UK. It wasn't easy, and after he had secured an old body builder, Thrupp and Maberly, established in 1790, Humber, who owned Hillman, became part of the fledgling group. The Hillman Minx was a great success for them, and fuelled by those profits, they merged Karrier Motors with Commer Cars to create the commercial vehicles side of the business, making vans and lorries. The most prestigious prizes, though, were Talbot and Sunbeam.

The brothers knew all about Talbot as Reggie ran a saloon model with the interior fittings tackily gold plated. And that's pretty much what they did to the company. Talbot, with their brilliant Swiss-born chief engineer Georges Roesch, built highly advanced, refined, fast and elegant cars. Sunbeam were famed for their high-profile Grand Prix success and land-speed-record-breaking cars. Oh, and their high-quality sports cars, which they sold to the few members of the public who could actually afford them. However, at a stroke, in 1935, the Rootes brothers devalued both marques by gluing their names together and then sticking them on to upmarket versions of Hillmans. Georges Roesch was incandescent with rage and left the car industry altogether to devote his skills to designing jet engines. Rootes weren't bothered – they just got on with making cars that people wanted to buy. Billy Rootes was a super salesman who built up his company into one of the most powerful and profitable vehicle businesses in the country. He is also credited with backing the shadow factory scheme of the 1930s which helped us win the war and give the car industry a head start after it.

Billy Rootes continued to buy companies after the war, taking on commercial vehicle builder Tillings-Stevenson in 1950 and much later in 1955 Singer, who had once been the third biggest manufacturer after Austin and Morris in the 30s but who had fallen on hard times by then. So Leonard Lord must have thought that bringing marques together was a good idea. However, that didn't stop him creating a brand new one. The man behind Healey was Donald Healey, an accomplished racing driver who had won the Monte Carlo Rally back in 1931 and had worked for Riley and Triumph before deciding to go it alone. Healey was determined to build a 100mph sports car with a Riley engine. To prove it, he drove his own Healey to an Italian Autostrada and topped 104mph. However, the car was expensive to build, and because it cost over £1,000 it fell foul of the government's punitive 1947 purchase tax on cars that cost four-figure sums. Healey admitted he needed a faster, lighter, cheaper car. By using the engine from the failure that was the Austin Atlantic, he created the Healey 100, and this is what Lord fell in love with at the 1952 Motor Show. Well, he probably wouldn't admit to that, but the car, renamed the Austin Healey, became BMC's corporate sports car. That happened even though the far more recognisable MG brand was now in the fold.

As with the failed Austin Sports, Jensen built the bodies of the Austin Healey and the running gear was fitted at Austin's Longbridge factory. The Healey got progressively larger engines over the years, even though the successor to the 100, the 100/6, proved to be slower before the 3000 in 1959 restored some pride and a 110mph top speed, on a good day. So you might possibly buy it as an alternative to a Jaguar, or because you wanted something prettier than a Triumph TR. Moving production to the MG factory at Abingdon was a sensible decision, while the one to make a cheaper Austin Healey seemed odd, because surely that was MG's job? Weird decision-making was at the heart of BMC at the time, and Lord was still determined to make inroads into the world's biggest export market by building American-friendly cars. He was also still smarting at the wholesale rejection of his Austin Sports, but his new best friend, Donald Healey, was there to help.

Having worked with the American Nash car company to make the Nash Healey (what else?) he introduced Lord to the company. Nash would later merge with Hudson to create American Motors and become the only American manufacturer with any interest in making anything smaller than XXL cars. At that time, they were developing a small two-seater with the idea of powering it with Fiat parts. Lord persuaded him that Austin had the willingness and resources to make it in Britain, which they duly did. The Metropolitan was a fabulously odd concoction of a car that mixed cheeky, almost Barbie Doll styling courtesy of the Yanks, with reduced dimensions, engines and economy courtesy of the Brits. It was a very strange car for the American market, and it could only really be described as rather girly, so that's who it was aimed at, especially with two-tone paintwork. If that was slightly confusing, then so were the names. It was sold as simply a Metropolitan and at other times as a Nash Metropolitan or a Hudson Metropolitan. When it was finally sold in Britain, from 1957, it became the Austin Metropolitan, although it never wore the Austin badge. In Britain, no one really knew what to make of it, because it was just an ugly, slow convertible or coupe, which fell all over the road. In Britain, though, there was a tiny market amongst the "weaker" (in the 1950s) sex.

For a while, however, this odd little car was an incredible export success. It became the best selling British-made car in America, and for just one year was the second best seller overall in that market, some way behind the Beetle. Here was proof that Austin and BMC could build something quite unlike anything they were used to and actually make a success of it. Production of the Metropolitan ran from 1954 to 1961, but meanwhile, BMC still seemed determined to duplicate what they already had, and to this end, Leonard Lord asked Donald and Donald's son Geoffrey to design a sports car based on the components used to make the Austin A35. The Healeys then developed a small sports car according to the instructions, and then it was handed over to MG to finish.

MG engineered out the most interesting feature: headlamps that popped up out of the bonnet. Sadly, it was a cost issue that nixed it, along with the realisation that it was something else that could go wrong and really, really annoy American customers when it looked as if their Austin Healey was winking at them. Instead, the lights were left in the up position, which gave the car a look of permanent surprise and led to it's permanent nickname, "Frogeye". Unveiled in 1958, the Austin Healey Sprite, as it was officially known, wasn't quick, but it was fun to drive and could be endlessly tuned to produce more power. It was cheeky, too, although not in a Nash Metropolitan way, in that real blokes could drive one of these. Subsequent models, including the MG-badged version – the MG Midget – would form the backbone of sports car production for the next 20 years. Although both the Austin Healey and MGs were popular and export earners, particularly in America, all these sports cars were low-production models. Not only that, but they relied on the conventional saloon cars for all the crucial parts. Yet the bread-and-butter model line up at BMC was something that always needed sorting out. It all looked good on paper, but the reality was something different. Britain and BMC still needed a Beetle.

Dad would never get to own a sports car, although he talked about it sometimes. But then he also talked about buying a speedboat. Although he had a real soft spot for Morgans that I'll explain in more detail later, he was much more of a Grand Tourer man. He wanted something comfortable and stylish, and in the 1970s he would have loved a Triumph Stag. We got as far as looking through the brochures with serious faces, but sadly he knew they were rubbish. More on that later as well.

At least Triumph had a reputation for being sporty, although that didn't extend to every model, as we'll find out.

Births
1950 Marauder
1950 Paramount
1951 Turner
1951 Russon
1952 Austin Healey
1952 BMC
1953 Lotus

Marriages
1952 Nuffield Oganisation (Morris, MG, Riley and Wolseley) to Austin Motor Company to form BMC

Deaths
1950 Invicta
1951 Connaught
1951 Lloyd
1952 Marauder
1952 Russon

New Arrivals
1952 Volkswagen

In the Car Park

In this Chapter you will have come across some of the following vehicles ...

Top left we have the MGTC, then on the right its successor the MGTD followed by, in alphabetical fashion the MGTF.

Top left is the Jaguar XK120 which looks rather similar to the pre-war BMW 328 which is seen here in full racing trim. Then below we have the Triumph TR range, starting with the TR2 and followed in numerical fashion this time by the TR3 and TR4.

Here's a bunch of sporting cars starting with the curious Riley RMC top left and
the equally unsuccessful Austin Atlantic next to it with its three headlamp set up.
The Austin A40 second row left was equally underwhelming whereas as the
cooperation with the American Nash company resulted in the twee Metropolitan.

Top row is the Austin Healey 100 and 100/6 with the 'Frogeyed' Austin Healey Sprite below that and MG's more conventional version. Somehow a Wolseley 6/80 is parked among the sports cars, essentially a giant Morris Minor that the company were keener to promote in export markets than the "poached egg" it was based upon.

5 Mayflowers to America and Ambassadors to India 1954–55
(although we do fast-forward to 1960 at one point)

In the garage: It's still a metaphorical garage, of course, but parked in the street is a Triumph Mayflower. Mind you we could have put it underneath a cover which thank goodness was especially easy for women to use. It was called the Skipper Auto Cover and was made from double-proofed canvas.

Like thousands of others starting new jobs in the early 1950s, Dad needed a car. Companies were realising that they could get more business done if they gave their reps the freedom of the road, and a car to go with it. Dad hated the word "rep", abbreviation for representative, but that's exactly what he was: a company rep, checking and installing display advertising at football grounds, shops and just about anywhere you could find a hoarding with a cigarette or beer advert on it. That required a driving licence, which Dad didn't have, but he was a fast learner. He was already used to moving vans and lorries around the yard of the cigarette manufacturers where he worked, and brother Charles provided the car and the finishing touches. Behind the wheel of a pre-war Hillman Minx picked up for just a few quid, Dad passed easily. The Minx, though, belonged to Uncle Charles, and anyway, Dad was going to work in something a bit more special.

The Triumph Mayflower was certainly special – in fact it was frighteningly unique. No other company would have been brave or stupid enough to make such an ugly and ill-conceived small car. Not only that, but it was based on misunderstanding the needs of an entire continent. Sir John Black, who ran Standard cars, owners of Triumph, had been told that the well-off American buyer loved Rolls-Royces. So the very idea of a half-sized Roller named after the Pilgrim Fathers' boat would clearly be a roaring success. Apparently he thought that there might be a market for "his" and "hers" Rollers, her Roller being the pocket-sized Mayflower. Unlike the Nash Metropolitan, which was just as petite and odd as the Mayflower, the Metro looked reassuringly American. The Flower just looked wrong.

The Mayflower enjoyed a British 1940s-50s styling fad that was generally referred to as "razor edged". As you might imagine, this meant sharp lines so that every panel was flat and some of them had straight creases in them. On big limousines it worked, and Triumph had their full-size Renown as proof. However, on a tiny car with two doors it just looked daft. Unfortunately, there was no such thing as irony or kitsch in those days to justify owning a stupid looking car. Triumph made matters worse by cutting the roof off 10 of them, which made them structurally marginal, so not only could owners hear pedestrians laughing at them, they could feel the whole vehicle wobble like a jelly. As an indication of just how desperate Triumph were to make the Mayflower more appealing, there were even an unspecified number of pick-up versions (a big open boot where the rear seats used to be) for Australia. That must have cracked them up, and probably led to a boycott by embarrassed sheep.

Dad didn't have any choice. This was his company car. He genuinely liked the mini-limousine look, with leather and wood inside, which isn't a bad way to start your motoring career, even if it was a second-hand one. The trouble was, he told me, it pretty much fell apart over a couple of years as he pounded up and down the A1 and shook it to bits. Dad's company then swept it into a corner and everyone forgot that they had ever seen it. Even though the Mayflower was slow and hilarious to look at, Triumph still managed to sell 35,000 of them over three years. Not many to America though.

Over at the newly created BMC, they had rather more to worry about than one disappointingly razor-edged saloon. Leonard Lord looked at the combined model line-up and realised that the 14 models on the price lists only shared nine engines. Putting Austin's A series engine into the Morris Minor helped to transform its performance and reliability, and undoubtedly increased popularity so that it had sold a million by the end of 1960. A special edition was badged as the Minor 1,000,000 and painted lilac. But even so, BMC had been determined to kill it off.

Although Lord Nuffield wasn't around any more to insult the Minor and its designer, Issigonis, there was still a residual hatred of the blameless car. Even before the creation of BMC, Morris was considering non-poached-egg redesigns. Leonard Lord was just as keen to change the look of the Minor, and commissioned a restyle, but with a bigger Austin B series under the bonnet. Even though the engine wasn't that big, it didn't make any sense to build a thirstier Minor in the current climate. That climate was the Suez crisis. Egypt's President Nasser nationalised the Suez Canal, forcing tankers on their way to Europe to pay high taxes or take the scenic route around the African Cape. Petrol was not just in short supply, but rationed, so small cars were back in fashion. These circumstances would lead to the development of perhaps the most important British car ever – the Mini. For the time being, though, it meant no big-engined Minor.

But Lord was not about to throw away development time and money. Plan B was to focus on overseas markets like Australia, which needed stronger cars – proof that, slowly, the British car industry was learning. So when an even bigger-engined prototype was made, Lord loved it so much he sanctioned UK production. That meant instead of this new super Minor replacing the original Minor, it went into production alongside it. But the super Minor wasn't going to be called an Austin or a Morris. Nope, BMC had a whole cupboard full of badges waiting to be pinned on any appropriate or even inappropriate bonnet.

Already the Riley and Wolseley badges had been used on identical models, so the Riley Pathfinder and Wolseley Six-Ninety were one and the same, as were the Wolseley 4/44 and MG Magnette. This practice was known as badge engineering, and as we have seen, it originated in America and was successfully copied by Rootes. Now BMC had the opportunity, and an armful of marques, to make it happen. So in April 1957, the Wolseley 1500 was intended as a well-appointed (wood and leather) small car aimed at the more mature buyer, and few months later, the Riley One-Point-Five had a more powerful engine, a wider range of colours and was aimed at the younger, sporty saloon buyer. Visually, these models were fuddy-duddy and just a bit too fussy when compared with the loveable poached egg Minor. So why bother?

Well, BMC could make more profit on the Riley and Wolseley, with their posher badges, than they ever could on a Minor. The actual sales, though, were not that impressive. The cheaper Wolseley made the biggest impression, proving that there was some demand for an upmarket Minor, and just a few more than 100,000 were sold by 1965. However, the market for a sporting Minor was much more limited, and a few short of 40,000 were made over the same period. But even as those models were discontinued due to lack of interest, the Minor continued to find a substantial haul of customers, and would live on for another six years. BMC may have rationalised components and bodies, but they didn't rationalise the names, and learned nothing from the marginal sales figures of their clone models.

In 1959 a range of Italian-designed saloons highlighted the fundamental problems that faced BMC. So while the otherwise identical Austin Cambridge and Morris Oxford models did well enough selling in hundreds of thousands, the marginally different Riley 4/68 and 4/72 struggled to sell 25,000. The MG Magnette was only a bit better, selling just short of 30,000, but the good value Wolseley 15/60 and 16/60 managed to get to the giddy heights of almost 88,000. So yet again, why did BMC bother?

The idea had been to maintain customer and dealer loyalty by continuing with these established names, but this was a pointless and expensive strategy. That's because the old buffers who'd owned a Riley or Wolseley before the war and wanted a familiar name on the grille of their car were dying off. Add to that the questionable relevance of making a performance MG version which seemed to be lost on most of the buying public who clearly preferred their sports cars as small and mostly open-topped. Even so, in 1960, BMC were making 500,000 cars for the first time, and had record profits of £26.9 million. So maybe they didn't have much to worry about, until, that is, you took a closer look at what the Americans were up to in Britain. Ford were making 180,000 fewer cars than BMC, but recorded a £33.7 million clear profit. So how on earth did they manage that?

At its simplest, Ford had just the one factory, Dagenham, while BMC were struggling to control more than a dozen plants, most inherited from the Morris side of the business when the companies merged. Also, Ford's model line-up was brilliantly simple – basically, you could choose from small, medium and large. Let's take a look at what was available in 1953, when BMC were offering a myriad models and badges. Firstly, you could buy a cheap and cheerful two-door Popular, at the time the world's cheapest car, for £390. The Pop had zero specification, although there was a single windscreen wiper and felt floor covering. It looked old fashioned, and could trace its very layout back to the Model T, but the old Pop lasted to 1959 and sold more than 580,000. Then there was the much more modern small Ford in the shape of the two-door Anglia, and slightly posher and medium-sized four-door Prefect. They had racked up sales of more than 1.5 million by the early 1960s. Then came the larger and lower-rent Consul and jazzed up Zephyr. That was it. Pop, Prefect and Consul. There were some variations on the theme, of course, as you could get an open-topped Zephyr and an estate version Prefect. Ford just added extra equipment and profit as the customer ordered it. Simple.

Interestingly, the large Consul and Zephyr models when launched at the 1950 London Olympia Motor Show were regarded as among the most advanced car designs in the world. Apart from the single-structure construction, everything was bolted to the body, with a new independent front suspension system that endures to this day. The engine was powerful but unstressed, which meant it would be reliable. It also had the smallest wheels seen on a British car at 13 inches, which undoubtedly helped it to handle more tidily. It was a thoroughly modern and comfy car, which was manufactured in larger numbers because of an innovative new way of making engines. Effectively, the Consul and Zephyr were the blueprint for all future family saloons. Some critics would ultimately see this as an indication that cars from then on would be undemanding, boring and built down to a price. A case of the customer simply accepting what they got, rather than demanding more.

This approach certainly served Ford well over the years, as they produced consistent best-sellers like the Cortina throughout the 60s and 70s. The lesson for BMC to learn was that having an understandable range of simple cars at the right price certainly helped sales and profitability. More important than that, though, the people employed at Ford were cleverer than anywhere else.

The concept of graduate recruitment, which seems commonplace now but was brand new in 1948, was at the heart of the change at what had been a stuffy and conventional company. Terence Beckett took advantage of the Ford's scheme in 1950 as he had the unusual combination of an economics degree and engineering qualifications. Ford were the only car company to offer a management training course, and Beckett took full advantage. In fact the course was cut short so that he could become the personal assistant to Sir Patrick Henessey, who ran Ford in Britain. For a time, Beckett kept an eye on the product and engineering side for his boss before being made styling manager. Then in 1955, he was put in charge of Product Planning. Here were two words, product and planning, that rarely shared the same sentence in British car manufacturing circles. Obviously it was another American idea, and highly appropriate that it should be given a run at Ford in Britain. In the face of much opposition by the engineering department in 1953, it would transform the way that cars were developed and lead to Ford's market domination for decades to come.

The reason for a planning strategy and a department to do this was pretty obvious when you looked around at what was going at our British-owned companies. These were run by autocrats who at times often seemed to be a nut and bolt short of a full engine. How else could you explain why Lord Nuffield drank his own urine in preference to introducing the Minor? Or Billy Rootes' offhand dismissal of the Beetle and Leonard Lord's ability to hold on to a grudge? Not to mention Sir John Black's preference for being towed around the factory grounds on skis at the first snowfall.

At a stroke, a planning department took the decision making process away from one bloke, usually with a knighthood or a peerage, who woke up one morning and decided that calling a car Mayflower, or maybe Atlantic, might be a good idea. There is an argument that having a committee stifled spontaneity and clever innovations, such as the Mini, and led to dull, worthy, so-called Dagenham Dustbins like the Cortina. The difference is that the Cortina made lots of money and the Mini never did. So however depressing it is to have planners and accountants cluttering up a car company, they can be a force for good, or at the very least survival. So how were the smaller, not so clever or profitable car companies surviving in the 1950s?

Standard were the smallest of the big six in Britain, although they had expanded during the war as John Black was an enthusiastic proponent of the shadow factory scheme that helped the country maintain production and win the war. He was knighted for that, but in 1944, before the war was over, Black was thinking of Standard's future and looking at Triumph. The receivers, though, had already approached William Lyons, who ran Jaguar, but he took one look at the books and didn't like what he saw. Black went to Lyons and proposed a partnership to take over Triumph. Lyons wasn't interested, so Black said he would buy it anyway and directly compete with Jaguar, which was neither a threat nor a promise as it turned out. Neither was it a good example of how to win friends and influence people. The new Triumph sports cars (essentially Bergerac's police car) looked clumsy next to Lyons' supple Jags, and the saloons obviously resembled the Mayflower, but bigger. On the Standard side of things, there was the Vanguard, whose lack of export success we have already poked fun at. Lucky, then, that his company built tractors.

Lucky is certainly the most appropriate word to use, as a series of extreme coincidences brought inventor Harry Ferguson and Black together. Ferguson's tractor design was unique because the implements for ploughing and all that were hydraulically moved, whereas previously it was all down to the farmer who had to manhandle them. Ferguson had briefly made the tractors with Ford in the States, but came back to Britain when the Northern Irishman came looking for a partner. Lord Nuffield wasn't convinced, although others within his company reckoned he had missed a golden opportunity. In desperation, Ferguson went to the Board of Trade, where Sir Stafford Cripps listened to the not unreasonable argument that more tractors meant more home-produced food so less imports. But it would also mean more exports of tractors, and all this would have been music to Cripps' ears. Ferguson asked for enough materials to make 200 tractors a day on the condition that Standard take on production. This was not favouritism but pragmatism, as the shadow factory adjacent to Standard was government property. Eventually, the tractors would use Standard car engines, and there was a 12-year manufacturing agreement which effectively guaranteed Standard's profitability. In the meantime, Ferguson had sold out to a Canadian company, Massey, to create Massey Ferguson. That company would eventually (in 1959) buy out the tractor side, leaving... well, leaving what exactly?

The one major obstacle in the way of progress was the slightly eccentric Sir John Black (I've already mentioned how, at the first snow of winter, he would be towed behind a Standard vehicle on a pair of skis). In 1953 he was becoming increasing erratic, one reason being a serious car crash when he was a passenger in a prototype Triumph sports car. That didn't stop Black from declaring himself fit a week later and leaving hospital. At the works Christmas do just weeks later, he did what every boss dreams of doing and said there were too many managers. But instead of sobering up next morning as we all would, he actually named who should stay and who should go. Brilliant. Obviously the Standard board didn't like it one bit. It took them until New Year's Day 1954 to get together and sack him. The entire board turned up at his house, and of course he had a butler who announced their presence. He asked why they were there, and they replied that they were there for his resignation. They even presented him with a letter to sign. So after 29 years as Standard's managing director, he left with £30K, a Bentley, access to a company Bungalow in Wales for holidays and the ultimate kick in the teeth: a Triumph Mayflower.

When Alick Dick took over as managing director, he was only 37 years old and the youngest boss in the industry, and he realised that he needed a partner to survive. He was related to Spencer Wilks at Rover, and they considered putting the two companies together to form the United Motors Corporation, or maybe Consolidated Motors as an upmarket rival to BMC. However, Rover had taken a close look at Standard's projected profits and they didn't make cheerful reading. Then talks began with Rootes about a possible R&S Holdings, but Standard found it unacceptable that the far larger Rootes Group would have dominated the combined board, so that plan was abandoned too. Standard were in serious trouble, but what about the others?

Well, Billy Rootes and his brother were still buying up businesses. Not only that, but they were also concentrating on foreign sales for growth and profit while all their rivals stayed at home. The adventurous Rootes brothers established factories in Canada and Australia. Billy even organised the first British Car Exhibition in New York in 1950. Meanwhile, they got on with snapping up old car marques like Singer in 1955 that had fallen on very hard times. This was the company at which Sir Billy had served his apprenticeship. Within a year, all the Singer models were discontinued, although the names survived intact to be used on other cars. So Singer as a manufacturer was no more, and Rootes turned the factory into a parts store.

Meanwhile, Rootes relied on the Hillman Minx as its main breadwinner, and gradually updated it. But the key was the adoption of one standard bodyshell in 1956 on to which they could begin sticking different badges. The larger models as represented by Humber didn't fare so well against the reliable Auntie Rover and the stylish and fast Jaguars, so profits were starting to slide. That was also happening at Vauxhall Motors, the only other American-owned car company in Britain.

Their losses could be explained by the fact that Vauxhall were investing in their future and were growing fast. Like Ford, they had a limited model line-up, and part of the reason was a single factory and body plant which meant they were limited on space. As a result, they had just three body styles and the engines were largely interchangeable. Their vehicles were also distinctive because of the influence of their American parent company. Vauxhalls looked like scaled-down Chevrolets, and the Victor was even exported to America to be sold through Pontiac dealers and went on to become Britain's best selling-model overseas. Keeping it simple, though, meant that profits per car were the highest in the industry at a remarkable £80 for a Vauxhall. Ford managed £45, BMC £35 and Standard just £30. Vauxhall's commercial vehicles business, Bedford, was equally strong, making more vans and lorries than cars.

BMC were also looking abroad to make more profits, becoming much more active not just in the business of exporting but also manufacturing on foreign soil. They were sending Completely Knocked Down (a bizarre term, abbreviated to CKD) car kits all over the world. By 1960, you could buy a reconstituted (Knocked Up?) BMC car in Argentina, Belgium, Ceylon, Colombia, Cuba, Eire, Egypt, Ghana, Holland, Hong Kong, India, Indonesia, Italy, Malaya, Mexico, New Zealand and the Philippines. Whereas completely manufactured cars were coming out of purpose-built factories in Australia, Canada, Rhodesia and South Africa. Sometimes these vehicles were identical to the UK models, although in some cases the steering wheel would be on the left. Occasionally they might also have different styling, more chrome, different lights or even an altered body, like the unique pick-ups for the Australian and Argentinian markets. Probably the most interesting thing about them, though, was the names, many of which sounded like long-lost colonial relatives. Morris Marshall and Austin Lancer were obviously military types, Morris Nomad never settled anywhere while Hindustan Ambassador was obviously going places in the diplomatic corp.

Actually, the Hindustan Ambassador is an interesting example of BMC's unwittingly creating India's very own people's car. The years following India's partition and the assassination of Gandhi were very uncertain, but Morris Motors came to an agreement with the Indian car manufacturer Hindustan Motors for them to import the Morris 10 as a kit. By 1949, they had moved on to the larger Morris Oxford, which was the same as Dad's second car, but it was badged as the Landmaster. The Morris Minor also found its way over, and it became known as the Baby Hindustan.

In 1957, Hindustan had moved on to the Series 3 Morris Oxford, which also turned out to be Dad's third car. It was tough and simple, so just as it managed to cope with the worst B roads in Britain, it could also survive the roughest of tracks in India. While sales in the UK were never that strong, demand on the sub-continent actually increased. This led to the wholesale purchase of the entire Morris Oxford production line. The "Amby" has become an icon in India, and proved its worth as the nation's taxi. It has remained in production for over 50 years, and has hardly changed, although the British engine has been replaced by a Japanese one. The Indian people's car always will be the Ambassador because it was sturdy, cheap to run and easy to fix. Qualities that we now take for granted in a modern car, but which were quickly forgotten as the 1950s became the 1960s. And it was about this time that my dad found himself in possession of a Vauxhall Wyvern.

After the peculiar Mayflower and a couple of dull but worthy Morris Oxfords, Dad bought himself a second-hand set of wheels that any Teddy Boy would have been happy to own. The Wyvern was pure early 50s Americana, being pre the silly fins era, with a bulbous body full of friendly curves but obviously built to a more handy British scale. There seemed to be a lot of chrome, and in the American manner, the gear stick was on the steering column.

I remember this car so clearly because it was the first car I ever drove. I was two at the time, and have the cine film to prove it. Obviously it was a special effects job, as Dad worked the pedals and I held onto the big plastic steering wheel. There was a bigger-engined model called the Velox, and also a really posh one with heaps more chrome called the Cresta. But Dad was happy enough with the Wyvern. It had loads of interesting details, from half-moon rear lights to long chrome inserts in the bonnet flutes (basically a groove in the bonnet) which had been a feature of the earliest Vauxhalls. Indeed that bonnet could be opened from the right or left hand side and be propped open like a grand piano or removed altogether. Clever.

I don't believe it ever let Dad down, although he eventually gave it away. My dad never sold a car, because he hated the whole process of people coming round to his house and kicking the tyres on his car and then offering some insultingly low amount for it. Even though my dad would go on to become a very successful businessman, the business of selling cars was something he never enjoyed. Especially when the person he gave the car to (a friend of a relative's aunt's son sort of person) complained that some of the tools were missing in his free car. Dad was still infuriated about it 40 years later, and it proved that he was right all along not to get involved in the grubby business of selling, or even giving cars away.

So if a Vauxhall Wyvern wasn't the future, just a flashy, chrome-laden diversion from the dull Austins and Morrises that dominated the austere motoring landscape of the 1950s, what cars were the British motor industry going to tempt my Dad with in the 1960s?

Still in the garage: After the Mayflower fell apart, in came a sturdy Morris Oxford which like the Mayflower was painted very black.

Births
1954 Fairthorpe
1954 Kieft
1954 Rodley
1954 Swallow

Deaths
1954 Healey
1954 Jowett
1954 Sunbeam-Talbot
1955 Allard

New Arrivals
1954 Skoda

In the Car Park
In this Chapter you will have come across some of the following vehicles...

Some models had started to look rather similar. Left is a Riley Pathfinder, right a Wolseley 4/44 with an MG Magnette on the next page looking rather similar of course, see if you can spot it.

Second right is the Wolseley 1500, bottom left a Riley 1.5 then an Austin Cambridge which actually looked quite different from Dad's Morry Oxford, which is in the garage. The later Oxford is next left which later went to India and became the Hindustan Ambassador. BMC's new Farina styled models included the Riley 4/72 on the right and the Morris Oxford version, left. Meanwhile Vauxhall's top of the range Cresta on the right looked very American while the Ford Popular at the bottom just looked very old.

6 Dockers, Hatches and a clever bloke called Colin 1955-60

(although I'm sure we go back to the 40s at some point in this chapter)

In the garage: There is actually a garage and a car to go inside it. Dad's first Morris Oxford can certainly fit inside, but as the vehicle outhouse belongs to an Edwardian house it is incredibly narrow. Getting out becomes easier as the cars change over the years.

According to Mum, living in the 1950s really wasn't that different from the 40s, or the 30s for that matter. In many ways, the post-war rationing was worse than the wartime rationing, and there was the Korean war and the cold war and then in the '60s only the Cuban missile crisis to look forward to. Essentially, it was a bit monochrome and bleak back then, and so were the cars. BMC made very conventional vehicles and so did Ford and Standard and everyone else. The big companies knew what the buying public wanted (something that ideally started most mornings and ran on petrol) and delivered it wholesale. There were few complaints. Anyway, the demand for cars outstripped supply, which explains why really quite rubbish cars like the Mayflower sold at all.

Indeed, daring to be different could have serious consequences. In 1946 there was precious little that was really new, or even needed to be new. Simply reintroducing the pre-war range as Austin and Morris did was greeted with relief rather than disappointment. However, in Yorkshire, two brothers, Benjamin and William Jowett, had been thinking rather differently. After specialising in simple, sensible and durable cars before the war, they stunned the whole world with their Javelin.

Here was a saloon car which showcased the latest automotive engineering innovations. That meant the suspension and engine were part of the car and not bolted to a separate chassis, making the whole thing lighter. Not only that, but the suspension and steering were state-of-the-art to make the handling sharp, while the smooth bodywork was very aerodynamic and the average cruising speed a substantial 80mph. The unique engine (it was a flat four, meaning that it was not unlike the VW Beetle engine, though cooled by water rather than air, if that's not too confusing) was very powerful for its size. Indeed, a convertible version called the Jupiter had a distinguished racing career.

The painful reality, however, was that Jowett should have stuck to making their Bradford van, a basic commercial vehicle whose considerable profits underwrote their business in the post-war years. Sadly, they had been a bit too ambitious, and the Javelin was a disaster. The engine broke its crankshaft occasionally, which is as serious as it gets in major mechanical failure terms. Also, Jowett's decision on cost-cutting grounds to fit its own gearbox wasn't too clever, as it proved unreliable. As demand plummeted, vehicle bodies were still being made at the same rate by an outside contractor. These piled up around the works in Bradford, which at one point even included Bradford City football ground. Here was one of the best new cars launched anywhere at that time, let down by lack of development and planning and the fact that Jowett tried to be far too clever by half. Certainly there was a demand for different and especially sporty cars, which some smaller manufacturers satisfied. Before we get to them, though, let's see how the big boys were viewing the future.

At Standard Triumph they had problems because the company that made its bodies was bought by BMC. Leonard Lord subsequently told Standard to clear off, but the company were contractually obliged to build the Standard 8. This was an ugly runt of car, which was their alternative to the Morris Minor, but with none of the charm. Here was a car that had to be replaced as a matter of some urgency.

The problem was that it would now have to use body parts made at different factories. So instead of bolting all the mechanical bits to the body, like the Jowett Javelin, it was decided to stick with the old technology and use a metal chassis so that the body could be built around that. Indeed, this also meant that the car could easily be assembled in developing countries. Independent suspension, which meant a smoother and more stable ride, was intended as part of the package and was usually only part of expensive rather than budget cars. Also a chance remark by one of the managers that it would be interesting to have the tight turning circle of a London taxi meant that, in the future, it wasn't only cabbies who would be able to do unannounced U-turns right in front of you. It was no wonder, then, that this new model's code name was Zobo. Not an entirely random choice, as it is defined as a Tibetan pack animal of indeterminate sex – a cross between a bull and a cow.

It could have ended up looking like a Zobo, too, when the man responsible for Standard's uninspired design for the last 30 years left in a huff (A huff is not a make a car but a very old Marx Brothers joke). This sudden departure meant there was a vacancy for a stylist. While Standard were wondering what to do, a freelance designer, Raymond Flower, turned up at the factory gates asking to buy a handful of chassis and engines for the Frisky Sport, a tiny open-topped car intended for what must have been the miniscule Egyptian market. Flower didn't get the job, but Standard were intrigued, not least because the bodywork of the car had not yet been designed, but Flower said it would all be ready in three months. Management effectively challenged Flower to do the same for them, giving him loads of parts from the Triumph TR3 sports car, and they chose a design from a sketchbook.

True to his word, Flower returned with a complete car within three months and for just £3,000. Standard did some detective work, which included talking to the lorry driver who delivered the car, and found that the Italian company Vignale in Turin had produced it, but more specifically that the stylist concerned was Giovanni Michelotti.

Standard acted fast and signed up the Italian company and asked them to do the impossible and cheer up the fading Vanguard, producing the Vignale Vanguard. When Michelotti left Vignale, Standard gave him a retainer to design all future Triumphs. Much more importantly, he was required to put a pretty body on top of the Zobo, which wasn't just going to be a saloon, but a whole range of vehicles. A two-door coupe, saloon, estate, convertible and van were all part of the line-up. At the end of 1957 the first prototype was delivered to the factory at Canley and managing director Alick Dick agreed with the rest of his management team that it was brilliant. As it was near to Christmas, they did the obvious thing and went to the works canteen where they got drunk. Now that's what I call a works canteen – one where you can buy a beer or two.

Standard were certainly happy and flushed with cash after selling off their tractor interests, and went on a spending spree buying up body pressing plants, tool makers and other companies to help secure their future. There was still one important decision to make, though, and that was what to call Zobo. Obviously it couldn't be called Zobo, could it? Well yes, they went one better and chose Torch. The Standard Torch anyone? Even in the late 1950s, a torch wasn't a particularly high-tech instrument, and that was something that Alick Dick must have been concerned about. He went to a management meeting one morning and said, "I've been on my boat over the weekend. It's called the Herald, so we'll call the new car that." This wasn't the only significant decision that was made, because the Herald would be badged as a Triumph. Effectively, the Standard name was being phased out and the future of the company now depended on one model: the Triumph Herald.

Michelotti had come up with a completely fresh design that looked sharp and modern and may have had fins like American cars but they were much more subtle. The entire front end hinged forward, giving an amazing amount of access to the engine. It was good to drive, economical and easy to maintain – the perfect combination in a small family car at the time. Unveiled the same year as the Mini, 1959, it is tempting to compare the two, but that would be to overlook one of BMC's most significant models in the hatchbacked shape of the Austin A40, which had arrived in 1958. Yes, you read correctly – a hatchback... well, a basic hatchback shape anyway, because the true hatchback would not arrive for another year. Like Standard, BMC had realised that in order to break away from the dull models they had been serving up in the 50s, they needed some Italian flair.

Now the A40 Farina may have looked simple, uncluttered and smart on the outside, but otherwise it was BMC business as usual, with an engine from an A35, and inside, instrumentation from that model too. The outside was pure Italian and the design house involved was Pinin Farina, hence the model's name. It pioneered the two-box shape, with a small one at the front for the engine and a big one for both the people and their luggage, and no boxy boot. Large doors meant that it was easy to get in and out of. The original saloon had a tailgate that opened downwards from waist height, while the rear seats could be folded back to give almost estate-car load capacity. In 1959, the Countryman model was a true estate car as the lower tailgate not only dropped down, but the upper one that incorporated the rear window could be lifted up. The A40 Farina symbolised a new era for BMC, and it meant that Pinin Farina would get a decade's-worth of work from them.

Here was a truly groundbreaking car, and obviously 20 years ahead of its time. The Farina sold in decent numbers, some 340,000 over the next nine years, but it was never seen as a particularly important car at the time. Oddly enough, neither was the Mini when it arrived, which may come as something of a surprise. Indeed, it was the Triumph Herald that took most of the attention, especially among the opinion-forming journalists of the day, who reckoned that it was the greater technical leap forward.

Before we get anywhere near the Mini, one man to look to for substantial technical leaps forward was Anthony Colin Bruce Chapman, who managed to avoid the mistakes made by Jowett. Colin was a very clever bloke who had left University College London in 1948 with an engineering degree and had already put that knowledge to automotive effect. Having attempted to earn some extra money to subsidise his student lifestyle by buying and selling cars, he found himself stuck with a 1930s Austin Seven. The Seven had been a tremendously popular small car, which was simple and easy to work on, so Chapman decided to strip off the saloon bodywork and replace it with something more interesting. Using aircraft construction methods, he combined plywood and aluminium to make a strong but lightweight body. Once it was complete, he registered the new vehicle as a Lotus, named after his girlfriend Hazel Williams (the future Mrs Chapman), whom he referred to as his Lotus Blossom.

A new car dynasty has been born, although Lotus Engineering was not fully established until 1952, when he set up shop in some stables behind his father's pub, the Railway Hotel in Tottenham, north London. The output was largely cars for club racers, who fitted the engine of their choice to the bodywork and suspension that Chapman supplied. His cars started to dominate the sport, so that he was able to leave his full-time job (he was an architectural engineer) and set up Team Lotus to go racing. The details and effect of that are dealt with elsewhere. His one true road car, which of course was also very handy on the track, was the Seven.

There wasn't very much of a car apart from four wheels and some aluminium bodywork – no doors, and just motorbike mudguards over the wheels. It was the car that, many years later, Patrick McGoohan would be seen driving during the opening titles of The Prisoner TV series. He was not a number, he was a free man of course, unless the other characters were calling him number six. Yet the Seven helped establish Lotus as a serious car builder, even if the Seven was regularly sold in kit form, which meant that the buyer was the real builder. With the hood up, or what passed for a hood, getting in and out was virtually impossible. It was uncomfortable, impractical, but utterly brilliant to drive. Encapsulated in one car was Chapman's complete car-building philosophy, which was less weight equals more: more performance and faster responses. It also meant that the customer did most of the work so that Chapman could make more profit.

In fact the Seven was to prove something of an embarrassment to Chapman, as it refused to fade away and interfered with his ambition to drive the company upmarket. That was the correct strategy, as there was more money to be made that way, and Chapman soon showed his intentions with the beautiful Lotus Elite in 1959. This small sports car with a fixed roof was a world first – a car with a glass fibre (plastic) structure which comprised the floor, body and centre section to which the doors, boot and bonnet were then bolted. The Elite drove like a dream and had great brakes, and its very aerodynamic shape meant that it used little petrol. The Elite might have looked perfect, but the reality was a bit different, as the noise generated in the plastic shell would send the driver and passenger mad. They would then begin to overheat because of the marginal ventilation, and there was no chance of cooling down because the shape of the door glass meant the windows could not be wound down. On top of that, the quality, whether factory- or customer-built, was never that good. For similar money, it was possible to buy a proper factory-built sports car by Jaguar. Even though the Elite was not cheap, Chapman reckoned that he had lost at least £100 a car. He was, though, a fast learner. He had to be.

No such dramas at Morgan. The fact that they continued to make staunchly traditional sports cars from bits of wood and metal had a universal appeal. They had paid attention to the Government's pleas to export, and found eager customers in both America and France. A good job too, because at home, the company struggled as the choice of more contemporary sports cars suggested that the car-buying public were tiring of the quaintly old fashioned cars. When the founder died in 1959 it was the end of an era. His son Peter Morgan took over, but the outlook seemed pretty bleak. However, at least they were still in business. Unlike Allard.

Competing against Jaguar was always a bad idea, as small-scale sports car manufacturer Allard found out. Its hand-built aggressive looking cars proved very popular in America, and the designer, Sydney Allard, even won the 1952 Monte Carlo Rally at the wheel of his own car. It was, though, a tough business, and Allard were just one of the small manufacturers who broke down.

By contrast, Daimler were Britain's oldest manufacturer, and far from small, having massive resources. So their survival never really looked in doubt. Established in 1893, they imported German cars at first, before making their own luxurious models and being adopted by the Royal Family as their official vehicle of choice (obviously the German connection helped there). Even though Daimler were bought out in 1910 by BSA, makers of motorbikes and rifles, the marque still had huge respect. And they didn't just make posh cars. They engineered technically advanced ones, too, having developed the semi-automatic gearbox, which meant that the driver simply pressed the accelerator to move off. That was clever, but the management team became less so in the 1940s. Sir Bernard Docker, whose father, Dudley, had created the whole BSA group, first became chairman of BSA, then of Daimler. Docker's dying father made sure that Bernard was appointed as the managing director of BSA. In doing so, he unwittingly initiated a soap opera that would make the company a laughing stock and bring about Daimler's long-term demise as an independent car maker.

In the brave new post-war world, Daimler simply had too many models, that were expensive to build and expensive to buy. It didn't help that purchase tax was raised to a swingeing 66.6 per cent (presumably by the devil), so the only answer was to export the majority of production. But things at home weren't going well. Even though they made vehicles that were fit for royalty, a wedding present Daimler for the future Queen Elizabeth developed a gearbox fault. That is thought have resulted in the Duke of Edinburgh's ordering a Rolls-Royce Phantom in 1950. So Daimler's core market was now under threat. Indeed their best-seller in the 1950s was called the Conquest, a small, dull, four-door saloon which, at over £1,000, was still more than twice the price of a more modestly badged alternative. Best-seller is a relative term, of course, as only 9,000 found the upper-middle-class homes of retired colonels from 1953 to 1958, so it was easy to overlook. Maybe that's why Sir Bernard Docker felt the need to let his wife design a Daimler or two. He even went to the bother of installing a drawing board in their Mayfair home.

Docker married Norah Collins, whose biggest claim to fame was that Sir

Bernard was her third millionaire husband, although exactly what attracted her to Bernard remains a mystery. Being an ex-dancing girl put question marks over her social standing at the time, but marrying Docker instantly made her a Lady. Sir Bernard also made her a director of Hooper, a famous coachbuilder that had become part of BSA. Lady Docker later recalled that she was "ashamed to discover, both at home and abroad, the superb Daimler was in danger of becoming a relic". She realised that Daimler needed to sell to buyers other than the aristocracy and fabulously wealthy, and needed to strike a chord with the motoring masses, but went about it in a very odd way. According to Norah, putting the marque back on the international map required a huge amount of panache and gold plate.

Now Bernard Docker certainly loved attention, and had built himself a huge open-topped sports car. Nicknamed the Green Goddess, it was the most expensive car at the 1948 Motor Show at Earls Court, with a price tag of £7001. Obviously Norah had to better that. Creating "The Gold Car" involved Hooper's taking the Limousine they had designed and adding an alarming amount of what is currently known as bling. The deep black paintwork had the side panels liberally covered in gold stars, while the silver chrome was replaced with gold plate and the interior was trimmed in golden camphor wood and gold brocade. It is easy to dismiss this as an exercise in poor taste and the desecration of Britain's best-known motoring name. However, Lady Docker had achieved what had once seemed to be impossible: she got everyone talking about Daimler, including my mum and dad. "We bring glamour and happiness into drab lives. The working class loves everything I do," she said. And she wasn't wrong.

Decades after the publicity stunt, my mother, who knew nothing about cars and never even learned to drive, would put the name Docker and Daimler in the same sentence. Dad used to talk quite often about the cars at the Motor Shows because he was actually there to see them in the precious metal. In the grey 1950s, Lady Docker and her cars were indeed a relief from the monotony of real life. Yes, people sniggered a bit, but they paid attention, which makes Norah a public relations genius. Trouble is, Daimler the company – and that means Sir Bernard – could not turn all this attention into sales. In one respect, this didn't matter as the BSA group continued to make healthy profits, so Norah kept on designing show-stopping Daimlers.

In 1952, a two-door Daimler was painted pale grey and powder blue, which certainly caught the eye. But it was the interior which made motor showgoers do a double take. Matched lizard skins, dyed grey-blue, from the seats to the steering wheel. Lovely. For 1953, the so-called Silver Flash had an eye-catching body and a questionable interior combination of black leather and red crocodile. Nora's last car was the Golden Zebra, which looked similar to the Silver Flash, but was longer and wider and cost £12,000 to build. Finished in ivory white, with gold-plated trimmings of course, it surpassed itself when it came to rare-breed interiors with zebra skin on the seats and a dashboard made of ivory. When asked why she chose zebra, Lady Docker replied: "Because mink is too hot to sit on."

Clearly, Lady Norah was one of the most quotable women who ever lived, but her extravagant lifestyle was becoming an easy target for the BSA board. Her brilliant idea of building a gold-themed showroom in Paris with one of her show cars as the centrepiece was the beginning of the end. Obviously she needed a dress to match, hence the bill for a gold-plated dress and mink-trimmed hat costing £20,000 that was charged to BSA. They objected, so to get more directors on her side, she managed to get her brother-in-law appointed to the board. But the Dockers had gone too far, and they were voted out of the company for good. Sir Bernard went and ordered a Rolls-Royce and Lady Norah bought a Bentley, claiming that she had always preferred them anyway. One of the most colourful episodes and motoring dynasties came to end. The Emperor and Empress had fiddled about whilst Daimler struggled.

They retired to the tax haven Jersey and survived by selling Lady Docker's jewellery and yacht while the irrepressible Norah took pot shots at her new neighbours, "They're the most frightfully boring, dreadful people that have ever been born." Sadly we would not see her like again in the British car Industry. There was palpable relief at BSA, of course, and they could get on with the business of not just promoting their cars, but actually selling them. This meant getting rid of another related company called Lanchester that sold even fewer cars than Daimler. The range of cars was reduced, automatic gearboxes offered for the first time and exciting new models like the Daimler Dart introduced.

Here was a sports car that could match any Jaguar for performance with its superb engine. But unlike a Jaguar, it was a frighteningly ugly open-topped car that was made of plastic. No wonder it never sold, and anyway, the American Dodge car company objected to the name Dart on the reasonable grounds that they already owned it. So it became the SP250, not because it could do 250mph, but for the more pedestrian reason that it was the internal company code name for the car. Despite being great to drive, the SP250 came to symbolise a company that couldn't get very much right. It had been aimed at Americans, but they recoiled in horror at the shape (deep sea Guppy), and the slight waywardness of its handling. So more were sold in the UK, and indeed the British police adopted it as their high-speed pursuit vehicle of choice. Although the BSA group made profits, Daimler didn't. But it had already caught the eye of the boss of Jaguar, Sir William Lyons.

Lyons wasn't drawn to Daimler because he thought he could make the SP250 look pretty. What he saw was a prestigious brand name, a million square feet of factory space and a skilled workforce. Anything else was a bonus. So when the very cordial negotiations between Sir William and BSA's Jack Sangster were over, a £10,000 discrepancy was discovered by a diligent bean counter. It was settled in a gloriously old-fashioned manner: on the toss of a coin. Sir

William won. Daimlers would never be the same again, and ultimately would become upmarket Jaguars with different badges and more chrome. For the moment, though, it was 1960 and the future looked bright for Jaguar and indeed for most manufacturers except for Standard. 1960 was a good year, too, with the arrival of a bundle of joy announced by the family doctor with the words: "Here's a little Adam Faith for you, Mrs Ruppert." Luckily I wasn't christened either Adam or Faith, or subjected to any of that cheery late 50s pop. It was 1960, my dad still had a Vauxhall Wyvern, while the Mini had been on sale for nine months and it wasn't doing very well.

Still in the garage: There's a replacement Morris Oxford which could only be one colour, black. It is followed by the rather less stuffy Vauxhall Wyvern. That's a boon when it comes to dealing with the narrow garage. That's because the front seat is a big bench thing like a sofa, and with no gear lever in the way, you can just slide over to either side. Easy.

Births
1956 Astra
1956 Berkeley
1956 Metropolitan
1956 Opperman
1956 Powerdrive
1956 Tourette
1957 Peerless
1957 Scootacar
1958 Britannia
1958 Elva
1958 Falcon
1958 Frisky

1958 Gill
1958 Ginetta
1958 Tornado
1958 TVR
1959 Gilbern

Deaths
1955 Rodley
1955 Swallow
1956 HRG
1956 Kieft
1956 Lanchester
1957 Dellow
1957 Tourette
1958 Frazer-Nash
1958 Gill
1959 Frisky
1959 Opperman
1960 Astra
1960 Britannia
1960 Paramount

New Arrivals
1959 Volvo
1960 Ferrari

In the Car Park

In this Chapter you will have come across some of the following vehicles and personalities...

Top left the rather advanced Jowett Javelin and on the right, a basic and rather ugly and crude Standard 8. Second row left is designer Michelotti's makeover of the Standard Vanguard to create the Vignale, but the Triumph Herald was all his and available in saloon, convertible and estate form. Bottom row the Austin A40 Farina is the first hatchback, then there is Colin Chapman. Next to him is the Daimler Conquest,

Top of the page is the boring Daimler Regency and below that a Lady Docker inspired Golden Zebra. Chapman's Lotus Elite and Seven are together and below them with two happy coppers in a Daimler SP250 At the bottom is the unchanging Morgan.

7 Minis, Imps, Anglias and a boxy Viva. 1960–1963

In the garage: It's the Wyvern, but one of those new Minis is going to turn up because it belongs to Uncle Charles and he and Aunt Florence live in the same house as we do, which is great.

Mini, the British people's car. The Mini stayed in production for 40 years, and more than 5 million were made. The Mini changed the way that cars were designed forever. The Mini dominated motor sport. The Mini even had its own feature film with top billing over Michael Caine. The Mini may have had celebrity owners from Peter Sellers and Spike Milligan to Clint Eastwood, but it was always our car. Commercially though, the Mini was a complete disaster.

As was the case with so many British families, our motoring lives were inextricably linked to the little car. Uncle Charles was an early adopter, me and my sister learned to drive in one, Dad bought a Mini Clubman in the 70s, and since 1979, I've never not owned one. The Mini story is an endlessly fascinating one. You could actually write a book about the Mini, and actually I'm one of the many hundreds who have. So there's no point. Here's what you need to know in seven bite-sized chunks.

1.The Mini was born of necessity. Sir Leonard Lord, that blunt leader of BMC, was upset. "God damn these bloody awful bubble cars. We must drive them out of the streets by designing a proper miniature car." That quote is attributed to Lord in March 1957, and just two and a half years later he would have a proper miniature car to present to the world. At the time, though, these were mostly German cars like Messerschmitts and BMW's Isetta, which really did look like a bubble on wheels. November 1956 saw the Suez crisis, which erupted when Egypt's President Nasser closed the canal of that name, and Syria cut the main oil pipeline that crossed their country. The crisis ushered in petrol rationing, and it really looked as though this dire situation would continue indefinitely. Not surprisingly, the British motorist (though not my own staunchly patriotic family) put their faith in the economical, motorcycle-engined, three- and four- wheeled bubbles. But Lord believed that a small and economical car need not be cramped and crude. His requirements were that this new BMC small car be smaller than any existing product and that it be introduced at the earliest possible opportunity.

2. Issigonis was a genius. We know this already because he single-handedly designed the brilliant Morris Minor. He joined BMC in 1955, and Lord had envisaged Issigonis devoting himself to advanced product design. That meant thinking outside of the box, before that terrible phrase had ever been coined. He was therefore the perfect designer for this project. Issigonis constrained himself even more by mentally drawing a rectangular box measuring 120 inches (3,048mm) in length by 48 inches (1,219mm) wide and high. He is reputed to have taken four chairs and drawn a chalk outline around them. He then decided that 80 per cent of the available space should be for the occupants and their luggage, which resulted in a passenger compartment of just 102 inches (2,591mm). Out of that tight brief came several brilliant solutions that made the Mini unique. First of all, the wheels were shrunk to an unusually small 10 inches (254mm) so that they did not intrude into the cabin. The suspension had to be rethought to fit it into such a small space. That left just 18 inches (457mm) to fit the engine. Issigonis's lateral thinking led to turning the engine around by 45 degrees. This meant that the gearbox, which was usually attached to the end of the engine, would have stuck out of one side of the bodywork and swiped pedestrians off the pavement. So his brilliant idea was to put that gearbox underneath the engine, as part of the engine, so that they shared the same oil. Problem solved.

3.The Mini was never styled. With all the mechanical problems solved, Issigonis could get on with the business of designing the bodywork, which from bumper to bumper was to be a mere 120 inches (3,048mm). Actually, the Mini was not so much styled as allowed to evolve around the mechanical components. Indeed Issigonis is quoted as saying: "Styling is designing for obsolescence." He was proved right when the Clubman, a later update to the Mini which involved grafting on a square nose, became dated in a decade and had to be dropped, while the original design soldiered on for another 20 years. Commenting years later, Issigonis put it perfectly: "The Mini was never meant to be styled. It is a function thing... A car should take its shape entirely from the engineering that goes into it... The thing that satisfied me most was that it looked like no other car." That was certainly true. Here was a shape which was the smallest, simplest and most practical way of accommodating four people. The rounded panels looked natural, while the seams that ran proud of the bodywork were part of making the Mini easier to build and therefore cheaper. Like the Austin A40, it was a simple two-box shape, but sadly with no rear hatch (that would come later, and from Italy). Finally, just like when he was finishing the Morris Minor, Issigonis took a few steps back and decided to increase the width by 2 inches (51mm). Firstly because it looked right, and secondly to add just a bit more shoulder room. Unlike the Minor, though, this did not require any spacing plates or obvious joins.

4. The Mini didn't get off to a great start. You could be forgiven for thinking that the Mini was an instant hit and saved the world, but it didn't. BMC brought the little car out in record time – just four months from Lord's orders to a wooden mock-up. By October 1957, two prototypes were ready for the road, and in July 1958, Lord was able to take a test drive and then tell Issigonis to get it in production within 12 months ("make the bloody thing"), which he did. Even by modern standards, that would be super quick and the first two prototypes were called orange boxes because they were painted in bright colours and thrashed around an airfield to find out their weak spots. Trouble is, the long hot and dry summer of 1959 meant that the testers missed one fatal flaw: water. BMC could not believe what they were hearing from customers who had been subjected to an unwelcome footbath. The combination of water and carpets produced a soggy, musty and distinctly uncomfortable environment. All sorts of bizarre theories were touted to explain the unusual weather conditions inside the new car. They eventually discovered that the flaw was the floor. A floor pressing overlapped the wrong way. That could be fixed, as could plenty of other niggles. Again, the Mini had its own microclimate as air was supposed to circulate through the sliding window, but it slammed shut. A locking window button was the answer, although more importantly adding a fresh air heater to the options list was also a cure. However, those window catches would work loose and chatter, so they had to be redesigned. Also, the exhaust fractured because the engine moved around too much, so a thicker pipe and stabilizing bar on the engine all helped. Then the rear brakes would stick on, but a new heavy-duty spring soon stopped that. So while none of these were really serious problems, they did nothing for customer confidence. But hey, if it's cheap enough...

5. The Mini was far too cheap. It cost just £497. At the time, the cheapest car in the country was a Ford Popular at £419, which wasn't exactly a bargain. That was an ancient design with a pre-war engine and a three-speed gearbox, and it looked like something your great, great granddad would drive. Yet the Mini was being priced to compete directly with it. Not only that, but the Mini also undercut the older and less sophisticated offerings from BMC, by being £41 cheaper than an Austin A35, essentially the model it was set to replace, and the Minor by a £93. Never mind pricing the bubble cars off the road – it made popular foreign imports look incredibly pricey. The equally small, but not so cleverly packaged, Fiat 600 cost £116 more, while the Renault Dauphine and Volkswagen Beetle were a whopping £219 more. Obviously BMC were more concerned about shifting Minis in high volumes than about making money. We know this because those clever people at Ford couldn't quite believe how cheap the Mini was, so they bought one, took it to pieces and costed every part. Ford calculated that BMC were losing £30 a car. If they had panicked, then the all-new Ford Anglia that arrived at roughly the same time could have been priced much closer. Instead, Ford had the confidence to make it a clear £97 more expensive. They knew their buyers and what they expected from a Ford. BMC didn't.

6. BMC had no idea who would buy the Mini. Issigonis rightly saw it as a people's car – something that the worker could park outside his council house and use to get to work and go on holiday in. Sadly, the complex mechanicals frightened them, and the teething problems detailed above didn't help their confidence. As a second car for the middle classes, or even aspirant first-car buyers, small meant cheap, which of course it was. The working class still bought their Fords and the middle classes stuck to Morris Minors and Wolseleys. My Uncle Charles, though, bought a brand new Mini in 1962, and he fitted Issigonis's profile perfectly, working at the docks for the Port of London Authority. He was attracted by the very low price and the fact that Auntie Flo was comfy and their niece and nephew could sit comfortably in the back. The technical cleverness, the style, or the fact that there was an Austin, rather than a Morris badge on the back, never mattered to Uncle Charlie, or anyone else. Indeed it identified further problems at BMC.

7. The Mini had too many names. When the Mini was launched on the August 26,1959, customers could choose between an Austin Se7en or Morris Mini-Minor. The Seven, or Se7en as BMC wrote but never actually badged it, was meant to conjure up an image of Austin's fantastically successful small car from the 1920s and 30s. Mini-Minor was meant to piggyback on the success of the Morris Minor. Actually, the Austin Mini might have been called the Austin Newmarket, as the company had a policy of using southern counties and towns to brand their cars. The trouble was that two names meant two distinct and expensive advertising campaigns, the Mini-Minor being "Wizardry on Wheels!" while the Se7en was "A new breed of small car!" So all they had in common was the exclamation mark. Even madder, though, was the fact that the cars could be sold in different showrooms. Many towns could have both a Morris and Austin franchise who were effectively in competition with each other, yet offering identical vehicles. Plus, there were also Wolseley and Riley versions badged as the Hornet and Elf respectively.

So the Mini still became a sales success, if not a profitable one, in spite of the massive mistakes that were made. It certainly helped that the Mini was great to drive, like a little sports car, and in turn it was adopted by racing drivers of the day, which led to the Cooper, although that is a story for later. Never mind about Austin or Morris, simply putting the name of a Formula One world championship winning car on it made all the difference. So Minis were adopted by the beautiful people of the time, and the middle classes finally realised that here was a great value car. Companies made fortunes from selling add-on accessories and unique parts. It seems that everyone had fun and made money except BMC. This fact was not lost on other manufacturers, which led to the saying "Mini cars make mini profits". It still holds true today unless you are BMW, highly profitable makers of the new MINI. Even when BMC had the opportunity to charge more with the Riley Elf and Wolseley Hornet, they blew it yet again. It wasn't just extra chrome, different badges and some bits of wood that made these models different; they had major body surgery too.

The clean, cute and functional bodywork was compromised by having a boot tacked on to the back, while at the front, a more traditional, old fashioned grille and a couple of moustache-like side pieces appeared. Lift the bonnet and the grille went with it. Now getting your head underneath a Mini bonnet is a challenge at the best of times, and suddenly there was a large chrome grille to gash your scalp on. At the back were little fins that in 1961 were going out of fashion. The intention was to add authority to the rear end and provide a better frame for a boot lid that was now hinged at the top. All that work meant there was less than 10 per cent more space. Also, the original Mini had a hinged rear number plate which hung down if the boot was overloaded. However, these ponced-up pseudo Minis had the plate screwed in place, so instantly you had a less practical car. It was also harder to park as that bigger rear end added a massive 8.5 inches (216mm) to the overall length. Here was a prematurely aged Mini that looked as though it was ready to collect its pension. It looks all very retro cool now, and has been a favourite classic in Japan for that very reason. At the time, it was aimed at the more affluent buyer, and in some areas this worked. But going to all that trouble was very expensive, and these Mini Limos sold in tiny numbers. It was an utterly pointless exercise in design excess that must have made Issigonis feel ill with embarrassment.

Much better variations in the Mini theme, and offering even more opportunities for profit, were the commercial variants. Leonard Lord had made good money out of the van and pick-up markets especially as the Morris Minor variants sold 325,000, so he wasted no time in getting the Mini van into the showrooms. It had zero specification – even the rear-view mirror was an option. Obviously tradesman loved them, but it was attractive to private buyers like my Uncle Charles. He liked the idea that it cost just £360 compared to the saloon's £497. The difference was the Purchase Tax, which was not payable on commercial vehicles. All Uncle Charles had to do was refrain from cutting windows in the rear side panels and keep his top speed down to 30mph, except on the new M1 where he could speed up to 40mph. That way it would qualify as a commercial for tax purposes. Auntie Flo was having none of that, though. There might have been plenty of room for the shopping, but a boomy old van... and where would her niece and nephew sit? Well, there was an after-market kit for rear seats, but that wasn't point. I remember talking to my brother-in-law, Jimmy, who knew a lot of mods in the 60s Those were the ones who would stay up all night and wear the sharpest of suits, and not all of them would ride scooters. In fact they rather took to Mini vans, regarding them as modern and smart. Oh yes, and they had a useful amount of load space for a dead Lambretta, or just to crash out in after a hectic weekend in Brighton. For a journey down to the coast, it was certainly a lot less draughty and more reliable than an Italian scooter. It wasn't just mods who loved Mini vans – so did the Post Office, the Police and AA patrolmen, not least because they finally got a proper weatherproof car instead of an uncomfortable motorcycle-and-sidecar combination.

Having stretched the Mini a bit to make a van, and also a pick-up, the logical next step was to fit windows and rear seats to create a Mini estate. The Austin version was called the Countryman and the Morris was a Traveller. The front was standard Austin or Morris Mini, but the rear had extensive exterior woodwork which the BMC marketing department had deemed necessary to cultivate an upmarket image. This was an extravagance that Issigonis was opposed to, but they refused his request to have it removed. This mock Tudor beam work did serve to connect the models with other BMC estates, principally the Morris Minor Traveller. The difference was that Minor Traveller actually needed the wood to hold the rear of the car together. For the Mini, though, it was purely decorative, the timber being simply glued on. Maybe to keep Issigonis happy BMC, offered an all-steel alternative which saved the buyer £19 and quite a few planks of wood. So here was a complete and very impressive range of vehicles which were sadly were never going to make a profit.

It was hardly surprising that Ford weren't keen on making a direct rival to the Mini and waited until the mid-70s to bring in the Fiesta. Vauxhall had their own plans for something more conventional. Standard Triumph believed that the Herald was as small as they wanted to get. So who in their right minds would even consider going into the small car market? That would be the Rootes Group.

To be fair, their decision to go into the bubble- car-bashing business was born before the Mini orange crates were even nailed together. In 1955, two clever development engineers were given a brief to look into the small car market and later on come up with a vehicle that could do 60mph and 60mpg while carrying two adults and two children. Given the unattractive code name of "The Slug", probably because it had a tiny and crude small engine that was located where the boot usually is, it must have struggled to get the car to 6mph let alone 60mph. However, the Slug fulfilled the economy criteria and was presented to Sir Billy Rootes in 1957. He hated it on sight, refusing to even ride in it, but the basic principle was accepted. It needed a better engine, and a lighter, aluminium one was located and installed along with much more sophisticated suspension. Even though it was a much better package, the Slug, which then became known as the rather more appealing Apex did not get the all-important thumbs-up.

Building an all-new car that was expected to sell in hundreds of thousands required lots of investment and ideally a new factory. With this in mind, Rootes had bought lots of land around Coventry near their existing plant with the express intention of developing it. Planning permission was always denied as government policy had remained unchanged since the 1940s: build new factories in deprived areas. Companies that did this were rewarded with all sorts of grants and incentives. So Rootes had no alternative but to establish a new factory at Linwood, near Paisley in Scotland, just eight miles from Glasgow. This location was also right next to a company called Pressed Steel, which already made bodies for Rover, Volvo and BMC Commercial vehicles. In theory, it made some sense, and the official announcement came in 1960 that Rootes would build 150,000 small cars in Scotland and export most of them. The government loaned the company £10,000,000 to make it all happen.

Progress was slow, and the Hillman Imp, as it was finally christened, was introduced in May 1963. Unlike the Mini, which had used an old engine, the Imp was completely new, with crisp styling, lively and economical performance with a clever innovation on the saloon that allowed the rear window to be lifted up and the rear seat folded forward. Yes, the Imp was a hatchback too. So how could it fail, even if it did cost £508, which was £61 more than the equivalent Mini?

Like the Mini, the Imp suffered from early teething troubles, but they proved to be rather more enduring and serious. The aluminium engine regularly overheated, causing the head gasket to fail, which was never a good thing. Not only that, when garages needed to work on an Imp, usually to replace a head gasket, some were resistant to use the specialist tools needed to work on an aluminium engine, which then caused damage. Also, whereas most cars used a throttle cable, the Imp used a clever pneumatic item which sadly proved too troublesome in service. Lubrication was not required on the steering, but unfortunately on early models the whole system seized up because of... a lack of lubrication. Later cars got much better, but the reputation for breaking down at every unwelcome opportunity stuck.

It didn't help that Rootes had been forced to build a new factory with an inexperienced workforce, hundreds of miles away from the company's headquarters. Also, the design may have looked smart, but technically it seemed like a step backwards. Putting the engine in the boot and driving the rear wheels was certainly sporty and led to the car getting the nickname "The Linwood Porsche" after a rather more expensive car which also had the engine in the boot. Meanwhile, the Mini was proving that it's front engine, front-wheel drive layout was the motoring future. The Imp was the wrong car at the wrong time that at its very best sold 69,000 in 1964 and never got anywhere near the 150,000 capacity. Rootes dealers had no experience selling small cars, and struggled against the more established Mini.

Being Rootes, there wasn't just the basic Hillman Imp. It came in all sorts of exciting flavours. There was the Husky estate, which was also available as a commercial van wearing a Commer badge. The excitingly named Hillman Imp Californian had a sloping rear roofline and no opening window tailgate, but it looked great. You get also buy essentially the same models with a Sunbeam badge as the Imp Sport and Stiletto, although they had tuned engines. If Sunbeams were the sporty Imps, then the Singers were the posh ones, and you could buy a Chamois, which had more chrome and some wood veneer, a faster Chamois Sport and a Chamois coupe. None of these models really helped matters. Here was a fundamentally good, though slightly complicated, car, which was built badly on borrowed money, and sadly, the ramifications for Rootes would prove terminal.

It's interesting then to look at what Vauxhall's idea of a small car was: basically a "box on wheels". The Vauxhall Viva must have been the car that inspired such an uninspired description of a nondescript car. The Mayflower had sharp edges, but at least it was interesting, whereas the Viva was made exclusively from flat oblong and square panels. In fact, I know just how nondescript it was because in the very early 1970s, my sister briefly drove one which had belonged to a distant member of the family. I recall that it seemed very spacious, and by that time, very rusty. When it was launched in 1963, this incredibly square car proved to be very popular, and 100,000 were sold in 10 months, a number that Rootes could only have dreamed about for their Imp. Not only that, this new car emerged from a brand new factory. Even though Vauxhall was an American company, it was still subject to the planning laws of Britain, so was obliged to locate at Ellesmere Port on Merseyside. Unlike Rootes, Vauxhall managed to get a workforce that was not experienced at building cars to produce a reliable and deservedly popular model. What was most significant about the Viva is that it was essentially a British version of the German Opel Kadett, also part of General Motors, who owned Vauxhall.

Once the Germans had developed their Kadett, it was Vauxhall who suggested that it might be a good idea to take advantage of the shared parts and spread the huge costs involved in developing a new car. So the British contribution was to put a box on top of the rather more stylish Opel Kadett. But it worked. Competition within the UK-based industry was on the increase. If Vauxhall could make a small car that everyone wanted, just think what a mighty international company like Ford could make. Ford, though, were happy enough with the Anglia and really didn't need the hassle and expense of making a small car.

Certainly Dad wasn't thinking small, because with the old Wyvern given away, he needed to find a replacement. It was late 1963, and he was buying Autocar and Motor to check what was on offer, plus the Daily Mail and Daily Express Motor show guides. I know because I've still got them, including the motoring mags. But should Dad believe everything he read in the press? And if he did, what did they tell him to buy?

Still in the garage: The Wyvern's been given away to some ungrateful twerp moaning about a few missing tools in the boot. Meanwhile, we get around in Uncle Charles's 1962 Mini.

Births
1960 GSM
1960 LMB
1960 Marcos
1960 Rochdale
1960 Warwick
1962 Gitane
1962 Heron

Marriages
1960 Daimler to Jaguar
1961 Standard Triumph to Leyland

Deaths
1960 Armstrong Siddeley
1960 Lea Francis
1960 Ogle
1960 Peerless
1960 Powerdrive

1961 Berkeley
1961 GSM
1961 Metropolitan
1962 Buckler
1962 Gitane
1962 LMB
1962 Warwick
1963 Standard

New Arrivals
1960 Saab

In the Car Park
In this Chapter you will have come across some of the following vehicles on the next few pages...

Minis, top left you have a Morris Mini Cooper S and next to it is the estate version the Morris Traveller then the Van and pick up versions. Below them are even more versions of the Mini with the posh Riley Elf and Wolseley Hornet on the left which has a boot, more chrome and walnut dashboard. Next to it is the military Moke.

Top left is the Imp in standard saloon form and next to it the exciting, fastback Californian. Below them is the Husky estate. Below that the very square Vauxhall Viva and underneath the reliable Ford Anglia that cost less to make than a Mini, yet cost more to buy.

8 Dagenham Dustbins, Giant Crabs and Maggie's Favourite V8. 1964–66

In the garage: We are still relying on Uncle Charles's Austin Mini, which is a doddle to get in the garage. But don't worry, a new large blue car is arriving soon.

Dad had lots of saloon car options in 1964, and it would have been easier to follow the crowd to Dagenham and buy a Ford Cortina. Launched in 1962, it rapidly became the fastest selling car in the history of the British car industry. But it wasn't earning any money for Blighty. Here was a company earning big bucks for America after buying out the last British shareholders for £150 million.

New models were already revitalising the Ford range as the Anglia was an ultra-conventional alternative to the Mini. This was followed by the Classic, which had the Anglia's distinctive cut-back roof, which seemed to have been dropped on top of a scaled-down American car. However, the company was keen to stress the home grown-ness of it all with the words "styled at Dagenham by Dagenham people". It was intended to plug a gap between the Anglia and larger Consul, but most people have forgotten that it ever existed. Motoring historians put it down as a rare example of Ford getting it wrong. The truth was the Classic was a stopgap model with a deliberately short showroom life. It may have been heavy and slow because of the Anglia engine under the bonnet, but it had an unfeasibly large boot. One Ford publicity shot featured a woman on a deck chair, in the boot, it was that big. The Classic was an irrelevance, though, because it was the model that followed it which created something of a sensation.

Ford's big claim was that they had invented a brand new type of car that bridged the gap between the small and large family cars. In marketing speak, that is C/D, but I don't think anyone has ever really understood this alphabetti spaghetti approach to vehicle categorisation. The Cortina was just a family car pure and simple, and it was born out of Ford of Britain's determination to remain independent. Sir Patrick Hennessy was the man in charge, and he responded to a Ford Germany and Ford America project to make a new small car for Europe. That was project "Cardinal", after a small North American bird, so Sir Patrick came up with his own project called "Archbishop" after a senior member of the church.

The Germans had a year's head start, and were developing a car that would have an engine in the front driving the front wheels, just like the Mini. Ford of Britain decided to stick with the tried and tested front engine and rear-wheel-drive layout, but then did really clever things with the body. Ford had developed a system that used complex aircraft industry stress calculations, and applied that to the car's structure. It suddenly became possible to save a lot of weight (equivalent to an adult passenger in the Cortina's case) by using less metal.

It was Ford's commitment to product planning which was the key to getting the Cortina in on budget and, according to legend (among accountants, anyway), it actually came in under budget by less than a pound. Not surprisingly, 200 technical cost estimators worked on the project, ensuring that it was financially sound. Quibbling over the cost of components such as the steering wheel, which was redesigned four times because it exceeded the planners' estimates by one very old penny, may sound petty, but it was crucial. The styling was by a Canadian called Roy Brown, who had made a hash of Ford's biggest-ever flop, the Edsel, in America. Dreadful name and a dreadful car, so presumably he'd been sent to Dagenham as some sort of punishment. So with this new model, he had to get it right. The Cortina was certainly inoffensive, but you could see it had American origins: clipped back rear fins and an arrow-shaped indentation that ran the length of the car. Hennessey was keen to call the car the Caprino, until further investigation revealed that it meant "goat dung" in Italian. Instead, they went for Cortina, which had been the Italian venue for the 1960 Winter Olympics.

What Ford had actually created here was not some alphabetical-niche-filling car, but a large car at a small car price. That's the reason why, for the first few years, the well-established name Consul was also put on the bonnet to emphasise that this was a larger car. It's nearest rival was BMC's 1100, and that was really a slightly bigger Mini. The Cortina was cheaper, larger and yet no slower than the smaller car. So it was no surprise that after one year, 250,000 had been sold both in Britain and abroad.

In the 1960s it was hard to get away from the Cortina. My Uncle Harry worked at the Docks with his brothers Charles and Ted, and to my knowledge, he drove nothing else, but then he did live much closer to Dagenham than the rest of the family. Meanwhile, my Dad had a Cortina estate for a short while, which must have belonged to the company he was working for. It was a De Luxe estate (Ford were brilliant at carefully considered and priced trim levels), and I know this not just because I am a sad anorak-wearing car spotter, but also because it was the only model offered with wood panelling. Well, it wasn't actually real wood panelling like you would get on Morris Minor travellers and the Mini Countryman. There was no chance of wet or dry rot with the Di-Noc plastic wood which was glued on to the sides of the estate. I found it fascinating. So fascinating that I had to save up and buy the Corgi model version, which I thought came with a plastic dog that lived in the back, but it was actually a tiny Golfer and his trolley.

For many, the Cortina represented lowest common denominator motoring, but Ford didn't care; they didn't need to make the Cortina sexy or cool because it was practical and cheap. But they did anyway. There was a GT with a tuned engine and wider wheels, but the masterstroke was linking up with Colin Chapman at Lotus. Ford drove lorries full of Cortina bodyshells to the Lotus works in Cheshunt, where they were fitted with performance engines, retuned suspension and lightweight body panels. It went on to great success on the racing track. I could only dream that Dad would get one of those limited-edition superfast Cortinas. In the end, he bought me a plastic Airfix Kit of the Lotus Cortina, which I remember destroying in some garden-based, matchbox-and-lighter-fuel-related fire.

So if Dad didn't buy a Cortina, which he didn't, what were the other options for the family car buyer? Rootes offered an absolutely massive choice of mid-sized vehicles. There was the Hillman Minx range, which also included the upmarket Singer Gazelle, and a sporty two-door Sunbeam Rapier. A slightly larger replacement for this range was called the Super Minx, which again came in Singer Vogue and top-of-the-range Humber Sceptre flavours. Incredibly, someone high up within the organisation decided to keep both ranges running together. Now as the range included estates and convertibles, it must have been a bewildering time for Rootes dealers, who already had to cope with unsold Imps. That explains why Dad regularly brought home a different Hillman each week. A local garage who serviced his car were a Rootes outlet, and must have been trying to convince him to part-exchange for something, anything, with a Hillman, Humber or Singer badge on it. I particularly liked the Super Minx models, which had more than a little dose of Americana in their styling, with little fins at the back and indicators placed on top of the headlamps. Dad liked them enough to collect the brochures, but they never tempted him at that stage to swap to any Rootes product. Well, not yet anyway.

Clearly Rootes were in trouble both on the product and financial front. The American car manufacturer Chrysler came to the rescue by purchasing a stake in the company, which required government approval. At least it meant that the company could get on with the business of building a credible rival to the Cortina. Meanwhile, the only model putting up a fight and seemingly winning was BMC.

Announced at the same time as the Cortina was the Austin and Morris 1100 (same car but different badge – you know the drill by now). It was BMC policy to release models at different times, but for some reason, Austin dealers had to wait just over a year for their version. At its simplest, this car was a Mini, but a bit longer and with something called Hydrolastic suspension. This meant that it was more comfortable and held the road better than any other car. Inside, the amount of room was a revelation, matching or bettering BMC's larger models. Such a car could only have been designed by one man, and that was Issigonis. However, he didn't have anything to do with the bodywork, which was a problem as he had no time for stylists, except for Pinin Farina. The Italians were responsible for some of the most beautiful cars in the world, and when asked to comment on the Mini, told BMC it was perfect and not to change a thing. On the 1100 they did a superb job, producing a clean and uncluttered design that must have pleased Issigonis immensely. Inside, he also got his way, because it was a minimalist's paradise in there with just a narrow strip of dashboard. This great little car had one big flaw though: its price. As with the Mini, BMC got their sums wrong, so they were always going to make a loss. It cost £592, which was a £1 more than the Cortina.

Yet in pure cars-out-of-showrooms terms, the Austin and Morris seemed to be a raging success. In fact, until 1972, the BMC car topped the sales leagues. But the Cortina was the faster seller, and it also sold many more in export markets. Incredibly, Ford took a really close look at what BMC were up to, and came to the conclusion that financial ruin wasn't far off. Ford boss Hennessy even telephoned the boss of BMC, Donald Stokes, to break the news to him. There was probably a bit of self-interest here, as raising prices would have allowed Ford to do the same and make even more profit. Indeed, that's exactly what happened with the next version of the Cortina. It cost more because Ford reckoned that the customers were better off and could afford it. Meanwhile, BMC continued on their own self-destructive course. That included offering a whole bunch of 1100 and later 1300 models with fancier badges. As ever, the posh one was a Wolseley, the faster ones were called Riley and MG, but they even made a Vanden Plas Princess version, which was the double posh one, more of which later. There were two-door, four-door and estate versions to choose from, but these days the car is best remembered as the one that Basil Fawlty thrashed with a branch.

Much less famous is the Vauxhall Victor. This was another potential purchase for Dad, and of course it made some sort of sense to replace one Vauxhall with another. Like the Viva, this was little more than a slightly larger box on wheels with lots of straight lines which buyers found reassuring after the American styling of the old car. Indeed, the last Victor to wear the badge had a reputation for rampant rust. They had virtually disintegrated before their owners' eyes, so the new ones had to be better, and they were. That didn't tempt my dad, though, because his first new car was yet another Morris Oxford. I was too young to argue, but I did go with him to the dealer to pick it up. The salesman was bald, seemed very old but probably wasn't, and informal enough to do without his jacket. There were plastic covers on the seats and that unforgettable new car smell, which was also overwhelmingly plastic. Cars in those days rarely had plastic dashboards, and the Oxford was solid metal and painted battleship grey. So what tempted Dad to buy it? Reliability. The previous ones were fault free, and he hoped that the new one would be the same. Working on one was a doddle, and if it didn't start because the battery was flat, you could poke a starting handle through a keyhole in the front bumper and wind it into life. It was also tough.

I remember being slightly unnerved to learn that Dad had been hit by a bus. It happened at a zebra crossing. Dad was stationary, but the bright red Routemaster double-decker rapidly closing in from behind was skating on ice. It thumped the rear of the Oxford, which shot forward and gave the poor bloke crossing the fright of his life. Dad, who had been watching the bus get gradually bigger in his rear-view mirror, was sort of ready for the thump. He got Routemaster whiplash, but was well enough to get out and inspect the damage. The bus actually looked worse off, and the Oxford simply needed a new bumper and rear light lenses. I remember looking at the bulbs in what was left of the lenses, and they were perfectly intact.

Dad said that they had to tow away the bus because the radiator had burst. It was a tough car all right, and endured another six years of big mileages for work and family holidays in places like Torquay, Yarmouth, Scotland and Ireland. The Oxford was certainly a smart old bus, with slightly dated though sharp lines by those arty Italians Pinin Farina. Obviously **BMC** offered a wide choice of models, with the Morris Oxford and Austin Cambridge at the bottom and moving up to Wolseley, MG and Riley versions. That meant five slightly different rear ends, front ends and interiors. Very complicated, but I know that Dad would not have paid any extra for those so-called "Farina" versions. No, if he wanted, or more to the point could have afforded, a more upmarket family car, he would not have been taken in by some bits of chrome and badgework – not on a **Morris**, anyway. He'd have wanted a Triumph or Rover, and by the early 1960s, their offerings were looking pretty impressive. At least Dad never bought an Austin 1800.

In 1964, the 1800 was one of the major car announcements of the year and intended to replace the myriad Farina saloons, but my Dad and many others were not taken in by what was in effect a super, supersized Mini. This was unmistakably an Issigonis design, and with its big MGB sports-car-related engine driving the front wheels, the rest of the body could be given over to looking after passengers. Inside, it was truly massive, and with its advanced suspension was a successful candidate for the Car of the Year gong in 1964. It was strong, compact and heavy, but with a smooth ride. Whereas the 1100 and 1300 had understated bodywork courtesy of the Italians, the 1800 was also styled by Pinin Farina. However, it was seriously meddled with in Birmingham. As a result it looked dumpy and uncomfortable, and quickly gained the nickname "land crab". Issigonis's insistence on a stark interior didn't help either.

Launched first as an Austin, the model was hard to find at the dealer and quickly gained a reputation for being less than reliable. So as the gearbox and suspension played up, BMC struggled to sell 22,000 in the first year. Indeed, more buyers opted for the old Farina saloons that comfortably outsold the all-new car. The 1800 did get better, finally acquiring a Morris badge, then a posh Wolseley one and even a sport "S" upgrade with a larger engine, making it a giant Mini Cooper S. Total sales over more than a decade amounted to just 373,000. This was a car which was technically and practically superior to just about every other model on the market at the time which failed to make any lasting impression. Obviously the buying public were happy with what they understood, either a Cortina, or a Morry Oxford like Dad's. Then again, car buyers were also going upmarket.

The last time we visited Triumph they were doing rather well with their Herald. Actually, it was really Standard doing rather well with their back-up marque, but they still needed a partner to survive in such a competitive market. Standard had abortive talks with Rootes, Rover and even American Motors, who we last saw selling the quirky Metropolitan that had been made by Austin, as an illustration of just how tight-knit the car making community was, and indeed still is. Perhaps it was an act of desperation that they ended up in the clutches of lorry maker Leyland.

As a commercial vehicle manufacturer, no one was bigger than Leyland, who had grown by acquiring the leading British marques. The last time they had made cars was back in the 1920s, so Standard Triumph looked like a good way to re-enter the market and stamp their no-nonsense approach on to the company. In 1961, when Leyland took over, much of the original board were sacked, along with 800 staff. Cost-cutting and efficiency were the priority as the business was rationalised. Joining the board was a certain Mr Donald Stokes. He would become an integral part of the new automotive order, a new British car dynasty that would change car manufacturing and the country forever.

Leyland's tough love started to work and put the car arm on a solid financial footing. For some time though, the main concern had been how to replace the Standard Vanguard, which incredibly was still on sale and looking very tired. The company even considered stretching the Herald into a four-door. In fact it seemed such a good idea that they did produce some prototypes. It probably would have been a decent rival for the Austin/Morris 1100/1300. Instead, they packed it off to India where, in later years, it was called the Standard Herald Mark III. Then they set about designing an all-new saloon, which was code named Barb. It was aimed at the "executive" market, a new breed of middle-management and entre-preneurs who wanted cars that were as thrusting as they were. The cars needed to be stylish and performance orientated, rather than just big with leather, wood and chrome trim. Indeed, a manufacturer in Bavaria realised that there was a profitable niche for cars that were sophisticated sporty saloons. If they hadn't then, BMW would have gone bankrupt. That was 1962, and the designer of this new generation of BMWs was Mr Michelotti. Previously seen making small Triumphs socially acceptable, he was now required to work his magic on a larger Triumph. Time wasn't on his side, as Standard had heard that their direct rivals, Rover, were also poised to enter the executive market. So the race was on.

The first thing Standard did was to lay its own name to rest. From now on, all the company's output would be badged as Triumphs. Even if Rover won the race to be first to launch their new car. The MD of Triumph, Stanley Markland, dismissed the Rover by claiming that his company was taking more time to ensure their car was perfect. However, Triumph didn't take the opportunity to change the model's name. These brand new aspirational models had the same millennial name, 2000. Actually, that referred to the size of the engine, but while one vehicle looked like the future, the other not only looked futuristic, it was technically one of the most advanced cars in the world.

The Triumph 2000 was the more conventional offering, using the engine from the old Vanguard, but in a more tuned form. The styling was as handsome as anything Michelloti would ever draw for BMW or anyone else, and it looked as good in the company car park as it did cruising up the M1 to an important meeting. And then there was the Rover 2000.

No one saw this one coming because Rover had only built solid and dependable maiden auntmobiles for the previous 30 years without incident. Well, that's not strictly true as they did take an odd diversion into gas turbine experimental vehicles. These looked and sounded like Jet cars, but it was a technological dead end, which is why they concentrated on the 2000. Here was a Rover that looked nothing like a Rover and, unusually for a new car (usually it is bits of old cars rearranged) was completely brand new: engine, gearbox, suspension and structure. Not only that, they also built a brand new factory in Solihull to make it. Beneath the sharp styling was a stressed steel skeleton to which the body panels and mechanicals were bolted. That was clever, and not unlike the Citroën DS, plus it also had amazing suspension, just like the DS. In case you are interested, it used coil springs all round; at the front, they were horizontally mounted, operating through bell cranks, at the rear supporting a de Dion axle on a Watt linkage.

Understand that? Well now you know why I've kept the technical explanations to the absolute minimum. Clearly it wasn't the Rover old guard who were responsible for all that. No, two young engineers, Peter Wilks and Spen King (first cousins, both related to Spencer and Maurice Wilks, if you remember, who were responsible for the Land Rover). They were backed up by Rover's managing director William Martin-Hurst, who encouraged innovation and eventually sent the Rover 2000 rallying and created a Rover-BRM Le Mans race car. Rover would never be the same again.

Then, after five years, the Rover 2000 became even more exciting when a new model joined the line-up. It was badged as the 3500, indicating that there was a much bigger engine under the bonnet. That wouldn't have mattered to anyone except the police, who ordered Rover 3500s in white and blue to patrol the motorways and catch criminals in old Jaguars. But in fact this engine, which originated in America, would become one of the most charismatic and important powerplants of all time. It would be fitted to some of the best and worst vehicles ever made, and would keep some of the smallest British companies ticking over for decades. So it is worth spending a little bit of time understanding how this V8 came to Britain in the first place.

It was lucky that Rover's enthusiastic managing director, Martin-Hurst, virtually tripped over it on a visit to a factory in Wisconsin. It was 1963, and he was trying to sell some of Rover's turbine technology to Mercury Marine, who made engines for boats. They were more interested in the diesel engine used in Land Rovers, which they wanted to adapt for a fleet of Chinese fishing junks. So these curious circumstances accounted for Martin-Hurst's being where he was and stumbling over that engine. It wasn't his first encounter with it, having previously driven a Buick Skylark in America which had the V8 burbling away, and having rather enjoyed the experience. Mercury were happy for him to take it away, as this was now an obsolete and unloved unit. Later, an agreement was made with General Motors to buy the design outright. So why did Martin-Hurst bother?

Here was a lightweight aluminium V8 engine (two banks of four cylinders arranged in a V shape, in case you wondered) that was small but complicated to make and maintain, which didn't seem too promising. Rover had wanted to fit one of its bigger engines to the 2000, except that they were heavy and lethargic. They had even considered gas turbine power too. However, this American engine was not much bigger than the 2000's engine, and it weighed six bags of sugar less. As a result, the car would go like a bomb. Of course it wasn't as easy as that, because Rover needed to do a lot of development work to make the engine suitable and to iron out the bugs that had made it a failure in the USA. So it may have come from America, but this V8 was certainly reborn in Birmingham. Indeed, Rover claimed that by the time they had finished with it, this engine was 75% British. From 1967 onwards, the Rover V8 would feature as the driving force behind so many uniquely British cars. Its first job, though, was to make sure that the Prime Minister got to Downing Street on time.

The first Rover to get the Buick engine treatment was the large Rover saloons, known universally by its internal codename P5, but with that engine it became the P5B. The B stood for Buick, and this handsome, understated car was quickly adopted by the civil service and royalty. Here was a suitably large car that managed to remain discreet, especially in a suitably dark colour. That suited the style of Harold Wilson, Ted Heath, James Callaghan and Margaret Thatcher, who had a fleet that were used well into the 1980s when the model had long since been discontinued. Indeed, both Maggie and Harold used the same car, and in a rear-seat armrest was a special ashtray designed for a pipe. I never realised that Maggie smoked a pipe, did you? As well as prime ministers, it was a favourite ride for both the Queen and her mum.

With the Rover 2000, 3500 and the Triumph 2000, which also got an engine uprate to 2500, it proved that there was a strong demand for this new breed of car for a new breed of executive. Companies like Ford wanted some of that profitable business, and expected their Corsair, a sort of posh Cortina, to fill that gap in their range, but it didn't. Ford were clever, though, and knew all about adding value to their products. They did this by offering subtly different levels of trim according to the badge on the boot lid. Company car park snobbery was born and, most significantly, with the next generation of Cortina, you could buy a 1600E. The 'E' stood for executive, of course. Fancy wheels, uprated interior trim and more powerful engine were all part of the package. You could also get a Corsair 2000E, and an even larger Ford Zodiac Executive. But as medium sized cars became all the rage, demand for the larger gentleman's car was declining fast.

BMC had it's fair share of big old barges that fell into that category. Incredibly, Austin had aimed to challenge Bentley after the war and specifically designed the "flying A" radiator mascot to ape Bentley's own "flying B" design. There was the Austin Sheerline, but then they also offered the Princess, which was handmade by Vanden Plas, a company that Austin had bought in 1946. In fact it became a manufacturer in it's own right in 1960. There was also a larger version of Dad's Morris Oxford with a larger engine, which was called the Austin Westminster, as well as the Wolseley 6-99, (later 6-110), a favourite with the police force before the Rover 2000/3500 came along. And then right at the top of the range was the Princess. There was loads of leather and wood and sound proofing and a regal grille with a little crown, or rather coronet, on the grille in black. These cars were built at BMC's Cowley factory and then sent to the Vanden Plas works at Kingsbury in London to get the posh bits bolted on. This wasn't good enough, of course, as BMC felt that they should be competing against the big Rover and Jaguars. At that point, discreet contact was made with Rolls-Royce, who were also thinking along similar lines and considering making something smaller. Both companies worked together for a while, and experimented with Rolls-Royce's more industrial engines that had been used in several military vehicles.

Launched with a suitably big fanfare in 1964 and was so self-important that it had one of the longest model names in history. The "Vanden Plas Princess 4-litre R" in italic chrome script took up the entire length of the boot lid. The "R" stood for Rolls-Royce, but that company had probably wisely decided not to take their version any further. Obviously much was made of the Rolls-Royce connection, but the engine wasn't quite as whisper-smooth and powerful as many expected. However, BMC Chairman Leonard Lord was happy to be chauffeur-driven in one until, that is, he was harangued by unhappy customers. It seems that the BMC 1 registration plate attracted rather too much attention. Although high sales were predicted, they never materialised, and by far the most successful Princess model was several sizes smaller.

This came about when Fred Connolly, who ran the Connolly leather empire, asked Vanden Plas to reinterpret a new Morris 1100 in a suitably luxurious manner. A prototype was put on display at the 1963 London Motor Show, and it caused so much interest that it was put into production. The front end was identical to the larger Princess, with a great big grille, and it had enough leather and wood to keep pretentious buyers happy. To avoid confusion with the 4-litre R, the coronet on the grille had a red rather than black centre. From then on, it was possible to buy a little and large Princess, which is exactly what our next door neighbours did.

Mr and Mrs Lewis had a double plot of land, a carriage drive, and a recently-built red-brick house. My understanding is that they owned a factory that made knick-knacks – the sort of pound shop rubbish that now has "made in China" on it. As a result, they had plenty of time to spend away on cruise liners, and when they did, in the interests of the community safety, Dad agreed to regularly move the Princess. The little one. Apparently, reparking the Princess regularly was supposed to indicate to potential burglars that someone was actually at home. Actually, it was me and Dad having fun in a small automatic car. After "driving" my dad's Vauxhall Wyvern, I had now moved on to actually driving the neighbours' little Princess. I was probably about seven at the time. Thank you Mrs Lewis.

The Princess badge was a boon to the BMC network as the car could be sold through either Austin or Morris showrooms. They appreciated the opportunity to sell a more profitable model which added a bit of class to the other rather plain cars on sale. By contrast, a Rootes dealer had a huge number of models to try to sell, in all shapes, sizes and badges. But when it came the large, luxury cars, there was just the one marque, Humber. Being Rootes, though, there were a variety of flavours to choose from. The big Humbers continued the model line that stretched all the way back to the Snipe that Dad and uncle Charles used on their honeymoons. By the 1960s, the luxury line-up comprised the Hawk, a slightly larger-engined and better-equipped Super Snipe, and at the top of the range, the Imperial, that among other things had a vinyl roof. Not that there were very many customers for these cars any more.

Over at Vauxhall, buyers would rather have small Vivas than anything bigger. So although the medium-sized Victor struggled, it was the much larger Cresta, the first Vauxhall with an American Chevrolet engine, that had a problem justifying its existence. Even worse, the top-of-the-range Viscount version only managed to sell in tiny numbers – around 1,000 a year – and that sort of figure didn't make any sense for a mass manufacturer.

At Ford, they had a knack of getting the numbers right, and their new Zephyr and Zodiac ranges from 1962 sold in suitably large numbers over a relatively short four-year life span. It was probably the most American-looking

Ford ever, and obviously benefited from weekly TV exposure on the BBC police series, "Z Cars". That was my favourite bit – the opening titles, which were dominated by the huge cheesy grille of a Zephyr 6 with a blue flashing light in black and white. Keen pricing and "Executive" badging all helped to make these "Z cars" popular. The follow up "Z cars", which also made the opening titles, were not nearly as nice to look at and consequently sold in much smaller numbers. Apparently, the new American head of engineering, a Mr Harley Copp, decided that bigger was better. The new Zephyr and Zodiac from 1966 were indeed bigger, but it coincided with the decision to fit a physically smaller engine. That meant that the massive bonnet on top of which you could probably play a game of five-a-side football, once opened, was filled with... well, nothing very much at all. However, Ford decided to fill the huge space with the spare wheel. At the other end, instead of a huge boot, there was an apologetic oblong bump. Inside, it was huge, but from the outside it looked silly. Proportionally, the Zeds were all wrong, and sales slumped. Here was another clear indication that the days of the deliberately large car were numbered.

I was uniquely placed to know exactly what was going on in the big car business because Dad's brother Joe was a chauffeur. He worked for the Port of London Authority, and later on, News Corporation. The best period was in the 1960s, when several Sundays a month, he would drop by on the way to or from work after first stopping on the Mile End Road to pick up provisions. That meant I was going to eat bagels and fresh prawns (but not the rollmop herrings in the jar – I didn't like the look of those). So it was a great occasion when Uncle Joe turned up, because not only did I get to eat exotic food, I also got to sit in a large, luxurious car. In the 1960s, it could have been just about all of those models previously mentioned, although mostly it was the big Rootes models: the Humber Super Snipe and Hawk.

Over the years, Uncle Joe's cars changed a lot, before settling down to be quite ordinary cars with large engines and lots of extras. In the mid-1960s, though, there were clearly too many manufacturers after the same buyers. Something pretty major was not just going to happen, it had to happen.

In the garage: Our comfy Morris Oxford.

Births
1964 Gordon-Keeble
1965 Peel

Marriages
1964 Elva to Trojan
1964 Rootes to Chrysler

Deaths
1964 Falcon
1964 Heron
1964 Ogle
1964 Tornado
1965 Scootacar
1965 Trojan

Best Selling Models – 1965 Country of origin in brackets.
Austin 1100/1300 157,679 (GB)
Ford Cortina 116,985 (GB)
Austin Mini 104,477 (GB)
Ford Anglia 84,589 (GB)
Vauxhall Victor 60,854 (GB)
Vauxhall Viva 58,884 (GB)
Austin 1800 52,503 (GB)
Triumph Herald/Vitesse 46.626 (GB)
Ford Corsair 44, 463 (GB)
Morris Minor 44,905 (GB)

Best Seller by Year
1965 Austin 1100/1300 157,679
1966 Austin 1100/1300 151,946

New Arrivals
1965 Honda

In the Car Park
In this Chapter you will have come across some of the following vehicles and personalities...

Top left is a Ford Classic with a lady on a deck chair in the boot, next is the Cortina this is the exciting GT model and second row left is the Deluxe Estate with plastic wood panels, then Germany's more advanced Cortina called the Taunus. Third row left is the Mark 2 Cortina in 1600 E for Executive trim. Next to it is the Cortina's main rival Austin and Morris 1100/1300. Row four has the estate, and then bottom right the posh Princess 1300.

Top row left the MG 1300 the high performance version while the Austin 1800 on the right was essentially the same as the 1100/1300, but bigger with a truly huge amount of sprawling room inside. Second row left is a Hillman Minx, next to that a Hillman Super Minx then the next row down a Sunbeam Rapier then a Singer Vogue, welcome to the confusing world of Rootes. Third row are the two advanced executive saloon offered by Rover on the left and Triumph on the right.

Above top left row the less sophisticated (than a Rover or Triumph) Ford Zephyr estate and Vauxhall Victor. See BMC's big limousines like the Austin Westminster left and the Vanden Plas Princess right on row five. One of Rootes offerings was the Humber Super Snipe (there was also a lower Hawk and higher specification Imperial). Bottom right is the Guv'nor the Rover 3.5.

9 1966 and all that, BMH, BMC, BLMC = BFG (B Faltering Giant) 1966-1970

In the garage: Morris Oxford. It's comfortable, reliable and even survives being hit by a bus, but is there something else pulling into the drive?

1966 was an important year, especially if you loved football and were English. I had a football with the official mascot World Cup Willy on it that I regularly smacked against next door's back window. It sometimes took a day or two to come back. Dad wasn't there with me to watch the boys in red and white on black and white telly at Wembley. No, he'd driven to Germany to build exhibition stands. Obviously he still watched the game, but in a German hotel room.

Dad and the bloke he shared a room with made quite a racket during the exciting match, and ended up dancing around the room when Geoff's last goal went in. The hotel was utterly silent but for a couple of English blokes going mad in their room. There was even a knock at the door from a perplexed member of the hotel staff to check that they were all right. Of course they were. English football would never feel this good again, and neither would the British, or more oprecisely the English, car industry. This was pretty much the beginning of the end.

Already there had been something of a merger and takeover mania, especially as manufacturers jostled to secure the ownership of companies that built car bodies. Because without a guaranteed supply of bodies, they would be left with a load of parts and nothing to bolt them to. With that in mind, BMC, who already owned Fisher and Ludlow, had bought another body manufacturer, Pressed Steel, in 1965, so other independent car companies had to stick together.

Jaguar were clever enough to realise that they needed partners, although on the face of it they were a strong company. At the head was a remarkable man, William Lyons, who had single-handedly built a motorcycle sidecar business into one of the most recognised and desirable motoring brands in the world. Not only that, he had acquired Daimler, their profitable bus manufacturing business, as well as Guy commercial vehicles and Coventry-Climax, who made forklift trucks, fire pumps and engines. They were, though, finding the cost of developing what would become the hugely successful XJ6 a financial drain. Lyons had no line of succession, either within the company, or his family, so it was essentially a one-man show, and he needed to secure its future.

In the summer of 1966, Lyons reckoned that BMC would be the best bet, so the two companies officially became British Motor Holdings (BMH). For marketing purposes, though, they stayed as BMC.

Rover, of course, had to do something or be left out on their own without a body supplier. At the end of 1966, they turned to Leyland, who didn't just buy Rover, but also Land Rover, with another car and military vehicle maker, Alvis, included in the package. The merger and acquisition activity did not end there, because in 1967, Chrysler finally moved into the driving seat of Rootes. For some time the number-three manufacturer in America had looked on enviously at Ford and General Motors' profitable operations in Europe. Having already acquired Simca in France from Ford, the weak Rootes Group looked perfect for a takeover. The products were not inspiring, a long strike had left the company disheartened, and each year they registered a loss. Lord Rootes was still there, but getting on a bit at 70, so clearly the family management wasn't working. Chrysler therefore stepped in and took a minority interest in 1964 that they progressively increased this until a full takeover.

At the time, though, the Labour government under pipe-smoking Harold Wilson were not happy that an American company had control of another part of the British motor industry. So it was the job of the pipe-smoking and tea-drinking Minister of State for Technology, Tony Benn, to intervene. Initially, the government had tried to prod both Leyland and BMC to make a bid for Rootes, and after that persuade them that working together would be better for the working man than being in competition with each other. Actually, both the head of BMC, George Harriman, and Leyland's Donald Stokes had sort of discussed closer cooperation in a half-hearted manner. The truth was that BMC were not doing very well at all. Their share of the home market fell massively between 1966 and 1967, which played directly into Leyland's hands. Harold Wilson invited both the company bosses to his official home at Chequers and engineered a collision course that culminated in an official announcement of the merger at the beginning of 1968 and which came to pass in May of that year.

Well, it wasn't exactly a merger; what we had here was the takeover of BMC by Leyland, hence the new name The British Leyland Motor Corporation

(BLMC). After what Leyland had done with Triumph and its general success at selling commercial vehicles all over the world, there didn't seem much to worry about. Donald Stokes was now fully in charge, although he kept Sir William Lyons of Jaguar on board as a Deputy Chairman. But this new British car dynasty were lacking in one key area: no one had ever run a car maker this big before. Suddenly there were 190,000 employees to worry about, and between the 48 factories (yes, there really were that many) the potential to make a million vehicles. Donald Stokes was alarmed to discover just how small or non-existent profits actually were, how little was being invested in new models and how disorganised some of the factories were.

Stokes and the BLMC board certainly had work to do, and that meant reorganisation on a huge scale. In essence, BLMC was divided up into seven divisions. Austin Morris provided the basic bread-and-butter models, which meant Austin, Morris and the sporty MGs. However, Austins would be the advanced ones, using the front-wheel-drive technology of the Minis to see off the more interesting imported cars. Morris would concentrate on uncomplicated mechanicals, but have more flamboyant styling. Well, that was the plan anyway. Then there was the Specialist Division, which included the middle-class marques of Jaguar, Rover and Triumph. That took care of the cars, but there was so much more to this huge conglomerate. General Engineering included the body maker Pressed Steel Fisher. Plus there were Truck and Bus and Construction Equipment, which is self-explanatory, and the Overseas division. Creating these new divisions was logical, but was to cause more problems and rivalries in the future. Probably the most momentous decision was ending the theory and practice of badge engineering, although this would take quite a few years to actually die out.

So what did BLMC actually do? They dropped the MG Magnette and Austin Westminster, but of course no one ever realised that they were still in production. Riley, another irrelevance, was also rubbed out. Then there were the cars that BMC hadn't quite finished developing just yet. The Austin Maxi was so far advanced and so much money had been spent building a new factory to make a new engine, that they were obliged to finish it off.

When the Maxi was launched in 1969 it looked like a very good bet. It was Maxi by name and maxi by nature. Here was a full-sized hatchback, still a huge novelty. It also came with a five-speed gearbox when four was the norm, and turning the engine around to drive the front wheels freed up acres of space inside. It was truly remarkable inside a Maxi, not least because you could fold all the seats flat to make yourself a double bed. Fold the seats forward and suddenly the Maxi became a 50 cubic feet van. It should have been a world-beater, or at least a Cortina-beater, leaving the Ford looking ordinary. However, at least the ultra-ordinary Cortina would not let you down.

An overcomplicated gearbox fitted to the Maxi led to problems selecting gears, the new engine was sluggish and prone to overheating, whilst the interior could not have been any barer or less welcoming. Claims that the car was "all-new", as they say in marketing speak, were countered by the clever dicks who spotted that the front doors had been donated by the unlovely 1800 "land crab". BLMC had to fix and pretty much relaunch the Maxi a year later. They had expected to build 250,000 a year, but never managed to get beyond 472,000 when it was finally laid to rest in 1981. The Maxi was never going to touch the Cortina, but that would never stop BLMC trying. Which explains the Morris Marina.

It is generally accepted that BLMC should not have even considered competing with Ford. They would be repeating the massive Mini mistake of underpricing and not relying on their technical superiority to set the model apart from the more conventional Fords. Indeed John Barber, who we previously saw at Ford carefully costing the Cortina, was now at British Leyland. He couldn't repeat the trick because purchasing parts was a chaotic affair. Within the industry it was a standing joke that BLMC paid more for their parts than anyone else, while believing that they were getting a great deal.

Against this background, we got the Marina. Here was the first all-new car built under the new regime. Did I just write "all-new"? Styling was by Roy Haynes, the man who had shaped the boxy but successful Mark II Ford Cortina. He had been recruited by BMC in 1966, so with him on board, together with Ford's ex-finance director, John Barber, who became managing director of BLMC, surely the company had a Cortina-beater on their hands?

Launched in 1971 (yes, I know this chapter is supposed to go up to 1970, but we'll stretch time a bit to include the Marina), the Marina had roots that could actually be traced all the way back to 1948. Scratch the surface of a Marina and underneath you would find a surprising amount of Issigonis's Morris Minor. Of course it wasn't as simple as that, not least because the gearbox was so old it would crunch into first gear. That meant modifying a Triumph gearbox and spending millions to convert existing sheds into a gearbox plant. Also, building the car at Cowley in Oxford meant that the facilities had to be updated to improve quality. In practice though, creating a quarter-mile-long conveyer belt to take the shells from the body plant to the main assembly line on the other side of the Oxford Bypass wasn't too clever. The track may have had a roof on it, but posting them over the rooftops on rails and exposing unpainted bodyshells to the elements was bound to cause paint quality and corrosion issues at a later date.

Maybe the name could have been more exciting, as Marina sounded like a maiden aunt. They did seriously consider Monaco, Machete and even Mamba. The very thought of getting into a Morris Machete is incredibly exciting, and undoubtedly would have had some appeal to the fleet market at which the Marina was aimed. Indeed it had it's work cut out, as the bigger-engined version took on the Cortina and Vauxhall Viva, while lower down the range it was supposed to take on Ford's all-conquering Escort. Trouble was, although BLMC had used a lot of existing parts, the whole thing had been rushed into showrooms with the paintwork still wet and about to bubble with rust. That reworked gearbox failed, while motoring hacks soon discovered that driving a Marina at speed was a very dangerous business. Thrown into corners, it was reluctant to turn, preferring to chuck you headfirst into a bush – or lending library if you were in a built-up area.

BLMC tried hard though, modifying the Marina and offering saloon, coupe, estate and van variants to catch all the possible markets. Different levels of trim mirrored what Ford were doing, but there the similarities ended. Ford were never threatened by the Marina simply because they could raise production almost at the push of a button and then offer higher discounts to the fleet buyers that BLMC coveted. As a result, the Marina never reached the projected production target of 5,000 a week. Compared with a Cortina, it was no more sophisticated and just as dull to look at, but it just wasn't made by Ford, which made all the difference.

At home, we briefly had a Marina Coupe on loan for some obscure reason. I think my Dad's car was in for a service and the dealer was desperate for him to drive the new Morris. Actually, I liked the idea of being seen in a sporty coupe, but the Marina didn't even have a vinyl roof. It was hard to see the point of a less practical, fairly grim looking two-door car when there was the rather good looking Ford Capri. Famously, the Capri was described as a Cortina in drag, and it was another object lesson for BLMC in how to make and, most importantly, market cars.

Essentially, the Capri was the European version of the Ford Mustang. The Mustang used tried and tested mechanical components, but all wrapped up in a sexy coupe body and with a seemingly limitless number of specification and engine options. A staggering 100,000 customers bought one in the first few months. Surely the same recipe would work in Europe?

Designed in Britain, the Capri was called project Colt for a while, and allusion to the American car, and then GBX, which made it seem a bit more home grown. With its long bonnet, thick rear pillars and low stance, in late 1960s Britain it looked utterly sensational. Being a Ford, it was also extremely afford-able. When unveiled in January 1969, it was promoted as "The Car You Always Promised Yourself". Back then, it really was. And unlike most sports cars which had complicated mechanicals, cost a fortune to look after and broke down a lot, this was a Ford.

Being a Ford also meant that there were 26 models to choose from when you combined the various option packs. Just in case you wondered, the basic L pack cheered up the exterior with chrome wheel trims, body side and exhaust trims, dummy air scoops and a locking petrol cap which was at least useful rather than decorative. The X-pack overhauled the interior so that the seats reclined and the rear passengers got individual seats and armrests. If you went for a GT then you could opt for an R pack, which added a leather-covered steering wheel, a map reading light on one of those flexible chrome stalks, plus front fog lamps, matt black radiator grille and matt black (or rather "sub gloss", according to the brochures of the time), on the bonnet, the panel below the boot and sills below the doors. Yes, you could create a Capri GT XLR as conclusive proof that Ford completely understood who bought their car. So no, you wouldn't want a Morris Marina Coupe would you? And another reason not to buy the Marina was the Ford Escort.

"The small car that isn't" replaced the Anglia in 1968, and was significant as it spearheaded the Europeanisation of Ford. Ford of Europe had been created the previous year, and here was a model built in both Britain and Germany. The Escort would have been called the Anglia but for the fact that the Germans reckoned that Anglia conjured up images of World War 2 East Anglian bomber bases, which wouldn't have been good for business. In Germany anyway. The Escort's distinctive front end had a dog-bone-shaped chrome grille, although the Ford spin doctors preferred "twin spatula" shape. There were five different models right from the off, from a basic De Luxe right up to the performance GT and Twin Cam models. Taking the engine from the Lotus Cortina and squeezing it into the Escort to create the Twin Cam was the sort of thing that could over-excite a young man. For my part, I cut out pictures of the ones that went rallying and stuck them in a scrapbook. More grown-up boys could actually afford to buy one, or at least a De Luxe and then put some wider wheels on it. Cleverly, Ford had created a car that everyone could afford, and if necessary, you traded up through the range to get the better model. Sporting Fords were born with the Lotus Cortina and Escort TC, and it proved to be a highly profitable decision, not least because the fast, sexy ones make the slow, boring ones look good. That was something that BLMC either forgot or didn't realise.

Now everyone loved the Mini, but they really wanted a Mini Cooper and Mini Cooper S even more. That was especially the case when the improbably small car started to win races on the track and in the forests. In fact everyone loved the Mini even more when it didn't win the Monte Carlo Rally in 1966 because the cheating French decided that the lights were at the wrong level. Disqualifying the first three Minis and the fourth-place Cortina, meant that a Citroën won. The Coopers, though, got a heroes' welcome. Despite that, BLMC hated the idea of paying royalties to outside firms. So the Formula One championship-winning car builder John Cooper, who got £5 a car, had his contract cancelled. Also, the charismatic Austin Healey name that had been created back in the BMC days was killed off for the same reason.

However, if there was one revenue raising line of models that BMC could rely on it was the sports cars. There was still a seemingly inexhaustible demand for little Brit sports cars in America. The Austin Healy Sprite, better known and identified as the Frogeye, became the more conventional looking Austin Healey

Sprite Mark II. It was joined by an identical (except for the badges, of course) MG Midget version. However, MG's bigger MGA was the model that needed replacing, something that BMC had been thinking about since the mid-1950s. Strapped for development cash, the designers turned to their promotional vehicles for inspiration. The EX181 had been designed specifically to break records in 1957, while a highly-modified MGA coupe had been prepared for the Le Mans 24-hour race in 1960. So they took the top half of the former and the bottom half of the latter to arrive at a brand new shape. With that agreed upon, the engine was more of a problem, because the existing MGA engine had too many reliability issues. BMC, though, were prepared to fund the development of a larger engine to use in the ugly "land crab" saloons. That made the new MGB a guinea pig, and what a pretty little guinea pig it was too, when launched in September 1962.

At the same time as the MGB was released to universal acclaim, BMC also revealed the MG version of the 1100 range, which was an indication of the badge engineering horrors awaiting the undead MG marque in later years. Meanwhile, everyone seemed to love the "B" even though the heater was an option, but at least fresh air was standard. It rapidly became the roadster you bought because you couldn't possibly afford a Jaguar E-Type. At £834.6s (that's six shillings, remember?) it was cheaper than the big, butch Austin Healey 3000 (£1,190), the blokey Triumph TR4 (£1,030) and about the same price as the slightly girly Sunbeam Alpine. Truly, this was the golden age of the great British drop top, and there was more. Competing against the MG Midget and Austin Healey Sprite was the Triumph Spitfire.

Although the Midge, Sprite and Spit were all on the same team by 1968, it hadn't started that way. First there was the Herald in 1959, which was styled by the wonderfully talented Giovanni Michelotti. He'd also styled a two-seat sports car based on the Herald's running gear. It was codenamed "The Bomb" and was intended as a rather more superior alternative to the very basic Sprite. Standard Triumph, though, didn't have the money to develop it, so a dust sheet was thrown over the car and it was pushed into a dark corner of the factory where it remained, unexploded. When Leyland bought the company, an executive spotted the distinctive shape, peeked under it, liked what he saw and instantly re-primed the project. They made it larger, more comfy and more luxurious (there were wind-up windows) than the Sprite. And as with the Herald, the whole front end tipped forward, allowing complete engine access.

Given that it was launched in 1962, no one is completely certain exactly why it was called the Spitfire. Using the name of the legendary World War 2 fighter aircraft certainly helped the car to get noticed, and is was pictured with the aeroplane in promotional photos. It is suggested that, as Standard, the company that owned Triumph, had made so many aircraft parts during the war, including those for the Spitfire, there was no objection. Anyway, it was a cute little car, cute enough for my sister to buy a brand new one in the late 70s, which shows you how long it was around. Four years after the convertible came out, Triumph put a sloping roof on top and a much larger engine under the bonnet to create the GT6. This was dubbed as the poor man's Jaguar E-Type, which has an equally long bonnet and general curviness.

MG had already tapped into this market by putting a roof on the MGB to create the MGB GT in 1965. One of the designers involved had worked at Aston Martin, and the idea actually was to make a poor bloke's Aston Martin. In 1967 they too put a big engine under the bonnet to create their own affordable E-Type. The irony was that, by 1968, Jaguar, Triumph and MG were under the same roof and competing for business. That caused problems for Triumph and MG, but Jaguar were more upmarket in the sports car game. Except that, when it came to the prestige car market, Rover and Triumph were just as ambitious as Jaguar to do well. That created rivalry which could have been a force for good, leading to healthy competition – but only if they weren't part of the same company.

Not only were there too many competing marques, there were also too many employees. A high-profile casualty of the reorganisation was Alec Issigonis. Although he still had an impressive title, Director of Research and Development, he was no longer the God of Longbridge. So no more highly advanced, strange cars then. There would be strange cars in the future, but nothing that would turn out to be very good. Certainly nothing in Austin or Morris showrooms to tempt Dad. It was 1969, and the Maxi didn't appeal, he was hardly going to wait for the Marina to turn up, and a Cortina was just a bit too common. This time, dad gave Rootes, or rather Chrysler, a chance. Those loans by the Rootes dealer when Dad needed a spare car had paid off. He opted for the company's own version of the Ford Cortina, otherwise known as the Arrow.

Well, actually it wasn't. Arrow was the internal codename, but it is a shortcut way of referring to a huge number of differently badged but otherwise identical models. In 1966 Chrysler took over Rootes just as this new range of saloons and estates were introduced. Chrysler were busy amalgamating 30 separate operating companies into two, and probably looked on in horror at the sheer number of versions of this one car they were going to try and sell. For me, though, when I found out what Dad was considering it opened up some very interesting possibilities. I knew that he wouldn't have gone for the fussy Singer Vogue, or smaller-engined Gazelle. They had extra chrome and wood trim, and Dad liked all that, but I reckoned it was an old man's car, as was the even posher and more expensive Humber Sceptre version. There was also a large coupe called the Sunbeam Rapier which would not have been practical, having just the two doors.

However, I already had a lot of respect for the most basic model in the shape of the Hillman Hunter, which had won the gruelling London-to-Sydney Rally in 1968. I had followed that race extremely closely, not realising that it had been organised to showcase the durability of British cars, even though foreign ones were also allowed in. The race was also meant to be an adventurous and positive event, as a counter to all the rioting in the streets that was going on at the time. At least a British-built car – the Hunter – won, and Chrysler were determined to capitalise on it by launching a special model. Yes, what Dad needed was a Hillman GT.

To the innocent eyes of a nine-year-old, the GT was no cynical marketing exercise designed to get buyers to pay extra for a tarted-up Hillman Hunter. No, it had sexy Rostyle wheels. Rostyle was the brand of really rather ordinary metal wheel that had an exciting moulded pattern on them comprising four silver spokes with four half spokes in between, like a clock face, on a black background. Rostyles looked like they belonged on a sports car, but they would be a crucial part of Dad's next car. That's how important Rostyle wheels actually were to me and any other small boy at the time who loved cars. Rostyles weren't just bolted on to family saloons that needed a sexy lift. More upmarket Rovers and fantastically expensive Jensens wore them too.

Apart from the wheels, there were also a couple of go-faster stripes down each side, and several badges that said GT. This was 60s shorthand for Grand Turismo. This GT was unlikely to do any grand touring – just get Dad to Surrey and back each day, and to various locations around the country for major exhibitions and maybe the odd summer holiday to Torquay. Most of all, though, when he took me to football on a Saturday at Hackney Marshes or Wanstead Flats, I'd be sitting in the front of the coolest saloon ever. Even cooler than a Ford Cortina Mark 2 1600E, which also had Rostyle wheels. But it was a Ford, whereas inside the GT were high-backed sports seats that looked a bit like executive chairs, except that they didn't swivel. No other car I knew of had such exciting seatage with an integral headrest.

However, the one thing that was very clear to me was that the GT looked nothing like the Hillman that had raced all the way from London, via Calais to Sydney. I knew that because I had been given the Corgi model the previous Christmas. That had diamond headlamps, a tool box that opened and spare wheels mounted on the roof. There were also spot lamps on the roof and front wing which swivelled. Most important of all, it had "Golden Jacks", a system that allowed you to take off the wheels and change them. You simply flicked a metal switch (which was gold, of course, and that became the jack on which the model stood.

Up front there was a red plastic "roo" catcher. Long before the days of 4 x 4s wearing bull bars, this innocent bit of ironmongery was only supposed to come in handy for the Australian leg of the rally. And just so small boys could experience the "roo" catching experience for themselves, a small plastic scale model of a kangeroo was included. It wasn't so much catching as bashing a "roo", which made it even more fun. Actually, I didn't really care that the production version didn't have the toolkit, or "roo" bars, or even the rear step plates welded on the back to help the co-driver (me, Mum or my sister) to bounce the Hillman out of a bog. Although at Hackney Marshes, that would have been incredibly useful.

So as part of my campaign to convince Dad that he really needed the GT in his life, I left magazine advertisements lying around the house for the car to the point where my Dad should have been subliminally inclined to sign on the dotted line for a Hillman GT without realising it. Imagine my joy, then, when Dad arrived home with a gold Hillman Minx. It was the lowest specification model on the price list. A Minx was effectively a Hunter with most of the ingredients missing, which wasn't much anyway, just as a Hunter was a GT with all the crucial parts not even on the options list. A Minx had the smallest, weediest engine, and I was already missing the solid, dependable Morris Oxford that had been passed on to Uncle Charles. I also think Dad was too.

On the outside, the Minx looked clean and nicely styled, but it represented all that was wrong with the British car industry that was content to produce the absolute bare minimum. Mechanically, it was crude, while the interior couldn't be any more synthetic, comprising the hardest, bleakest and cheapest plastics known to science. As a further taste of things to come, the company that made it, Rootes, were now foreign-owned.

Welcome to the 1970s.

In the garage: There's now a gold Hillman Minx which is underwhelming, and it hasn't got any GT badges on it. However, in my rather smaller car collection there is the Corgi London to Sydney version with the removable wheels and a red "roo" bar and everything.

Births
1966 BMH (British Motor Holdings)
1966 Unipower
1967 Trident
1968 British Leyland Motor Corporation (BLMC)
1968 Piper
1968 Davrian
1969 Enfield

Marriages
1966 Alvis to Rover
1966 Jaguar to BMC to create BMH
1966 Rover to Leyland
1968 BMH to Leyland to create BLMC

Deaths
1966 Turner
1967 Alvis
1967 Gordon-Keeble
1967 Peel
1968 Rochdale
1969 Elva
1969 Riley

New Arrivals
1966 Porsche
1967 Toyota
1967 Mazda

Best Seller by Year
1966 Austin 1100/1300 151,679
1967 Ford Cortina 165,300
1968 Austin 1100/1300 151,146
1969 Austin 1100/1300 133,455
1970 Austin 1100/1300 132,965

In the Car Park
In this Chapter you will have come across some of the following vehicles and personalities...

Left is Donald Stokes who we probably should have pictured in the last chapter, but here he is and the first car the newly formed BLMC was responsible for, the Austin Maxi. All the seats folded flat to create a double bed, how useful.

Top Left on the second chunk of pictures is the Morris Marina, then the coupe. Below those an Escort GT and a Lotus Cortina. Third row is the Ford Capri and a Sunbeam Rapier. Fourth row is a Hillman GT and an upmarket Humber Sceptre.

Sports cars with the top row left MGA, then MGB, MGB GT on the second row with the Sunbeam Alpine next to it. The Triumph Spitfire and Triumph TR4 are at the bottom.

10 Commies, Aggros, Snags, Dollies and the arrival of the Snob Roader 1970–1974

In the garage: Still that Hillman Minx, which is starting to look a bit red and rusty around the edges. Mind you, a 1963 Austin Mini Super De Luxe turns up, bought by my sister off her friend Regina. Several years later I spray the roof matt black.

In the 1970s everyone was on strike, apart, it seems, from Mum and Dad. It was homework by candlelight, telly went off early and wearing flares was compulsory. Apart from glam rock, it was fairly grim, and of course if I haven't mentioned it already, everyone was on strike. The industrial strife of this era was, of course, another crucial factor in the downfall of the British car industry. 1971, when the ruling Conservative Party introduced the Industrial Relations Act, was actually the worst ever year for industrial upset and an act of parliament didn't make any difference. The thing is though, poor labour relations were nothing new, and dated back a very long time. Indeed it all dates back to when the business of making cars was a curiously seasonal activity, especially between the wars.

What happened was that new models were introduced between August and October and then displayed at the London Motor Show. Well, these weren't exactly new models in the sense that that they actually existed. These were usually cobbled together as display items, which was highly appropriate as they would be put on show at Earls Court in a sort of beauty contest. At that event the manufacturers would then take their orders, which then meant they could plan their production schedules over the winter. After being stockpiled, these new cars were distributed to dealers in March and the selling season would last until the early summer. Meanwhile the workers would be laid off until they were required to go back and build new models. That meant they got summer jobs, so to speak, but generally they earned high wages because of the seasonal nature of the job and because they benefited from overtime payments if production needed to be increased. So working in a car factory was a good job, but it wasn't one that was dominated by trade union activity. That didn't happen in until the second world war.

A series of agreements that allowed more unskilled workers to do jobs which had been solely for the skilled were then pushed through, as it was crucial to get more women into the factories to make planes and tanks and armaments. Not only did the unions agree to this, but they managed to negotiate reciprocal deals whereby a skilled toolmakers would be paid at least the average earnings not only of the production workers in their own factory, but throughout a particular area of the country. Here was the root cause of spiralling wage demands that would hamper the industry for the next generation. The dynasties in charge of each car company suddenly found that there was a new tier of often competing unions that they had to deal with. In peacetime this situation got even worse, especially when new models were introduced or new factories opened.

However, I don't want to go into huge detail on all this as I think you may get as bored as I would, rattling on about piecework, acronym-heavy union names and what went on during those interminable beer and sandwich meetings between government and union leaders which were constantly on the news at the time. I bought a great book from a charity shop years ago called "Ford Strike" by John Matthews, published in 1972 by Panther Press, a more right on version of Penguin. Not surprisingly, it's a paperback about a strike at the Ford factory in Dagenham, which happened in 1971. It was written from the "workers" point of view and it told me all I needed to know about industrial relations and what a humourless, scary and sanctimonious bunch the union leaders and their supporters were. What makes this book funny (when it is a deadly serious polemic on the evils of global capitalism) is the fact that its previous owner, who presumably paid the full 40p cover price, had annotated various paragraphs. He reads like a working class Tory, which is what Dad became, who underlined swear words in biro and wrote sarcastic responses to some of the book's more extreme Marxist claims.

There is much detail about the fairly petty grievances that led to mass walkouts and summed up the gulf between management and worker. Something as simple as going to the loo without permission was a big deal for both sides, and inevitably led to a walkout. Then there were the convoluted scenarios that saw a foreman doing a material handler's job: handling material obviously because the handler wouldn't be doing any handling. Then the material handler refused to handle said material again, in protest at the unauthorised handling. He was suspended and everyone walked out.

Over at BLMC a no-search policy at the Longbridge factory meant entire engines and numerous other components would routinely be liberated in the backs of Austin 1100s whose headlamps were presumably pointing at the sky. Then there was the employee at Daimler who stole a unique set of prototype wheels and fitted them to his Ford Anglia. It didn't take Sherlock Holmes to spot them in the car park. The stories were rife right through the industry, and it is a miracle that any vehicles got made.

So all you need to know is that there were a lot of stupid, meaningless strikes that affected production, quality and customer confidence during the 1970s. Just as there had been during the 1960s and 1950s really. Trade unionism was to blame, as was an inept and weak management structure. Closer to home, Dad had not just been a passionate union member, he also became leader of the Tobacco Workers Union in the early 50s. After the war he had rejoined cigarette maker Godfrey Phillips, where many of the family already worked. Now although the union could be a force for good, Dad saw at first hand the pettiness, minor corruption and debasement of working class values that characterised the way some union officials operated. He became disillusioned, and when he left the factory to learn to drive and get behind the wheel of a Triumph Mayflower, he also left behind the union and the Labour party, never to return. Like everyone else at the time, he moaned about "the bloody unions", but at least he did so from a position of some authority.

There might have been loads of industrial trouble and strife, but the British Leyland Motor Corporation (BLMC) looked to be in a fairly healthy state. In 1970 they sold a not unimpressive 788,737 cars. Meanwhile a rather smaller statistic hardly registered on the motor industry radar, as 4,291 cars arrived in Britain from Japan.

Significantly, as the Japanese manufacturers made the most of their "just in time" production techniques which had been in place for over 20 years, BL struggled. Oh yes, "just in time" operates in exactly the way it sounds. The parts needed to make a car are delivered by the suppliers as the car is being built. With no costly stockpiles to worry about, the Japanese could get on with the business of building better cars for less money. By contrast BLMC was an operational nightmare, and because of the constant industrial strife, they maintained more than one supplier for items like exhausts. Also those parts would be of variable quality and were not always priced very favourably, so again, it was a major achievement that any cars got built at all. Still, the British manufacturers weren't looking that far east at the competition, and neither were their customers. No, they were peering behind the iron curtain.

In the late 1960s and early 1970s it was the Czechoslovakian, Polish, East German and Russian cars that made British car buyers think twice about buying British. Hungry for western currency and a labour rate that was either minimal, paid in cabbages, or free in the gulags, these cars could easily undercut an Escort or Marina. Not only that but they could then load up their vehicles with extras that would usually be on the options list. Heated rear windows, radios, fog lamps, more comprehensive tool kits and exciting things like that.

The first model to come to the British car buyer's attention was the Russian Moskvich, which meant "Son of Moscow" and was a medium-sized saloon and estate car that even Dad looked at half seriously, entranced by the longer than usual specification list. These cars had their origins in a pre-war Opel Kadett – war reparations, but for the Russians this time. It resembled a Morris Oxford in a rugged and no-nonsense way. Moskvichs even went racing on the track and on rallies to prove how tough they were, even though they were truly terrible to drive. However, if you were ideologically aligned with Iron Curtain cars then you wouldn't worry if they weren't that great to drive. That is the only explanation as to why anyone ever bought the East German Wartburg.

Try saying "I've got a Wartburg" without creating an unofficial exclusion zone. And if the name didn't put you off, having to add two-stroke oil to the petrol like an old motorbike meant that you created a smoky and smelly atmosphere wherever you went. It is incredible to think that it was made in the former BMW factory that had been trapped on the wrong side of the curtain. Then there was the Trabant. Equally East German, and only nominally available in the UK, it was conclusive proof that the communists couldn't do cars. Except for the Czechoslovakians, that is.

Skoda had a long and illustrious history and, as has already been pointed out, heavily influenced (were ripped off) the design of the Volkswagen Beetle. So although they didn't get a free hand under communism, their cars were at least interesting. The ones coming to the UK were packed with extras at no extra charge. Indeed, a Skoda 1000MB appeared two doors down in 1969. This was a surprise as the owner of the car wasn't just well off, but multi-millionaire super-rich. However, the playboy bachelor at number 3 wasn't in the habit of flashing the cash around. Even though his father who lived with him was a minor shipping magnate and always wore a black overcoat and bowler hat, they owned a red Mini. So when the old man passed away I expected to see a Jensen Interceptor, Aston Martin DB6 or E-Type appear. But no, the Mini was swapped for a Skoda.

Ron, who lived at number 3, was a modest, shy and retiring bloke who lived the frugal life. He enjoyed rambling, in the countryside rather than in conversation, and regular continental holidays with a lady friend. So if a man with unlimited resources preferred to buy from a Czech car company because he got so much more for his money, such as two extra doors, an engine in the boot and seats that reclined into a double bed, what hope was there for the British motor industry?

Actually I don't think they were too bothered. BLMC could relax as the best selling car in Britain was the Austin/Morris 1100/1300, which kept the Ford

Cortina in second place. Overall though, and taking foreign sales into account, the old Mini was the company's best seller being built in Australia, Belgium and Italy. As has already been explained, these small cars didn't actually make much in the way of profits, so BLMC were determined to make changes. Having failed to create a new best-seller with both the Austin Maxi and then the Morris Marina, they had to do something different. However, it was a company within the huge conglomerate who made the next quantum leap in car design, and it was so good it's still with us. I am talking about the Range Rover.

The strange thing is that Rover had kicked the idea of a posher Land Rover around for some time. Indeed, if you go all the way back to 1948, a coach building company called Tickford put an estate car body on a Land Rover in an attempt to civilise the Landie. It wasn't a big hit, mostly because, at £949, it was furiously expensive. You could probably buy a country estate for that, plus £200 of Purchase Tax was added because it was classed as a car. Catch 22, though, was that it was also regarded as a commercial vehicle and limited to a top speed of 30mph. Hardly surprising then that it didn't catch on. Rover though did experiment with the concept and called their prototypes Road Rovers. Trouble was, these were based on cars, so were just two-wheel drive and had boxy bodies that looked like sheds.

However, a bright engineer called Charles Spencer King noticed how well the Rover 2000 car performed with coil springs in the suspension and reckoned that the same would work on a Land Rover. At the same time a chap called Graham Bannock in the marketing department noticed the way that off-road vehicles in America were no longer being bought soley by farmers and cowboys. He reckoned that the 4x4 would become a fashionable urban accessory, and he couldn't have been more right. The key ingredient that made the Range Rover so good was that they fitted their V8 engine rather than something underpowered and weedy. So it had permanent four-wheel drive, unlike the rest of the Land Rover range, and that made it unique to drive. The brilliant styling was the result of an extremely square prototype being tidied up by stylist David Bache. Also by accident they had created a timeless classic with a Lord of the Manor driving position. The result was part dual-purpose vehicle, but mostly a four-wheeled status symbol.

Even if Rover believed that it would be building site professionals like architects and surveyors who would be the main customers, remarkably the Range Rover turned out to be an alternate executive/luxury vehicle. However, the first examples were sparsely equipped precisely because Rover expected them to lead a tough life. So inside there were wipe-down plastic seats and pull-out-and-shake rubber mats. It took them a full 10 years to add a set of more practical rear doors and then another decade to offer an unapologetically indulgent luxury model. Going upmarket took a very long time, but in the short term, they couldn't build enough of them.

With a new decade came the opportunity to make some more significant changes to existing model line-ups and maybe start to organise them a bit better. So for the 1970 model year the company dropped the competing Austin and Morris badges on Minis, so they became just Minis. Not only that, BLMC were now more determined than ever to make some money from their tiny best-seller and maybe even replace it. Indeed, those puny Wolseley and Riley versions, the Hornet and Elf, proved that it was possible to charge more if there was enough chrome and equipment to justify a price hike.

The difficult task of restyling the Mini fell to Roy Haynes, already responsible for the right-angled Mark II Ford Cortina and the rather underwhelming Morris Marina. Not surprisingly Haynes went down the square root (pun intended) to boost luggage space. The prototypes apparently looked a bit clumsy and lumpy and were rejected, except, that is, for the front end. They kept the boxy front which made the Mini 4 inches (102mm) longer, a bit heavier and, as a result, slightly less economical. They called it the Clubman, which cost £45 more than the original cute-faced Mini 1000 and actually did quite well. The buying public simply lapped up any new version of their favourite car, even if the front end resembled a very dear old friend after some ill-advised plastic surgery. It always looked like the afterthought it actually was. Owners though will tell you that they didn't skin their knuckles anymore when carrying out routine inspections under the bonnet. Inside, the Mini had been dragged into the 1970s by actually putting the instruments in front of the driver, rather than in the middle. The seats also had more padding, while fresh air ventilation came courtesy of simple eyeball vents at either end of the dashboard. What must have horrified the now powerless Issigonis was the installation of new fangled wind-up windows. Instantly they robbed the car of the hugely practical door pockets. BLMC management, though, couldn't believe it had taken so long to introduce such a simple update.

If the Clubman was at least acceptable – indeed my Dad did eventually buy one in the late 70s – one version visibly struggled to be taken seriously: the 1275GT. It had the unenviable task of replacing the legendary Mini Cooper and Cooper S. Although both models were available concurrently for a while, the reason given for introducing the GT was insurance. Mention Cooper and insurance companies would instantly raise their premiums. Actually, the insurance companies regarded it as a Cooper in Clubman disguise and the premiums stayed the same anyway. John Cooper, whom it affected more than anyone else as he was no longer going to be paid a fiver commission per car for the use of his name, suggested that something subtle like E should be used if insurance was the real reason for replacing the Cooper. Of course it wasn't, and even worse, the 1275GT turned out to be slower than the model it replaced. Arguably BLMC had killed off one of their most charismatic and marketable brands. Brand management, though, wasn't exactly a BLMC strong point.

Compromise and fudge were starting to dictate new model policy. In 1972 the final BMC related model was launched as the 2200. In theory, it should have simply worn the advanced engineering Austin badge. In reality it also had Morris badging too because Morris dealers didn't have much to sell apart from the mediocre Marina. So BLMC probably thought sod it, lets have a luxury one as well, which meant there was Wolseley version, too. So after trying to reduce the number of badges they were multiplying again. The 2200 was a real dogs' breakfast of old BMC parts using the structure and suspension of the unlovely "land crabs", effectively an engine and a half from the Austin Maxi and lots of bodged re-engineering to make it all work. Sadly no one really needed a slow, thirsty, dated but spacious saloon like this. Just over 20,000 of both Austin and Morris versions were sold in three years, which was pathetic. In fact 25,000 more buyers preferred to get themselves the better equipped Wolseley 6 version. Obviously BLMC should pay a bit more attention to their upmarket models where there would be more profit opportunities.

So just as the ill-fated 2200 was launched in 1972, a restructuring of the Specialist Car Division was announced. What this actually meant was an integration of Rover and Triumph, while Jaguar continued in its own independent way. Sir William Lyons stood down from his old company on the day of the announcement, having been incredibly and cleverly protective of Jaguar. Indeed when Leyland bought Rover in 1967 there was a super Rover saloon to rival anything made by Mercedes and using that reworked V8 engine. However, with the creation of BLMC a year later, such a vehicle would have been an obvious threat to Jaguar and their just announced XJ6 model. But development of this luxury saloon continued while Sir William's presence on the board meant that he could constantly make a nuisance of himself. This pressure paid off as just six months from launch, when millions had been spent on development, the board caved into pressure and called off the big new Rover. Not only that, but Lyons managed to scupper Rover's proposed sports car which had a V8 engine sited in the middle of the car. The P6BS, as the prototype was known, looked as though it had been styled with a set square, but this could have easily been sorted. BLMC and Rover would have had a Porsche rival if it weren't for Lyons.

Things were even worse at Triumph, because they were told by BLMC management that they would not be allowed to develop a replacement for their 2000/2500 models. No, that would be Rover's job, although Triumph would help out by coming up with alternative engines. At least Triumph had the Stag. Here was a brand new model that was a heart stoppingly beautiful four-seat convertible with a removable hard top. BLMC intended it as a credible alternative to a Mercedes SL, and also had high hopes for the American export market. After styling the Triumph 2000, Giovanni Michelotti thought that a sporty convertible based on it would work. It was called project Stag, a name that it kept through to production. Powering the Stag was Triumph's own V8 engine, essentially two smaller engines joined together. The creation of this V8 is significant because when the companies merged and Leyland took on Rover, they already had a V8 engine. Car companies even then rarely had use for one large powerful engine, let alone two.

Apparently attempts were made to put Rover's fully-developed engine into the Stag, but it was claimed that it didn't fit. The truth is that there was a lot of professional pride at stake, and the Triumph engineers were keen to keep their own engine under the beautiful bonnet. Unfortunately, the engine was not powerful enough and had to be uprated, and there were all sorts of extra delays and also an over-complicated production process. Incredibly there were three BLMC factories involved, which wasn't good for quality as bodies were shunted around the Midlands before final assembly. However, that was a minor inconvenience compared with the horrors awaiting unlucky Stag customers.

Here was a beautiful car with a beastly, undeveloped engine. It made a wonderfully throaty burble, not unlike a vampishly beautiful woman who smoked 60 fags a day. Otherwise there was little going for the car, and it never seemed to get very far because basically the Stag broke down a lot. If you want the details, well the cylinder heads – and there were two of those – would warp. That caused the cylinder head gaskets to fail, leading to a catastrophic loss of coolant. Not only that, but a timing chain – and there was only one of those – would stretch. Once stretched, it would jump off the cogs, which meant that the valves and pistons would collide rather than missing each other. It was a disaster and it was no wonder that it was soon nick named the Triumph Snag. The irony was that subsequently, many private companies offered Rover V8 conversions which seemed to work perfectly well. Clearly a missed opportunity for inter marque co-operation. This certainly put Dad off ordering one in the mid-70s, and he wasn't alone.

Triumph wasn't having a lot of luck as there were reliability issues across their range. Apart from the troubled Stag, their model range was a throwback to the 1960s with the Spitfire and TR sports cars, and in the case of the Herald there was still the whiff of the 1950s. The TR range, which in 1969 had made it's way to number 6, was restyled in Germany and became an even more brutish and blokeish sports car. It looked solid and modern while the old Herald, with its quaint little rear wings and cute chrome hoods on the headlamps like an ageing 50s starlet, was overdue a facelift. The company already had the 1300 introduced back in 1965, which was a sort of upmarket Austin/Morris 1100/1300 with a similar front wheel drive layout, but not as cleverly packaged. As with all the other successful Triumphs, it was styled by Michelotti. For 1970, though, all the Italian stylist did was add some extra bodywork to the front and rear to make it bigger. It also got a bigger engine and was called the 1500. Meanwhile the engineers took a step backwards and front-wheel drive was replaced by rear-wheel drive on the 1300. It kept the old rear, got the new longer front and a new name, Toledo. This was all very confusing, offering a jumble of vehicle formats and model names when Triumph had clearly squandered an opportunity to become BMW.

Not only did Triumph share designer Michelotti with BMW – he had styled the model that revived the German company in the early 1960s – but both had a sporting pedigree. By the 1970s, BMW had a range of models that shared similar styling that positively encouraged buyers to trade up through the range as they could afford and possibly need a larger vehicle. Not only that, but they would also produce what was effectively a road-going racing car with a performance engine and style that succeeded in making the more ordinary models look even more desirable. That was very clever, and something that even big manufacturers like Ford did when they created the Lotus Cortina, or went racing at Le Mans with the specially created GT40. It's the best way of advertising really. For BMW, it meant that they could charge more money for their cars which appealed directly to well-off enthusiasts. Already Triumph has created the 1300TC (the TC didn't stand for Top Cat as some friends at my primary school genuinely believed, but for twin carburettors). Now carburettors mixed air and petrol before feeding that into the engine. So two carbs meant that more fuel was going in and the car would be faster, which was a good thing, of course. Triumph, though, took three years to replace it with the 1500TC, which confusingly enough by 1973 had become a rear-wheel-drive model. This too was a good thing. All BMWs were rear-wheel-drive, which was always regarded as the "sporty" car layout, sending the power to the rear wheels for better balance.

The way was now clear for Triumph to become a Brit BMW. Sadly they failed to do this with a model that was only mildly less disastrous than the Snag, sorry Stag. First of all Triumph created another new model out of two existing ones. The basis of the new Dolomite was the 1500's front and rear end plus the Toledo's rear drive. It should have launched back in 1971, but obviously labour disputes delayed everything and the Dolomite was slow to arrive. When it did, the Dolly as everyone called it, was a smart, classy, well-appointed car that would become a blueprint for some of British Leyland's and Rover's later models. It would sell in respectable numbers and was so good that Dad bought two of them. However, one of them really wasn't that brilliant, and full breakdown details will follow in a later chapter.

So using the Dolomite as the basis, Triumph decided to take on BMW. Already buyers would happily pay a small fortune for a BMW 2002, a fast, small saloon car. In 1973 they could pay a lot less – £1,740 – for the Triumph Dolomite Sprint. By contrast, the basic 2002 was £2,399, although it wasn't as quick as the Sprint. Indeed to match the performance you had to trade up to the 2002 tii, which cost £2,799. The Triumph certainly looked the part, that is to say a BMW, but without the distinctive double kidney shaped grille. Indeed, if you had replaced the Triumph badges with BMW ones, glued on that grille and junked the wooden door cappings and dashboard of the Brit, you would never have spotted the difference. Even the Dolly's bonnet flipped forward in the same way as the BMW's. That meant you didn't have to crouch underneath a metal tent to stare at a darkened oily old engine. No, you could stand proudly with your back straight and arms folded admiring the incredibly sophisticated power unit in the harsh light of day.

The engine used in the Sprint had been designed by Triumph for Saab four years previously. It was the same one that they had joined together to make the Stag's V8 engine, with predictably poor results. It had also been installed in non-joined-together form in the basic Dolomite, but Triumph really excelled themselves when they developed it for the Sprint. Making the engine larger in capacity rather than dimensionally meant it was more powerful, but the key to even more speed was a 16-valve cylinder head. All you need to know is that this effectively doubles the usual number of valves and it was executed in such a clever way that it won a Design Council award in 1974. The bottom line was a top speed of 115mph and 60mph arriving in just under 9 seconds, making it a snail by today's standards but as quick as the hot hatches that would dominate the market a decade later. It was quicker than Triumph's own TR6 and the MGB, which were supposed to be sports cars. The truly compact executive saloon had been reinvented as a potent sporting saloon that undercut BMW and beat them at their own game.

Triumph must have been watching what Ford did to make their cars look sexy, and after the 1600E and Hillman GT this became another candidate as Ruppert family transportation – in my imagination, of course. What was quite an old design suddenly looked relevant again, wearing a front spoiler, alloy wheels, vinyl roof and twin side stripes. This makeover was the early 70s equivalent of your dad growing his sideburns and hair a bit longer, investing in a pair of hipster trousers, stack heels and something medallion-shaped for the neck area. Dad only indulged in a few of those. It certainly worked with the Dolly Sprint too, the added bonus being the high technology under the bonnet. However, like the Stag, it wasn't a lucky car. 1973 may have been a great year for fashion, but it was a terrible one for petrol and peace.

That Arab-Israeli war in October 1973 sent oil prices soaring, which meant that any high-performance car which used slightly more fuel than it should was less in demand. It didn't help, though, that the engine was a bit rubbish. Like the Stag, the Sprint overheated, and if you remember, that caused cylinder head gasket failures. This wasn't entirely the Sprint's fault as the owners really should have topped up the radiator with special corrosion-inhibiting coolant rather than plain tap water, just like in BMWs. Actually, it did have a lot more to do with that award-winning engine design, which was possibly a bit too clever for its own good. According to engineering boffins, the retaining bolts on one side of the aluminium cylinder head went through at a slight angle rather than being completely vertical. That meant that it didn't secure the top of the engine to the rest of it as tightly as it could have. Not only that, it pulled the top of the engine very slightly askew when it got very hot. It didn't help that build quality wasn't quite as wonderful as it could have been, either. So what you had with the Sprint was a high-maintenance machine. It got better, and this was never a disaster on a Stag-like scale, but it was another demonstration of the curse of the BLMC, which turned a marque once famed for reliability into one that clearly wasn't. It didn't help that the whole Triumph range really was now quite old and not due for any urgent updates, or replacements. So Triumph was effectively dead.

Never mind though, because BLMC could finally show the world what it could do from scratch. Obviously, the Austin Maxi could be explained away as the Austin Tragedy, an old BMC project that should have been re-engineered and restyled, if only they'd had the time and inclination. Then there was the Morris Marina, which was really the Morris Mistake, a rush job, nothing more than a dull re-skin of the lovable poached egg that was the Morris Minor. So in 1973, the strike-torn and terrorist-threatened Britain finally got the car it deserved: the Austin Allegro. And my Uncle Charlie bought one.

If any car summed up an era it was the Allegro, which arrived when the workers building them were on a three-day week and their wages had been frozen. Not that they let those small matters affect their dedication to producing a top-quality product. Yes, these were shoddily built saloons, but then the workers hadn't been given a top quality product to work on. That was despite the design stretching back to the creation of BLMC itself in 1968. Here was a car that they couldn't possibly afford to get wrong because it was intended to be the replacement for their bestseller, the Austin/Morris 1100/1300 and all those other differently badged spin offs. They had all managed to keep the Cortina in the number-two sales spot throughout the 60s, until the Ford became number one from 1970 on. So all the Allegro had to do was outsell the Cortina. Easy.

First of all, the front-wheel-drive layout was carried over from the old car, but they changed everything else. Fluid suspension was replaced by gas, which was more compact and promised a smoother ride. The Allegro was also big enough to take the larger engines from the Maxi, as well as the smaller ones from the old 1100/1300. All this was contained by a design that could best be described as dumpy. When it was on the drawing board, though, as penned by another ex-Ford man Harris Mann, it looked rather smart. Sadly, Mann's clean lines were interfered with and blobbified in the design studio, so that it latterly became known as "The Flying Pig". It may have been the fact that they needed to plumb in bigger engines and the heating system from the Marina, which meant making more space for all this extra stuff. Indeed, going down the rotund body route was in retrospect a mistake because at the time, car styling was getting noticeably sharper, like the soon-to-be-launched Volkswagen Golf.

Apparently the Allegro was more aerodynamic going backwards than forwards, but this is one of many Allegro Urban myths. Rather than boffins actually putting an Allegro in a wind tunnel, this is probably based on some back-of-an-envelope calculations. Actually, many cars would be more slippery if spun around, but it suits the comedy car reputation. Far worse was that the Allegro's slippery rear end had a boot. This seemed very misguided, as the hatchback was about to become a very big thing in Europe – see again the multi-million-selling Volkswagen Golf. The reason why the Allegro was denied a rear door was internal politics; it was deemed that the Maxi should be unique.

So if the Allegro looked odd on the outside, it was also decidedly weird on the inside. Fitting a heated rear window as standard was probably an initiative designed to distract the buyer away from the fact that the steering wheel wasn't exactly wheel shaped. In fact, it was described as a "quartic" steering wheel, effectively a rounded square. Apparently it was based on a throwaway doodle produced by brilliant designer David Bache. He'd been presenting concepts on behalf of Rover-Triumph and it was picked up by BLMC senior manager. The quartic fitted in with the new high-tech image being carefully crafted for the Austin marque. Actually, they had failed to understand what Bache was getting at, and created a crude interpretation. We know this because it wasn't until the Rover SD1 was launched three years later when the more carefully crafted profile of four arcs joined together passed unnoticed and never caused a problem. It was suggested that the "square-wheel", as it probably should have been called, was introduced because insufficient room had been allowed between the driver's legs and the base of the wheel. There was some truth in that because compared with the model it replaced, it certainly felt a lot less roomy. The rear seat cushion was actually cut at an angle to allow passengers to get in more easily. Meanwhile, the quartic steering wheel certainly caused problems, when even the highly trained police drivers repeatedly crashed their Allegro Panda cars, unable to pass the wheel smoothly between hands as they had been taught.

It is amazing that the constabulary managed to get the Allegro up to ramming speed. Allegro, if you know your music theory, means fast and lively, but this Austin was anything but, as the new car's performance failed to match that of the old 1300. Magazine road tests showed that it took longer to get to 60mph and it was actually 5mph slower in top-speed terms. This is probably explained by the fact that the Allegro was heavier and bigger, but even the bigger engines from the Maxi didn't make the car feel any more urgent.

The incredible thing about this litany of design and development mistakes is that they were warned it could all go horribly wrong. BLMC took the brave decision to invite a select group of journalists to give the Allegro a "once-over" before it was actually launched. They questioned the quartic wheel and the distinct lack of character at the front end. Obviously no one listened. As a result, the Allegro sold fewer than the car it replaced. Whereas the lovable old 1100/1300 managed to consistently sell comfortably more than 100,000 every year, the very best that the Allegro could manage was in 1975 when just 63,339 new ones were parked on suburban driveways. To put that in perspective, in 1973, the very last year that the 1100/1300 was on sale, more than 59,000 were sold. Not only was the Allegro wrong in so many ways, but it also gained a reputation for being the Austin Aggro due to poor build quality and less than impressive reliability.

Urban Allegro myths and legends multiplied, largely focusing on the blobby bodywork's overall structural unsuitability. That meant that the rear windscreen could pop out if the car was jacked up in the wrong place with a trolley jack. It was also reckoned that if you were reckless enough to attempt to tow anything behind an Allegro, best not to engage reverse gear, because if you did then the doors would burst open. There was certainly some truth in those rumours, and some also believed that if you attempted to tow an Allegro it would bend in the middle. However, one of the most alarming occurrences was being overtaken by your own rear wheel. That happened because the rear wheel bearings were prone to failure. Often this was the result of over-tightening, and once they broke the wheels would indeed come off.

In 1974 BLMC finally did something about the Allegro's dull front end: they made it uglier. As the rather cute and classy Austin Princess was phased out, in came the Vanden Plas 1500. It was just an Allegro with a large engine and a huge chrome grille that gave it a massive piggy snout. Vanden Plas was the name of the coachbuilder whose London workshop the Allegros were sent to for the shiny bits to be bolted on. The extra chrome, leather seats and wood veneer scattered around the cabin were a welcome distraction, but the very best thing about the Vanden Plas is that it came with a proper, fully circular steering wheel. BLMC never officially admitted they got it wrong, and the standard Allegro got its own proper round wheel the following year. The Allegro, though, had to get even worse before it could improve slightly. In 1975 the Allegro estate, which had just two doors as well as a tailgate, could have been the belated hatchback which saved the day. Instead it was another supremely uncomfortable styling exercise that only succeeded in looking like a miniature hearse.

Uncle Charles and Aunt Flo had moved from our house when they bought the Allegro, so at least we didn't have the shame of having it parked outside. The Allegro replaced his Mini, and it was a quartic wheel one, too. I can remember sitting in the back and looking at how awkward it looked when turning into corners. It didn't look smooth and it didn't look natural. Uncle Charles didn't like it one bit, and bought himself a conventional replacement. He didn't have the problem of rear screens popping out, or doors popping open, which would have alarmed Auntie Flo. I think, though, he did have some wheel-bearing issues though and it was never a very reliable vehicle and I believe it was abandoned in East London with the keys in the ignition. Well it probably wasn't, but it felt like the Allegro just disappeared and wasn't even recycled within the family, as usually happened. Fast-forwarding a few years, the huge irony is that I ended up giving Uncle Charles my first car, a Mini. It had already belonged to my sister, who still denies to this day that she charged me £50 for it. That Mini was already a decade older than the Allegro, but it was 10 times as good. These were bleak days for BLMC, when their cars were so bad they were easily replaceable by obsolete BMC models.

This was a worry for me as Dad was due for a change. But the unloved Hillman Minx would be replaced by what exactly? BLMC's products were a national and even international joke that lost nothing in translation. Dad didn't buy Fords, although the so-called Coke bottle styling of the Cortina looked quite good. There was always an outside chance of going back to Vauxhall of course, but the Vivas were too small and the Victors just looked big and clumsy.

So for the first time in my life I was worried about the future. Not about the collapse of a society that was permanently on strike and descending into pinko-communist anarchy. Not about England's failure to qualify for the 1974 World Cup. No, I was worried that there wasn't a British-built saloon car that would be good enough for Dad.

Still in the garage: Hillman Minx and my sister's Austin Mini.

Births
1970 Clan
1970 Costin
1971 Arkley
1971 Panther
1972 Jensen Healey
1973 Caterham

Marriages
1970 Rootes/Simca to Chrysler Europe

Deaths
1970 Austin Healey
1970 Singer

1970 Unipower
1971 Enfield
1971 Marcos
1973 Fairthorpe
1973 Gilbern

Best seller by year
1970 Austin 1100/1300 132,965
1971 Austin 1100/1300 133,527
1972 Ford Cortina 187,159
1973 Ford Cortina 181,607
1974 Ford Cortina 131,234

In the Car Park
In this Chapter you will have come across some of the following vehicles and personalities...

Communist cars from top left the Russian Moscvich, the East German Wartburg. Second row is the equally East German Trabant and next to that the Czechoslovakian Skoda.

Top left is the Range Rover and after that a brace of Clubmans, saloon, the 1275GT Mini Cooper replacement and finally the estate. Last row is the Austin 2200 'Landcrab' and next to that the much prettier Triumph Stag.

Top row left is a Triumph 1300, next to it the later Toledo model. Next row is Dolomites the 1500HL and the Sprint.

Left is the BMW 2002 which was designed by Michelotti, just like the Dollies. Then there is the Allegro, the Vanden Plas version and below, the Quartic steering wheel that caused all the trouble and finally the supremely awkward hearse-estate.

11   Ryder, some Big Bumpers and a Foreigner in the Family 1974–1976

On the drive: The Hillman Minx gets parked on the drive sometime in 1974 and doesn't move for two years. That's because there's a new car and it wasn't built in Britain causing much fluttering of curtains and conversation around the neighbourhood.

I must admit that I didn't really see this car coming. I was definitely looking the other way and I think I may have briefly been distracted by girls, football and Led Zeppelin. One day I looked out the window and there it was, an Audi 100LS, and it belonged to us. It was tremendously exciting to see such an exotic car up close. Its styling was simple, understated and classy. Even more than any of that, it seemed to be very solidly put together. There was almost as much plastic as the Hillman Minx, but it was a different sort of plastic. Some of it was coloured to look like wood, which normally would not have been a good thing, but it was strangely inoffensive. Plus, the Audi interior benefited from some strategically-placed chrome and probably the hardest-wearing beige upholstery I have ever encountered. The 1.8-litre engine made it the most responsive car ever to transport the Ruppert family. It also had front-wheel drive, which proved that large family cars with a Mini style layout were the future. Also, being the 1970s, it was brown. But it was a good brown – a scrummy, deep chocolate colour that really suited it. Not a dull, depressing BLMC one. Four brightly polished chrome hubcaps made the wheels gleam. The finishing touch was the grille, which had four interlinked rings of confidence. I remember this car so clearly not just because I was older, but because in three years' time it would become the first car I ever drove. Although technically I'd steered my dad's Vauxhall Wyvern for the purposes of a short cine film and operated Mrs Lewis's Princess 1100 in next door's drive, the Audi would be the first car I legally drove on the Queen's highway.

Now the Audi wasn't a Mercedes, it was actually much better than that – more youthful, less staid and more affordable. BMWs weren't yet on the radar in the UK really, and the original 5 series was also furiously expensive and not as handsome. The Audi could be regarded as a posh Volkswagen, because they owned the firm. VW, unlike BMC and BLMC, knew how to use the parts available to them, and anyway, they were skilfully building a distinctive and upmarket brand which today couldn't be stronger. Back then though, I never heard anyone refer to it as a pseudo VW, even though you had to go to a Volkswagen showroom and walk around a Beetle near the front door to place your order.

Obviously there was the more obvious Rover or Triumph 2000 option, but Dad didn't want another British car. The Hillman Minx's overall averageness, plasticity and synthetic aroma could no longer be tolerated. Unlike a lot of car owners, Dad could take advantage of the company car situation. He was now a director of an international exhibition company and could have whatever he wanted within reason. On that basis, I would have preferred it if he'd gone for an Audi 100 Coupe – that did actually seat four and looked just slightly like an Aston Martin DBS.

Dad's choice of an Audi sprung not from disloyalty, or even the fact that he'd driven a series of terminally dull British-built cars, but was a reflection of the fact that he knew there was a wider world out there. Since the late 1950s he had travelled extensively throughout Europe and more recently the middle east. He'd seen the Audi in it's European habitat and liked what he saw: a sophisticated and smart set of wheels. Cars like Audis, Mercedes and BMWs didn't just look good, they didn't break down either and may have been no better equipped than an Iron Curtain Wartburg, or Birmingham-built Maxi, but were beautifully bolted together. And anyway, this wasn't Dad's first foreign car; the Vauxhall Wyvern was American, as was the Hillman Minx, Hillman being owned by Chrysler at the time.

Although buying a non-British-built car was catching on, it was still a slightly odd thing to do. In fact I'll indulge in a bit of time travel and go back to 1974. I am now leaning out of the window of Nightingale Secondary School, which is destined to be bulldozed and replaced by a housing estate (what else?). What can I see in the car park to my right? Well, loads of British-built cars. Most seem to be Austin/Morris 1100s in saloon and estate form, and just about affordable on a teacher's salary. The same goes for a few Cortinas and inevitably a Mini. Oh yes, and an Escort and a Viva and a posh Triumph 2000 which belonged to the headmaster. I remembered that car very clearly because I got a lift to casualty in that. After all these years the true story can be told as I went through a reinforced door while mucking about with my school pals. Running in the corridor wasn't allowed of course, but ratting on your mates was a far more serious offence. I said I slipped, and that led to the headmaster telling me not to bleed on the cloth upholstery of his Triumph. In an age before rampant compensation culture, the school claimed I was wearing "fashion shoes", which of course I disputed. I wish I could say that having stitches in my bottom and a pair of trousers cut to shreds was worth it for a ride in the most expensive model in the car park. But I can't. The Triumph was a very underwhelming experience and I was relieved that Dad hadn't bought one of those.

That school car park represented a perfect cross section of UK car ownership, being small, medium and just a little bit foreign. Yes there were two Renaults, one a Renault 6 parked near to the main entrance and the other a Renault 16 up the other end by the bike sheds. Fairly predictably it was the French teacher who had the 6. This was a better equipped version of the Renault 4, which was itself Renault's interpretation of the peasant's and student's choice, the Citroën 2CV, but not nearly as lovable or wacky. Our French teacher not only drove a French car, she looked French too. Elegant, smartly dressed and very thin with short dark hair, she resembled Audrey Hepburn, who of course was Belgian. Her husband was just as cool and taught guitar. Years later I even bought one of his books called "How to play Rock Riffs".

The Renault 16 at the other end of the car park belonged to the school communist, although his official title was careers teacher. He looked as old as Trotsky would have been if he hadn't been stabbed with an ice pick in Mexico in 1940. He was a grumpy old sod who among, the recruitment posters for the post office and the red army, had piles of magazines that resembled a Russian Country Life. The gist was how wonderful it was behind the Iron Curtain. To cap it all, his advice could be summarised as don't work for anyone because the capitalist system is evil. I don't know how he got away with it, but he did. He should have been driving a Moskvich or a really crummy Wartburg, but instead he chose a Renault, possibly out of solidarity with the students and workers who took to the streets of Paris in 1968. This is a roundabout way of saying that there were only two hatchbacks in the school car park, and they both belonged to the two most distinctive and interesting members of staff. So if you owned a foreign car at this time, you weren't like everyone else and – dare I suggest it? – that you could think for yourself.

So while 1974 had been pretty good for the Ruppert family, the motor industry in general and BLMC in particular were careering rapidly downhill. Just to recap on the circumstances that created a basket-case of a country, just about everything can be blamed on October 1973 when the Arab-Israeli War broke out. The knock-on effect was reduced fuel supplies and a price that multiplied fourfold. To conserve fuel stocks, Prime Minister Edward Heath introduced a 3-

day week on 1ˢᵗ January, and there was a blanket national 50mph speed limit. The trade unions didn't like it and we got the miner's strike in February 74. Heath called an election that he lost and Harold Wilson and the Labour government were back on board.

That meant everyone went out and bought super-economical Minis, and that became BLMC's best selling model, leaping ahead of the grim Marina. The Mini had been designed to tackle the first energy crisis created by Suez, and it was rising to the challenge again 20 year later. Obviously the minimal Mini profits were not going to help company finances, and throughout 1974 the company desperately tried to find additional finance to keep going. BLMC didn't just talk to bankers – they also turned to the government. The Secretary of State for Industry, Tony Benn, who had so much to do with the creation of BLMC in the first place, made a statement to the House of Commons on December 6. Among the platitudes that the company was crucial to the economy as a manufacturer and exporter, he also made it clear that long-term there was likely to be some degree of public ownership. Obviously they weren't going to rush into this, although they did guarantee £50m of bank lending. The government wanted a full report on exactly what sort of state BLMC was in and what its prospects were. They could have asked Dad, or any man or woman in the street what was wrong, and they would have come up with a very cogent explanation of where BLMC was going wrong. Instead it was the usual suspects, the great and the good and the ennobled who were to comprise the team. Former Industrialist Sir Don Ryder was already the government's pet industrial adviser, and he was going to write the report.

Meanwhile as Ryder was scribbling away, yet another ill-conceived model was about to roll out of BLMC's factories. Here was proof that bad things certainly do happen in threes. After BLMC had created the mundane Marina and the all aggro Allegro (the Maxi was a BMC creation, remember) there came the frankly wonderful to behold Wedgies, the 1800 and 2200. Codenamed Diablo, these models were certainly devilishly handsome compared with the "land crabs" that they were directly replacing. The idea was to retain the same generous interior dimensions, but at the same time upgrade the interior, from bed-and-breakfast basic to something rather more three- or four-star. Harris Mann, who had styled the Allegro, was let down again by having his design "frozen" several years before launch and the proposed hatchback cancelled. His wedge-shaped design was certainly striking and not a bit like a dreary Cortina. Trouble was it really did look a bit too wedgelike with its tail high in the air sweeping down to a long bonnet. If the car had been any good, the distinctive styling would have probably helped. Unfortunately, it polarized opinion into the love it or loathe it, while the general cynicism towards BLMC products meant the 18-22 series, as the Wedgies were officially known, meant they never got an easy ride.

First the bad news: badge engineering was back. After deciding to do away with all those differently flavoured versions of what was essentially the same car, BLMC now offered you three Austin, three Morris and Wolseley badged wedges for your money. This was mainly because Morris dealers needed a model above the Marina. For the meantime though, you could tell them apart because the Morris versions had four headlamps, reshaped bonnet and a bolted-on mini grille, like a BMW, but not nearly as classy. In addition, the better equipped, big-engined Wolseley had its famous badge right in the middle of the grille, which lit up at night. This was advertised as "The car that's got it all together", but obviously the marketing was all a bit confused. This was confirmed when in six months, all the badges were dumped to be replaced by one name: Princess. The Wolseley badge disappeared forever, while the four-eyed models were 1800 and 1800HL and the trapezoidal lamps from the Austin went on the bigger-engined 2200HL and HLS. That didn't change much because the build quality was still dire and the likelihood of breaking down still quite high. Water leaks and collapsing trim were just a couple of issues. More serious were drive shaft problems on 2200 models, and these models were even taken out of production to be sorted, which was a seriously expensive course to take. The Wedgie story was far from over, but by this time everyone was more concerned with the contents of the Ryder Report.

As you would expect, it stated the fairly obvious: that Leyland had bad management, outdated machinery and appalling industrial relations. Fixing all that would cost a fortune, estimated at £2,800 million over seven years by the chancellor of the exchequer, Denis Healey. If they didn't go through with this, then the British car industry would die, which including all the associated companies would cause at least a million job losses. No government could afford the latter, so it was a case of getting the public to subsidise the former. Harold Wilson told the House of Commons that they would effectively be taking the company over. BLMC ceased to exist on June 27, 1975, and it was renamed British Leyland Limited, which means from now on I can finally refer to it as BL.

The boss, Donald Stokes, was kicked upstairs to become president, despite being routinely blamed as the architect of the company's downfall, having brought all these companies together under Leyland's lorries. The truth was he did take on more than he could cope with, and there just wasn't the quality of management to run this sprawling empire. Add to that some of the questionable decisions regarding marketing and design, plus the Arab-Israeli war, and they were pretty much doomed. Running a car company isn't an easy business, but they only had themselves to blame for the Stag, Allegro, Maxi, Marina and Princess. So what was Ryder's brilliant solution?

On the face of it, BL were set to continue much as they had done before by competing on both the volume (taking on Ford) and specialist (still make sports cars and Jags) areas of the car making. Ryder's really big idea though was to turn the company into one integrated business. That was meant to address the fact that the company offered far too many competing models. He recognised the need for better research and development facilities, along with better industrial relations. However, the real trouble was that Ryder would base his recovery plans on figures and projections that were plainly wrong. He regarded the 1975 production levels as "depressed" as the whole of BL made just 605,000 cars that year. He reckoned that the number would increase to 843,000 by 1980 and on to 961,000 by 1985. If only... If only the model line-up had been that appealing. Obviously Ryder had never tried to jack up an Allegro, change gear on a Maxi or drive anywhere in a Stag without 10 gallons of bottled water. Indeed he made no recommendation about closing factories. Even MPs, who love forming committees, produced their own report on the Ryder Report called "The Motor Vehicle Industry". They also identified the costings as being quite fanciful and projections as being over-optimistic. Indeed they identified the folly of putting all the car marques in one basket with a BL logo on it. This committee also realised that unless higher output and sales were achieved, there would have to be redundancies. But it was all too late.

Ryder's words were effectively law, and he would implement them when he was put in charge of the newly formed National Enterprise Board (NEB). BL was now some great big amorphous car company, and at the 1975 Earls Court Motor Show all the company's products were lumped on to one exhibition stand. That did not go unnoticed in my house as Dad was building stands for IPC magazines at the time. He was there with an exhibitor's pass every day leading up to the opening. Dad only then needed to go back on the last day to oversee the stands being taken down. The thing was though, he had a son who was, despite the appearance of girls, football and Led Zeppelin, still mad keen on cars. That meant he would take me up to Earls Court on a Saturday and we'd get in for free. Lanyards around the neck hadn't been invented then; it was proper lapel badge with "Exhibitor" written on it.

No queues, just straight into the brochure-collecting experience. That was the whole point of going, simply to see how many shiny brochures you could cram into a plastic bag. Being with Dad though was extra special because absolutely everywhere was open. Even the officious ex-forces commissioners who delighted in keeping the massed ranks of snivelling schoolkids and their dads off their patch visibly wilted at the sight of an exhibitor's badge. I could and did sit in every single car that I wanted. Obviously the fully-open stands like BL's and Ford's were still a scrum, but it was the roped off areas which held the most interest. At this point I am supposed to wax on about how marvellous it was to see lightweight Porsche 911s and really rather red Ferraris, but I can't. I did have a thing about Lamborghinis though, and owned a Matchbox Espada (although actually it was the Marzal prototype from 1967, trivia fans, that eventually evolved into the Espada) and obsessively collected pictures of the

Countach. Now the Espada was a four-seater, which meant that it was just right for our family transportation. The Countach would be something I could store and possibly grow into driving. And then there were the Alfa Romeos that I would doodle endlessly in my school textbooks. And no, I don't remember those stands as well as I do some others.

Obviously I would love to have been at the Motor Show on press day, the first day it is open for motoring hacks and the media, especially as from 1971 minor sports car maker TVR introduced the exciting concept of nude models. Sadly, press day, when the models would make the most impact, was always a schoolday. However, I can remember going up there on some late afternoons, but presumably the models had got cold and gone home. We would always spend quality time on the stands that Dad built, and he knew so many people that making progress was sometimes difficult. I remember clearly Cyril Lord, the father of Babs Lord, who was the pivotal blonde member Pans People just in case you don't know. For teenage schoolboys, this was the only reason to watch Top of the Pops. Why watch mediocre groups and singers aimed at girls mime to their hit when it was much better to see attractive young ladies literally interpret these songs. My personal favourite wasn't Babs but the rather more brunette Dee Dee, Ruth and Cherry. I didn't tell Mr Lord that though. He was a director at Kumficar, who were after-market accessory specialists in an age when car manufacturers hadn't realised that there was money to be made out of selling seat covers, mats and stuff. That explained why we always got some natty colour-matched car seat covers, but never on the Audi, because it didn't need them and it would have looked weird. Like putting plastic wood trim in a Morgan.

I was always able to check each year whether or not Morgan had changed materials because Dad loved going on their stand. I believed that there was an outside chance Dad would actually buy one. He would have waited five to six years without a problem. Here was a car that Dad could keep forever and, most important of all, let me drive and look after in later years. A hand-built British sports car made out of wood and aluminium just like the old days probably underpinned his love for the model. Indeed, Dad had said that there was an uncle once-removed called Jimmy McCormack who had done rather well for himself as an inter-war crooner (singer). He met a sad end during the war, but he earned enough to buy a sports car during the 30s. There is every chance that the car could have been a Morgan 4/4, but then there were dozens of models that fitted Dad's description of a low-slung, long-bonneted sweeping-wheel-arched sports car. It was certainly difficult to miss because it had "Doobie Be Bop" or something similar stencilled down each flank. To Dad and his brother Joe, it was fantastically exciting to see a sports car up close. It was even more thrilling to go for short rides around the utterly unmotorised streets. I think the Morgan must have reminded him of that car.

I usually tugged Dad towards the Plus 8 model, which had the V8 engine from Rover which was an intoxicating combination of raw power and ancient cart-building technology. It was an anachronism in the mid-1970s, but compared with the futuristic Triumph TR7 offered by the newly-nationalised British Leyland, it looked... well, normal.

Like other forthcoming models, the TR7 had been developed under the old BLMC regime and was released first in America, because it was designed for that market and to replace the MGB. It was the result of a competition between Triumph and MG. The boys at MG, or rather those based at Austin's old factory at Longbridge came up with a really advanced sports car with its engine in the middle, advanced suspension and styling that can only be described as Ferrari-esque. Over at Triumph they went down a more conventional route, which meant engine at the front driving the rear wheels. Triumph were the winners because in America that's what the company needed to combat the simple and, most importantly, reliable offerings from companies like Datsun and their 240Z, which had made tremendous inroads into that profitable market. Also, because it was feared that safety legislation would effectively outlaw the open-topped car, it had to have a hard top.

So Triumph won the competition, but bizarrely the two ideas were combined into one and Harris Mann was brought in to wave his wand of wedge shaped magic over it all. Yet again, his adventurous styling on the drawing board was compromised when it was finally made into metal. Not everyone was convinced by the styling, especially as the car had a bit too much ground clearance as if it was expected to be used off-road. The stylistic reservations were shared by design greats like Giorgetto Giugiaro, who was responsible for the original Golf and was obviously a bloke who new something about iconic shapes. Sadly there is no way of verifying the following story, even though he wrote a foreword for a book I wrote on Golfs, but he didn't speak English and it seemed cheeky to ask him. However, it is alleged that, at the 1975 Geneva Motor Show, he took a long hard look at the TR7, especially the sharp body line that curved its way from the top of the rear wing down to the bottom of the front one, and with impeccable comic timing and in Italian said, "so they did the same on the other side."

Now that could have been pure sarcasm, in which case it is incredibly funny. However, within the design community it has been general practice to do alternative styles on either side of a scale or full-size model. So it could have been general surprise, in which case it remains funny and becomes even funnier when someone told him this was a finished vehicle and not a concept. The point is, the TR7 looked a very odd.

However, launching the car into the hyper-critical American market first wasn't a great idea as fussy customers picked up on the lack of build quality straight away and so sales didn't live up to expectations. Not only that, but the Liverpool workforce at Speke went on strike for four months in 1977-78, which lead directly to the cancellation of a Sprint model which would have had the Dolomite's advanced engine and also a Lynx model which would have been a hatchback version. There were more knock-on effects as the ultimate TR7, which would be badged TR8 and have the V8 engine under the bonnet was delayed for two years. Not surprisingly, the Speke factory was shut in 1978 and production moved to Canley in Coventry. Oh yes, and just to help continuity, TR7 production was shifted yet again in 1980 to Rover's factory in Solihull. The rumoured banning of all convertibles by America never happened, so the prettier open version was finally allowed to accelerate off the drawing board. Actually by the end it had been developed into a decent sports car and it was Triumph's most successful TR, but it was also the last Triumph sports car.

Back in the mid 70s, although BL were bravely hoping that the TR would become a worldwide hit, at least they had a whole bunch of 1960s sports cars that they could rely on. The Triumph Spitfire was still about, and also the MG Midget and slightly larger MGB roadster and GT coupe. In fact BL loved them so much that they decided to give them a little face-lift. Already the MGB had to endure black plastic rather than chrome grilles, and nasty blue swirly BL badges were stuck on the wings. The ultimate indignity, though, came in 1974 when great big bumpers were bolted on the front. It wasn't just bumpers, but a whole new section that also replaced the grille. It was a bit like Hannibal Lecter's muzzle, but not quite so pretty. Enthusiasts referred to the new section as rubber bumpers, but as every anorak knows, they were actually plastic – polyurethane to be precise – with added steel reinforcement. It was those pesky Americans who insisted that all cars be able to withstand a 5mph knock without damage. So as a result, the MGB got a new front and rear end, which was available in any colour you liked so long as it was bleakly black. If that didn't look bad enough, the US also had new headlight regulations. Rather than redesign the front of the car, BL simply raised the suspension by an inch. Not only did it look really daft perched up in the air, it also meant that, combined with those much heavier bumpers, what had once been a tidy car to drive became a lurching, boatlike menace. The Americans probably would not have noticed the difference as they never went around corners, but real sports car lovers were appalled. BL even made the situation worse by deleting some crucial suspension parts to save money.

However, if the MGB looked bad with it's new appendages, the tiny Midget looked particularly deformed. At least the Spitfire remained unmolested as the chrome bumper had already been relocated more centrally and prettily into the middle of the grille back in 1970. Apart from unwise bumper additions, what was really slowing down British sports cars at this time was the Americans, again. Their anti-pollution regulations meant that the engines needed to be modified, and that meant making them go slower. For the Spitfire, that meant getting the bigger 1500 engine from the Triumph Dolomite, which was actually a good thing.

MG purists, though, were horrified to discover that not only had their baby Midget been disfigured but it also got the same engine transplant as the Spitfire. The British sports car was losing its identity and sales in the biggest export market (USA), to more reliable and exciting offerings from Japan. The Brits, though, could always be relied upon to buy the badge. BL certainly had their troubles, but they still had a lot of misplaced customer loyalty and taxpayers' money to keep them afloat. Chrysler weren't so lucky.

Chrysler struggled in the mid-70s and were losing a lot of money. In 1975 Sir Don Ryder, who had enough on his plate trying to sort out BLMC, was asked by Tony Benn to take a look at the state of Chrysler. It wasn't a pretty sight as there were few customers for what was now a very dated model range that still included the unloved Imp and Dad's Minx, although the Hillman and Humber brands were due to disappear forever. The Chrysler 180 was a very odd, largish saloon that was supposed to be the new Humber, but mostly it was ignored by every serious car buyer. Not surprisingly, the American bosses wanted to get rid of the company which scared the government so much they called for a meeting and even Prime Minister Wilson turned up. That meant substantial government loans and, in return, guarantees by Chrysler to keep on building cars in the UK. The Avenger, which hadn't done too badly as an alternative to the Vauxhall Viva, had its production switched from Coventry to Linwood in Scotland. However, Coventry got to make the 1976 Car of the Year in the big bland shape of the Alpine, previously only made in France. At least it was a practical hatchback. Mostly, though, all these changes meant that the lacklustre cars were all rebadged as Chryslers by 1977, which didn't help sales one bit. In fact it had the opposite effect.

On our drive, we still had the red and gold Hillman Minx. The red wasn't an original part of the finish, but bubbles had soon arrived to complement the gold paint, and when they burst, crumbly red rust spilled out. Dad hadn't driven it since the arrival of the Audi, and two years later, in 1976, I had half-heartedly tried to tackle the rampant automotive acne, only slightly worse than my own. With a patience that would come in handy in later years as I tried to keep old British cars roadworthy, I would carefully apply Kurust, then mix and apply Plastic Padding filler before painting it with a zinc undercoat.

That was good practice, but my main motive was that there was also an outside chance that perhaps the Minx might be my first car. If so, then I could make it look like a GT or even a proper recreation of the London-to-Sydney Corgi model with "roo bars" and everything. However, it was now 1976 and the hottest summer since records began, which meant that progress was so slow that Dad was going to give it away to my elder cousin's husband. He turned up with a Cortina one evening and found that it was seized pretty solid. It made horrendous deathly rusty scraping sounds as it was towed away, and we never found out whether he got it going again, and frankly no one cared because there was going to be another new car in our lives. Yes we were going to become a proper two-car family.

I had for the last few years been at the forefront of brochure collection for the Ruppert fleet. Outside of privileged motor show visits, I'd write to manufacturers and most excitedly of all go into showrooms, where I felt strangely at home. To their credit, I was never ejected on my ear as some scruffy schoolboy after a glossy for nothing. Indeed, when Dad did follow up my collecting expeditions with maybe a request for a test drive or further information, they'd always mention me, and in a good way. Obviously I knew my showroom etiquette and how to play the game. We were also lucky that there was a great big BL showroom down our high street. It was an Edwardian building that had masses of floor space and was heated by little gas fires in winter that made no difference whatsoever. The concrete floor was painted a creamy colour, and all the cars had paper mats underneath them with droplets of oil on them. Potted plants were dotted around the area, probably to fill up unused space rather than for decoration. The plain brick walls were painted white and relieved by colourful BL posters telling customers how wonderful their cars were.

So why did we need another car? After all, the Audi was brilliant. Well Mum wanted to learn to drive. Or more accurately, I think she liked the idea of driving and thought it would be a useful thing to know how to do. However, driving a car had never been a necessity. She knew all the bus and train routes and could walk all day without taking a break. Like most of the women of her generation who were born and raised in London and had survived the war, driving really wasn't an issue. In fact none of my aunts and the majority of my many uncles never even bothered to take a driving test. Mum reckoned that she had spent so much time in the passenger seat telling Dad whether or not anything was coming the other way at busy junctions that actually driving would be a doddle. She thought learning to drive by osmosis was perfectly possible, so consequently she didn't concentrate.

With Dad, that was fatal, as he would never hold back in telling anyone where they had gone wrong. So I think Mum lasted about half an hour, or about half a mile, before getting out of the car and walking home. My sister was patience personified, but after one or possibly two lessons, she retired from the driving instructor business.

Apparently Mum would have been a brilliant racing driver, always taking the tightest line around corners and even on occasion going right over the corner in true British Touring Car style. She wouldn't care if there was someone standing on the corner, mostly because she didn't realise they were there. No wonder my sister was as white as sheet with a look of abject terror in her eyes.

Mum would not unreasonably see something interesting going on and focus on that rather than something more important like steering. She was a beautiful, clever woman who had a capacity for hard work that was truly astonishing. She could excavate large areas of garden, mix concrete and shift tons of rubbish all while her son looked on admiringly, patiently waiting for her to finish so that she could cook his tea. The last thing mum needed to do was drive, even though it would end those long waits for the 101, 66 and 148. Dad, though, did the decent thing and gave her the opportunity. He knew that gears might be a multi-task too far for mum, so the car had to be fitted with an automatic gearbox. Even in the mid-1970s that was something of a novelty, especially on smaller cars. Tucked in the corner of the showroom, though, was a beige vehicle that seemed perfect.

I'd brought home the brochure, and it featured a mountain range, so it could only have been the Dolomite. We went into loads of detail about that model in the last chapter, but it wasn't a Sprint – no, this was a 1500HL. At least dad was backing Britain again. He could also have considered the Ford Fiesta, the American company's belated entry into the tiny shopping car market which at least had a hatchback. At the time, though (1976), there was no automatic, and for Dad, the Ford badge was a major obstacle. The most obvious foreign alternative was the Dutch-built Daf, a remarkably simple car with constantly variable transmission called Variomatic. Essentially that means one gear that adapts to the road conditions, and technically it involved a giant rubber band. That almost meant it was one of the slowest cars you could drive. Perfect for mum then, and I remember poring over the brochure with cartoons explaining how it worked the remarkable success the car had enjoyed in rallying. A racing pedigree, no less, even if it was competing in a class of one or two, both Dafs. But Dad could afford more expensive cars now, and believed that the more you paid the better it would be. Actually, the 1500HL, apart from some early guest appearances by rust, was a genuine credit to BL build quality. No, really it was.

The fact that it was a standard and not a Sprint Dolly didn't bother me too much at 16. I only had a year to wait before I would be let loose on the road, and knew that I would need to be satisfied with something more modest and less important to dent. I'd also grown up a tiny bit, and now knew that stripes didn't make a car faster or make you look any cooler. Long before irony became socially acceptable, the Dolly had a chintzy charm with it's tasteful wood- and chrome-decorated interior. As with BMW, there was a coherent family resemblance thanks to that clever Italian, Michelotti. You could see the Stag instrument layout in the dashboard and the larger, smarter Triumph 2000/2500 in the rest of the styling and cheekily cut off tail. Even more excitingly, I was beginning to learn that Dad was in the market for a new large car. I knew that it wouldn't be the Triumph 2500 because that was heading for the scrapyard.

Inside BLMC, Triumph had been told as far back as 1970 that they wouldn't be making larger cars any more, at least not on their own. Rover had been forced to defer to Jaguar, which meant they couldn't make any big saloons. But they could develop something smaller with Triumph. Consequently Rover's replacement for the 2000/2500 had its codenamed changed from P10 to RT1, which stood for Rover Triumph. That didn't last long, though, because it finally became the SD1, which stood for "Special Division", which was effectively team Rover and Triumph. Whereas the old Rover 2000 and 3500 were highly advanced and groundbreaking models, the SD1 was going to be far more conventional technically. Stylistically, though, it was going to be unique.

BL were now after the Mercedes and BMW buyer, which meant a big four-door saloon should have been on the drawing board. Instead, there was a huge hatchback. That was odd considering the underwhelming performance of the Austin Maxi, and the only other medium-sized hatchback of note was the Renault 16, which hardly bothered any Merc or BMW. The SD1 certainly looked sensational, and from the enclosed headlamps to the sharp bonnet shape and the double bodyline running down each side, it bore a strong resemblance to a Ferrari Daytona, but with three more doors. Englishman David Bache had done a sensational job, while inside they had managed to introduce the Allegro's square steering wheel, but without causing offence. The "Ovoid" wheel, looked very mid-1970s, while the rest of the interior was slightly sophisticated bachelor pad, with the instruments perched on top of the dashboard in their own Bang and Olufsen style Hi FI binnacle. Also under the bonnet of the first cars launched in 1976 was the faithful Rover V8. It was so wonderful that it was crowned European Car of the Year 1977. So what could possibly go wrong?

Just about everything really. It was launched just a month after the TR7, and BL were hopeful that their luck would turn, and it did. Demand outstripped supply by a truly massive amount. This was despite building an extended factory at Solihull, which was wider than strictly necessary as local residents had objected to its becoming any higher. Just under 7,000 were made in 1976 and a few more than 12,000 in 1977. You would have thought that as they made so few in that time, maybe quality could have been a bit better. No. Never mind that it seemed to be thrown together, it started to rust around its wheel arches and the lip of the hatchback. The electric windows and central locking would play up, while those groovy looking instrument binnacles had bits falling off. At least customers could rely on the good old Rover V8 for reliability.

In case you wondered what Triumph were up to, well they were developing a new range of smaller engines for the SD1. Unfortunately they weren't very good. The 2300 and 2600 not only burned loads of oil but they burned pistons and suffered head gasket failure, too, which were all really bad things. Apparently all this was down to a lack of testing and development. That was a pretty sorry comment on a company who established their reputation on solidity and reliability. Just as Triumph's reputation had been trashed by BLMC, BL was now running down Rover, and the frequent strikes didn't help either. During 1977 there was a tool makers' dispute at the Castle Bromwich plant which built the SD1. All that didn't stop Dad booking a test drive, but at least it was in a V8 and we are dipping into 1977 here.

I went along too, and sat sulkily in the back as only a non-driving teen could. It made a lovely sound though. The car burbled as I slouched, and Dad took it for an extended drive down the A12. Nothing fell off or rattled and it seemed much more luxurious than the sparse Audi, but certainly not better put together. The Rover had a lot more oomph, though. Enough oomph for dad to start asking the right questions about colours and delivery. My sneer turned into a distinct but well-hidden smile. However, the conversation took an unexpected turn for the worse. Of course they would love to take dad's money, but delivery would not be the formality that we had hoped for. There were delays which could run into weeks, maybe months, unless, that is, Dad coughed up £500.

You don't blackmail my Dad. He told the salesman what to do with that request and then went home to write a stiff letter to BL. This became an incredibly familiar pattern over the coming years. It made Dad feel better, but sadly it never really got him anywhere. What bothered my teenage mind more than anything was, if Dad wasn't going to buy a Rover SD1, what would he actually go for?

Still in the garage: Audi 100LS, while on the drive is a Triumph Dolomite 1500HL Automatic.

Births
1975 BLMC nationalised as British Leyland
1975 Princess

Deaths
1974 Bond
1974 Clan
1974 Costin
1974 Gilbern
1974 Piper
1975 Enfield
1975 Wolseley
1976 Jensen

1976 Jensen Healey
1976 Sunbeam
1976 Humber

Best Sellers – 1975 Country of origin in brackets.
Ford Cortina 106,787 (GB)
Ford Escort 103,817 (GB)
Mini 84,688 (GB)
Morris Marina 78,632 (GB)
Austin Allegro 63,339 (GB)
Vauxhall Viva 54,792 (GB)
Hillman Avenger 38,877 (GB)
Triumph Dolomite 30,119 (GB)
Austin Princess 29,067 (GB)
Hillman Hunter 28,966 (GB)

Best Seller by Year
1974 Ford Cortina 131,234
1975 Ford Cortina 106,787
1976 Ford Cortina 126,238

In the Car Park
In this Chapter you will have come across some of the following vehicles and
personalities...

Top left the Audi 100 Coupe that looks not unlike an Aston Martin DBS on the
right. Second row is Renaults with the 6 on the left and 16 on the right.

Top left is the wedge shaped Princess and on the right the Wolseley version that was made for one year only. Below that are Morgans, on the left is a Plus 8 in a motor show context with no small Ruppert in the driver's seat and next to that the not so quick 4/4.

Below is a Datsun sports car, this is the 260Z version which was proving such a bit hit in America. The Triumph TR7 was designed to take on the Datsun with it's controversial styling. Second row Triumph Spitfire on the left still looks stylish whilst the MGB next to it has to endure those big bumpers. The MG Midget on the bottom row looks even worse. The New Rover SD1 is set to be the saviour of British Leyland.

12 Hatchet Jobs, Turning Japanese and a Small Angry Schoolboy 1977

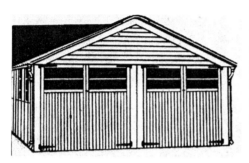

In the garage: Audi 100LS, while on the drive is a Triumph Dolomite 1500HL, plus a small blue 1963 Mini returns to the household and will be under new ownership. It looks like we are going to need a bigger garage.

Michael Edwardes actually arrived in November 1977 at the end of this chapter, but I thought it would be good to introduce him early on. He was rightly regarded as BL's last hope and seemed to be everywhere at the time, scowling. That wasn't surprising considering the mess this company was in. Heavy losses, chronic labour problems, outdated designs, inefficient factories and low productivity were just parts of one huge problem. Michael Edwardes would also have to deal with a lot of letters signed by Mr RD Ruppert. None of them complimentary.

Edwardes looked a bit like a small, angry schoolboy, but he was the pivotal BL chairman who both secured the long-term future of BL and the British-owned car industry, but also unwittingly sowed some of the seeds of its ultimate demise. At 47 years old, he was regarded as young and dynamic. At 5ft 2in, he was just a few inches south of Dad, and the South African's previous job had been chairman of the Chloride Group, that manufactured batteries. In a busy five years he had closed down plants and chopped the workforce from 192,000 down to 108,000, so he was obviously a no-nonsense manager. Edwardes was essentially a political appointment, as BL was now state-owned, and his boss was Labour Prime Minister James Callaghan. The deputy chairman was tough talking and acting Canadian Ian MacGregor, who would later take on the miners. Two men then who wouldn't be mucked about and on the face of it, this could be the shock treatment that BL needed.

At the time I didn't care what Edwardes was up to as I was now more concerned with getting to 17 years old, then getting a car, and then getting a driving licence, in that very strict order. I couldn't actually make time move any faster, but a car suddenly became a matter of urgency when my first girlfriend part-exchanged me for someone with wheels rather than a bus pass. It had all been going so well, but as the hottest summer on record became a pretty nippy autumn and winter, it was probably the sensible thing to do on her part. I was resigned to the situation until I found out that he drove a Hillman Minx. I didn't exactly own one, but I had been battling the rust on the dead one in our drive. If she could have been patient and waited for me to pass my test and get that Minx into shape, we might have been celebrating 30 years of marriage. Or a divorce with a rotten a broken Minx cited in the proceedings.

Dad, though, wasn't in any huge hurry to buy a replacement for the Audi. In 1975 he'd started his own company, realising that the only way to make a decent living was to do what he'd been doing for a lifetime, but for himself. From then on, Foresight Publicity Services Limited bought all our cars, including the Audi from Dad's former employers. However, with the Dolomite now with my sister, Dad reckoned that something smaller might boost mum's confidence and give pedestrians more of a chance to leap out of the way.

Now if you were in the market for a small automatic car in 1977 there was a new breed of vehicle that some marketing analyst would ultimately christen "supermini". Meaning it was small like a Mini, but actually just a bit larger, with a door where the bootlid used to be. In 1976, Ford seemed like the most surprising company to build a small, practical, hatchbacked and front-wheel-drive car. After all, they were the ones who had taken a Mini to bits, scratched their collective heads and concluded that BMC were mad. Why build a car at a loss? And anyway, the smaller the car the smaller the profit. Being Ford, though, they were unlikely to get a gamble like this wrong. Project "Bobcat" was a European project that was designed in Italy and ultimately would be built at various Ford plants around the world, including Britain, Germany and at a brand new factory in Spain. Here was Ford's first front-wheel-drive car, and it had the engine turned sideways just like the Mini, and one of the smallest units that Ford had made since the 1950s. This was a pricey project, but that made it all the more important to get it right as the fuel crisis meant cars like this were what people like Dad wanted to buy.

When the Fiesta came out in 1976 it was a very tidily styled, simple and attractive little car. Ford made 307,600 of the blighters at Dagenham until 1983, so it was also a successful little car. Dad didn't buy one though, because it was a Ford and because you couldn't get an automatic transmission.

Then there was Chrysler of course, a company previously known as Rootes with a whole bunch of different badges stuck to the same bodies. Chrysler had managed to get things slightly right by using a British-designed hatchback body and fitting an old French engine from Simca to create the Alpine which was enough to make it Car of the Year 1975. That was despite the wafer-thin bodywork corroding to dust within months and the engine getting noisy and needing an overhaul. The relative success only encouraged Chrysler to make another version of the Alpine but smaller, coming up with the Horizon, which was at least was better to drive and snatched another Car of the Year gong for 1978. From the Horizon they downsized still further to make the three-door Sunbeam in 1977. No prizes for this model, but here was a car which was effectively financed by the British government and built in Coventry. The Sunbeam was based on a shortened Avenger, and therefore had rear-wheel drive, which meant that it was sporty to drive and would lend itself to "hotter" versions. The smallest one though had an engine from the Imp, so it wasn't that quick. Not a bad looking car, although I only paid attention when it won rallies and had more stripes, lights and serious engines like the Ti and Lotus Sunbeam. It was a non-starter for Dad though, after the Hillman. There was no room for a tinny hatch, which again could not be bought with an automatic gearbox.

Over at Vauxhall they created what could have been a monster. They took the engine and gearbox from the Viva and bolted it into the European Opel Kadett floorpan. On top though they grafted on a distinctive pointed nose and a hatchback tail. This was 1975, and the whole package went down extremely well with British car buyers. Like the Sunbeam it had old-fashioned rear-wheel drive, which again meant sporting success. The HS model had light alloy wheels, a lovely lippy spoiler on the tailgate and a deep one at the front. It looked brilliant and was one of the first truly hot hatches. But Dad was never going to get one of those because it obviously didn't come with an automatic gearbox.

Although it was possible to get excited by car makers in Britain building small shopping hatchbacks, the shape of superminis to come was the Fiat 127. Although there was also a conventional two-door saloon, the one that everyone wanted had the all-important tailgate at the back. Launched in 1971 and available in UK showrooms a year later, it wasn't that pretty compared with the Fiat 500. It was certainly basic, but it set the standard for super clever packaging that everyone else would copy. Some 80 per cent of the floor space was available for passengers and their luggage, a bit like the Mini.

The Fiat, though, wasn't quite as popular in the UK as the Renault 5 from 1972. It's styling was certainly better and it was probably the definitive suburban shopper. Not so good looking was Peugeot's 104 hatch, which arrived in 1973 and didn't make much of an impact. Likewise the Volvo 66. Unusually for the company, it wasn't an estate car with warehouse-carrying capacity – no, it was much smaller than that. As owners of the idiosyncratic Dutch Daf brand, Volvo took a tiny estate car which was effectively a hatchback anyway, and re-engineered and rebadged it for the middle classes. It would have been perfect for Dad, especially as it could be bought with the rubber band Variomatic automatic transmission which was ideal for Mum. That wasn't good enough for Dad to buy, and neither was the real Volvo, the 345, which was offered from 1976.

Yes, the Europeans really embraced the whole hatchback thing, and probably the most successful model of all was the Golf in 1974. Volkswagen had finally developed a successful car that wasn't shaped like a Beetle. The VW Golf would have been the perfect buy for Dad, as would the slightly smaller Polo from 1975. Indeed there had been an identical (but for the badge) Audi 50 version which never made it to the UK. So posh hatches were around in the earliest days, and pointed the way ahead. But again, a lack of automatic gearboxes at the time influenced Dad's decision-making process. So he chose the smallest car that British Leyland built, which had a clunky automatic gearbox and, more to the point, a titchy boot rather than a fashionably useful hatchback. The thing is, though, it really didn't have to be that way.

There were two Italian connections to Leyland which could have resulted in their leading the world yet again in small car design. Alec Issigonis's last complete project for the company was the 9X in 1968. It was a remarkable 6 inches shorter, but 2 inches wider than the Mini. The engines were new and had something called a hydrostatic gearbox, a highly advanced automatic that adapted to the driving conditions and would not be fitted to cars for another 20 years. Most importantly, at the back was a tailgate. When researching a book on the Mini many years ago I looked through Issigonis's own files and found a report on the Autobianchi Primula. Here was a Fiat-based car that bore a strong resemblance to the 9X which had front wheel drive like a Mini and a hatchback. Clearly he had been influenced by this obscure model.

Issigonis had his prototype ready in 1968, but the new BLMC management knew how little money the original Mini had made and did not want to make the same mistake again. So although it was supposed to be introduced at the 1971 Motor Show, it never happened. Issigonis became very bitter about the cancellation but kept a 9X as his own car. Indeed he produced all sorts of clever improvements and even ran small diesel and steam engines, realising that alternative power would be the future. How right he was. But Leyland kept on making the old Mini. Or did they?

In Italy, home of the Fiat 127, a company called Innocenti had established it's reputation building the Mod's favourite motor scooter, the Lambretta. Founded in 1933 by Ferdinand Innocenti, the company decided to build the Austin A40 under licence in 1960, significantly the first mass-produced car to have a tailgate. The company then had a long association with BMC and built their own versions of popular models. They took the Austin Healey Sprite and put two handsome coachbuilt bodies on top, to make a unique convertible and coupe. Yes, that was the great thing about the Italians: they would put their own creative spin on the existing design, even when they had drawn it in the first place. So the Italian Austin/Morris 1100/1300 was given some subtle touches and even some rectangular headlamps that made it look like a mini Mercedes. As for the real Mini, Innocenti took a crack at that in 1965.

With the mechanical and some body parts imported, they created the Innocenti Mini-Minor 850. The grille was different, plus there were reversing lights and indicators bolted to the wings. Even better was their own Cooper version, and even later, the Mini t, which was their estate model, and the Mini Matic (what a great name for the automatic gearbox version). However, when Ferdinand Innocenti died in 1972, BLMC stepped in and created a new company, Leyland Innocenti SpA. That led to wholesale model name changes and a new British boss, Geoffrey Robinson. The very best thing to happen, though, was the Mini Cooper 1300. While in the UK it had been killed off for financial, political and quite spiteful reasons (no longer wanting to pay John Cooper a fiver per car), there was no such issue in Italy. Innocenti had never been party to the agreement. So while the UK had to put up with the watered-down 1275GT, Italy got the full-fat Cooper 1300, which had the Cooper S engine and the original styling, not the blunt-fronted Clubman version. However that still wasn't the best thing to come out of Innocenti. That honour goes to the Mini 90 and 120.

Coachbuilders in the England had been putting a third door into Minis since the early 1960s. Radford famously built several for Peter Sellers and The Beatles including a rear seat that flipped forward so that Ringo could get his drum kit in the back. Wood and Pickett were another company who would do whatever their customers asked, at a price of course. Most significantly, BMC built three Mini Cooper S models with a rear door. One was famously sold onto the then Transport Minister Earnest Marples. But after getting heaps of publicity, they thought no more about hatchbacks and Minis, unlike their Italian subsidiary.

Bertone were the well-established stylists who came up with the smart square-cut three-door that looked as good as and possibly better than it's hatched contemporaries. Underneath that practical bodywork was standard Mini running gear, yet it was only marginally bigger than the booted Mini. If you want the stats, it was just 2.6 inches (66mm) longer and 3.5 inches (89mm) wider, with the 90 version having the smaller engine, while the 120 had almost Mini Cooper S power. Anyone who spent any time under the bonnet of the standard Mini would have been surprised and possibly delighted to find the radiator at the front, rather than squeezed in the right-hand corner. Not so many skinned knuckles then, so there should have been some very red faces at BL. Here was a small, Mini-based car with a tailgate and rear seats that flipped forward to make a usefully large luggage area. That was what all Europeans were buying at the time, and all BL needed to do was price it right.

Indeed, the little Innocentis were imported to the UK in 1975 and tested by

BL with a view to adding them to their model line-up. It would have made sense, as the majority of mechanical components came from the plant at Longbridge and even some of the body pressings. The company actually got as far as drawing up plans to offer a limited run of 5,000. But apparently production costs would have been too high, so the project was canned. This probably did have something to do with BL's realising that profitable pricing was one key to success. But it was still an odd decision as they had already spent a large fortune on developing the model. So why not persist with it? Certainly British buyers would have coughed up a few pounds more than the standard Mini for something that was unique, more practical and just as good to drive. However, BL had their own small hatchback project under development and so wanted to focus on that. It would eventually become the Metro, but more on that later. The other very good reason why the Innocenti never made it here is that it would probably have fallen apart.

Certainly the ones brought in privately didn't last very long because of the low-grade Eastern Bloc steel that the Italian motor industry favoured at the time. So in our wonderful climate they, along with sundry Fiats, Lancias and Alfa Romeos, rapidly turned to dust. Now BL's troubles were bad enough, and an Italian-built car in the range could have finished them off even sooner. Certainly there wasn't a lot of money about at the time, and that probably contributed to Innocenti's bankruptcy in 1975. Fiat wanted to buy the concern, but a much smaller manufacturer, De Tomaso, beat them to it. Progressively, the hatchback became much less British when a Daihatsu engine was fitted in 1982, although it was now called the Mini III. Then it became the Innocenti Small and finally Fiat when they got their hands on the company and their Anglo-Italian rival was discontinued. What could have been? Well, we could have had one sitting on our drive, but Dad bought the next best thing: a Mini Clubman automatic.

Here was the most modern Mini you could buy at the time, although all that was really different was the blunt-fronted styling and the instruments shifted from the middle to where the driver sat. Dad, though, decided to give the chocolate-coloured car a twist, and ordered mudflaps that had a BL logo stamped on them and groovy "bumper bars". These weren't the aggressive killer bits of iron that became fashionable on off-roaders in the 1990s. No, ostensibly these were to protect your Mini in the car park, but really they were cosmetic chrome additions to the front and rear that rich people bought for their posh Minis. They even had a designer label and in this case a gold sticker that bore the names of Messrs Wood and Pickett. So if you couldn't afford their full-on makeover with leather, sunroof, wooden dashboard and all that, you could at least get the bumper bars, so we did.

Buying a Mini despite the proliferation of hatches wasn't an unfashionable move – indeed times had never been better for Britain's favourite small car. Its absolute peak had been 1971, when the standard Mini and Clubman sales topped

320,000 and it was the third best selling car behind the 1100/1300 and was never out of the top five right into the 1980s. So although the Mini had missed the Suez crisis that inspired it, in 1973 this model was in the right place at the right time. So with three-day weeks, national 50mph speed limits and even miners' strikes, nervous, frightened and frugal car buyers turned to an old friend. Mini sales in the 1970s could not have been stronger, and BL were furious. The loss-making Mini overtook the then rather new Morris Marina as their top seller for 1974. In fact the same thing happened again in 1979 when petrol prices soared after the Iranian Revolution. BL's best seller was the Mini, with the Marina and Allegro bringing up the rear. So the Mini was the car you bought in a crisis because you could rely on it to be economical and practical. But it wasn't irreplaceable. Those so-called superminis were coming.

So if the shape of things to come was a hatchback, it was also increasingly likely not to come to the UK and even more likely to come from places that were even further away than Europe. By the mid-1970s there were plenty of "Jap" cars to choose from, especially at the smaller end of the range. A Datsun Cherry came with a hatchback and more to the point had the same front-wheel-drive packaging as the Mini, but it also had better brakes and quite sophisticated independent suspension. The Toyota Corolla Liftback had a hatch, but the smaller Starlet would not arrive until 1978. Mazda had the 323 from 1977, and there was the Colt Mirage a year later. So there was no shortage of hatches with front-wheel drive from the far east. Yet again it was the automatic gearbox factor that influenced Dad, but there was still some resistance to buying Japanese.

Firstly there was the war. Although all the fighting Rupperts spent the second world war in Europe and North Africa and Iceland, there was the feeling that the Japanese soldiers had been a "particularly" cruel. Whereas only some of the Germans had been Nazis, to car buyers of my Dad's generation, the whole Japanese army had been Nazis. Dad didn't entirely subscribe to this view as our music centre was made by Hitachi and he would be an enthusiastic buyer of Sony music systems, Panasonic and Mitsubishi Televisions (and numerous Seiko watches) on the basis that they were the best. At the time, though, most Japanese cars weren't the best to look at. They could look weird – weirder even than an Allegro, or just terminally dull; there was no in-between. The Datsun Cherry was a stumpy little thing with two of the biggest rear blind spots in history courtesy of there being metal where the rear windows, or rather more of the rear windows, ought to be. Any visual oddness simply distracted buyers and drivers from the car's dullness. Plus, they had more chrome than was strictly fashionable in the later 70s and over-elaborate wheel trims that looked like novelty plates. Most of all, though, the Japanese packed their cars with useful extras like radios and heated rear windows. They played the value-for-money card brilliantly and far better than the Iron Curtain countries. You got so much more car. The absolute icing on the new car cake, though, was that Japanese cars didn't break down. They would start first time, every time, and the engines would rattle away to record huge mileages without being taken to bits. A feature of the 1950s and 60s had always been the "decoke". After 50,000 miles the Car Mechanics reader would follow the instructions, unbolt the head of the engine and clean off the sooty deposits. They would also grease the required nipples every few thousand miles to keep everything lubricated properly. Japanese cars needed less looking after and would just get on with the business of working.

The first buyers to spot these tremendous benefits were the Indian Asian immigrant communities. Without the Buy British baggage of the indigenous population but with an ability to spot a good deal when they saw it, they not surprisingly bought Japanese. And later on, when they could afford it, Mercedes. I'll base this social observation purely on living in East London and noticing what people drove, and also because of what went on next door. Mr and Doctor Nayani were reassuringly middle class, and turned into the best and longest-lived friends my parents ever had. I was more interested in their cars, which I remember being a large blue Nissan Laurel, followed in later years by an endless succession of Mercedes.

In the mid-1970s there was only one reason for not buying a Japanese car and that was because it shared one major problem in common with Brit and Euro cars of the era: rust. Except that Jap cars could be much worse. Steel that was even thinner than Italian cars of the time, combined with a UK policy of covering icy roads in corrosive salt, meant rust. Also Japanese cars didn't need to last that long in their home market as tough MOT regulations meant they were replaced after a few years. Over here, though, they kept on running, even when the body panels looked like paper doilies. So people still laughed at you if you bought Japanese. They laughed at your lack of style and cheapness, but of course they would be wrong. Short-term, long-term, in fact any term.

Our little Clubman turned out to be a fine little car. The paintwork wasn't brilliant, but the 70s chocolate brown paint seemed thick enough. And Dad had taken the precaution of paying for the car to be Ziebarted. This process involved caking the underside with black rubber sealant. You also got a sticker on the windscreen that featured a shield and the brand name Ziebart. It seemed to work, although the stuff was everywhere and leaked out of the car's pores (panel-gaps) for years afterwards. Then it went hard and flaked off. But that Mini never became a rot box even when it was passed down the family line and Uncle Joe drove it into the early 90s. So at the time we had a lot to be happy about, even though an automatic Mini made jerky and, it has to be said, noisy progress while you inhaled parfum de Ziebart. Not that I drove the Clubman much in 1977 because I had to stick to the gears in my £50 1963 Mini Super de Luxe.

Super de Luxe these days would mean sat nav, climate control, solid alabaster inlays and the finest cowhide known to man. In 1963, Super Luxe just meant fancier bumpers, wheel trims and a couple of extra instruments – water temperature and oil pressure gauges. In 1977 it also meant more added rust as the paint bubbled in key MOT failure areas like the floor and sills. My Mini did have one feature that in the noughties, in an extraordinary backward step, has become de rigueur for the fanciest supercars and is now trickling down to more humble models: an ignition button. In 1977, all that faffing around – inserting a key, then pressing a button – was regarded as quaint and very dated rather than something cool, as by that time, most other cars already had a new-fangled key that did the job in one easy action. However, this wasn't the car I first drove on the Queen's highway. That honour belonged to Dad's Audi. I thought I did quite well after stalling a couple of times. Dad, though, seemed genuinely shocked that I couldn't drive flawlessly within the first few yards. He was a hard man to please, and he expected me to be as clever as he was. This was a man, though, who during army service went on a return train journey to army barracks accompanied by a fellow Sergeant who asked if Dad played chess. Finding out that he didn't he taught Dad the moves and then never won a game. The fellow NCO never spoke to him again.

I could put up with Dad telling me where I had gone wrong, but at least I wasn't being taught by Uncle Charles. His docker's vocabulary had traumatised my sister, although it both amused and educated me as I sat quietly in the back as a seven-year-old along for the ride. At least my sister suffered no lasting damage because when she took me out she never swore at me once. She also took me to my first driving test.

I can't blame Marion, because I got to the test centre in a very relaxed frame of mind, but I do blame condensation. Everything was going extremely well until reversing around the corner, which I regarded as my specialist manoeuvre and an opportunity to score extra pass points. In all the excitement, though, and because it was a cool October afternoon, my rising temperature combined with an examiner conducting an emergency stop in a vehicle without safety belts caused the climate to change.

Inside my Mini, the windows steamed up. Even though I had the small stub of black electrical tape attached to the bottom of the rear window where the edge of pavement would have been. That was an old trick, and in ideal conditions it would have worked, but that day it was useless. I reversed by touch, and as the Mini's tyre rubbed the kerb I knew I'd blown it. Not surprisingly the first thing I did the next day was walk, yes walk, to my local motor accessory shop and buy a DIY heated rear window kit. I cleaned that rear window for ages so that even the merest suggestion of grime had been removed and the thin foil strips would be able to stick tenaciously to the glass and then conduct vital warmth to that rear window. In fact I've still got that rear window, and occasionally gaze through it with a feeling of dread, disappointment and defeat. I am sure that Michael Edwardes must have been feeling at least one of those things as he gulped and realised just what a huge task he had taken on.

Still in the garage: Audi 100LS, plus a Mini Clubman Automatic and that old Mini.

Deaths
1977 Hillman
1977 Trident

Best Seller
1977 Ford Cortina 120,601

In the Car Park
In this Chapter you will have come across some of the following vehicles and personalities...

Top left is the Ford Fiesta and next to it the Chrysler Horizon which was made out of the Avenger bottom left. Next to it is Vauxhall's entry into the hatchback market the Chevette.

Top right is the Volvo 66, although in a previous life it had been badged as a Daf from Holland. Volvo came up with their own small hatchback, the 345 parked next to it. Second row is the Fiat 127 regarded as the first supermini, but the obscure though equally Italian Autobianchi Primula had been around since the middle '60s. BMC owned Innocenti made Austin/Morris 1100s look different in the third row left whilst next to it was their own hatchback based on the Mini.

Top row are the Toyota Corolla and Datsun Cherry, then bottom left the Mazda 323, all hatchbacks. The Datsun Laurel isn't a hatch, but it is a big, comfy saloon.

13 (Unlucky for one Daimler buyer) Mad Bad and Dangerous to Drive, a most unstable Sovereign. It must be 1978

In the garage: Audi 100LS is about to be replaced by something rather grand. Meanwhile there are a couple of Minis running around, the automatic Clubman and the 1963 Mini Super De Luxe.

By February 1978, Michael Edwardes had come up with a plan that meant there would be plenty of changes and yet more reorganisation at BL. After years of trying to rope all the different marques and companies together there were now going to be five divisions, with Austin Morris making the mass market cars and Jaguar Rover Triumph the upmarket stuff. The rest of what was an incredibly large grouping of related engineering companies were corralled into BL Components and SP (Special Products) Industries and Leyland Vehicles for the buses and lorries. Edwardes was most determined though to get rid of the Leyland association and keep it to the commercial vehicles where it belonged. So out went British Leyland Limited and in came BL Limited. The emphasis was now going to be on the individual marques. It was all change yet again.

Edwardes became best known for facing up to and consequently facing down the unions. In his plan, at least 12,000 jobs would have to go, and although it was claimed that much of it would be natural wastage anyway, he did actually close a car plant. This was unheard of in the post-war era, and it was Speke number 2 factory, which had built to a consistently low standard the Triumph TR7. With production transferred to Coventry and 200 detail improvements made, the TR suddenly had better prospects. Sadly the knock-on effect of the factory closure was an end of several interesting projects that could have helped a recovery. The replacement for the unreliable Stag was the Lynx, which would have been a sporting hatchback which everyone may have loved and bought. An SD2, effectively a smaller Rover SD1 but with Triumph badges, also bit the dust.

That Lynx would have been an alternative to the Reliant Scimitar and something that Princess Anne and Dad could have bought. As a bit of a diversion here, the Reliant Scimitar was a brilliant example of how inventive the British car industry could be and how some of its smaller players managed to have a major international impact. Incredibly, a company best known for making three-wheeled vans out of plastic created one of the most charismatic and unique sports cars ever, though they could not have done it without the help of the Duke of Edinburgh and the managing director of a company that made cosmetics. That bloke was Boris Forter, the former MD of Helena Rubinstein who made things to make ladies even prettier, so he obviously had a few bob. He'd spotted something called an Ogle Mini SX1000 coupe at the 1962 Earls Court motor show. It was a Mini with an interesting plastic body, which got him thinking. Forter asked Ogle Design to create something bigger, better and faster.

The result was based on a Daimler SP250 V8 sports car and called the SX250. Meanwhile Reliant were finding that their Sabre 6 sports car, which looked like a Triumph gone slightly wrong, wasn't selling. They'd noticed the SX250 and made some discreet enquiries, because it looked a lot better than their Sabre and could easily replace the bodywork. That became the Scimitar GT. Meanwhile those clever designers at Ogle had been commissioned by Triplex Safety Glass to make a car that would be mostly glass. Although they might have liked to have started from scratch, they took Reliant's GT, cut the top half off and then involved glass.

Ogle produced a lot of drawings, but by far the cleverest was a four-seater sports car which for the Triplex people offered an interesting solar energy versus ventilation issue that applied equally to family saloons. Basically, it would be a rolling demo vehicle for their Sundym heat-absorbing glass product. By not going for the easy sloped-back sports car option Ogle had come up with a glasshouse estate car. This meant loads of demisting potential with the minimum of electrical consumption. Everyone was happy, especially Triplex who designed special glazing sections so the minimum of supporting glass fibre was required. They used their heat-absorbing glass (which was green tinted) to counter any solar heat issues, while a wire-heated windscreen, which later became a feature on rally cars to help them combat sub-zero temperatures, kept it clear. Here was the GTS, which stood for Glazing Test Special, and was shown at the 1965 Earls Court Motor Show to widespread acclaim. It was then loaned to the Duke of Edinburgh, which was a very clever PR move and meant the whole concept stayed in the public eye for even longer.

Ogle's Chief designer, Tom Karen, was now working closer with Reliant, and inevitably the GTS would find it's way into their range, including an estate car designed for the Turkish car market. Launched in 1968 with a Ford engine and rebadged as the GTE, it was an instant hit. It was the perfect example of a car that buyers didn't know they needed until they saw it, like the Range Rover. It was sheer brilliance, and the tiny company was swamped with orders. The first example of the so-called lifestyle estate for those who wanted to get from their central London pad to their country pile fast. Plus they wanted their luggage on board too. It helped that Princess Anne was given one for her birthday present by her dad, the Duke. It was the perfect Sloane Rangermobile, even though the term didn't exist yet and anyway they would soon take the Range Rover to their town and countrified hearts. There was still a market for a classy sports car, and the point is that the Triumph Lynx could have taken over from where the Reliant left off. Dad might even have bought one – he certainly asked me about the Scimitar in the early 1980s, but by then the quality wasn't very good at all and regrettably I told him so. Killing the Lynx was symptomatic of a British car industry, which was starting to lose its ambition, its way and its confidence. That was mostly because they were making obviously sub-standard products.

I think as a family we had been very lucky up to this point with our recent selection of BL products, which hadn't broken down very much at all. The Triumph Dolly seemed quite old fashioned, but in a good way, and the beige (Honeysuckle in the catalogues) paintwork's major drawback allowed us to monitor the progress of rust without looking too hard. The Mini wasn't really suited to an automatic gearbox, so that it sounded even more fractious than it normally would have. Although none of them was very spectacular to own or drive, even though in early 1978 I was in no particular position to make judgements or to pass comment in any capacity other than as a passenger. Yes I still had to pass my driving test, but the opportunity came soon enough on a bitterly cold February morning.

My sister was doing something rather more important – like working – but Dad made sure that he was available to accompany me to the testing station. That journey didn't go very well. Firstly it was snowing. Then as I skilfully turned a corner into Woodford Green, the car skidded very sideways. I managed to catch and correct the situation, which I thought demonstrated exemplary car control. Dad, though, rightly asked what the hell I was doing. Skidding. He wasn't very impressed, but at least I didn't fling the little Mini around like I was in the Italian Job. No, I hinted it possibly had something to do with the wintry conditions, and then drove carefully into the wire fenced testing centre car park and bounced over the ruts next to the driving school Ford Escorts. We got out and then very rapidly got back in again. This time Dad was driving. The offside rear wheel was completely flat, so we darted to the nearest petrol station, which just happened to be opposite. Dad didn't just inflate the tyre – he over inflated it so that it looked like a cartoon one.

Now reparked and relocated in the temporary hut that passed for the driving test centre, I sat on a stackable school chair next to the other spotty hopefuls. If

I had felt a tad nervous at the beginning of the day, I was now in a state of utter dejection. I knew that an unroadworthy car meant instant failure. I bottled it all in and just sat motionless next to Dad, although a girl was quietly sobbing two chairs down. I couldn't bring myself to look, but just stared at the floor and thought "third time lucky". Oh yes, and about the next most important thing that could happen in 1978, and that was Dad buying a Daimler.

I knew Dad liked Daimlers, and one reason was that it wasn't a Jaguar, although by the middle 1960s they had certainly become Jaguars but for the badge, the distinctive crinkly grille and extra chrome. Cleverly Jaguar charged a lot more for very little. Dad had a brochure for the Daimler Majestic Major, which was the last true Daimler saloon. It featured an artist's impression of a grey haired dapper gent who looked like short-lived PM Anthony Eden and his elegant very un-Docker-like Mrs dressed for Ascot, driving this big limousine. Yes this was a big car you wanted to drive yourself, even though it looked like something a bloke with a cap should be steering. The Majestic Major, though, had a lightweight V8 engine which was powerful and, as it turned out, a bit too much of a rival for Jaguar's own large saloons. Back when the brochure was handed out at some early 60s motor show Dad couldn't have afforded a Jag or a Daimler. But things had changed for us all, and despite the generally grim economic outlook, the fact that Dad did a lot of work for multi-national companies in Europe and the Middle East meant he could now buy a Daimler if he wanted to.

Dad was dealing with our local BL outfit, who had already tried to charge him £500 for jumping the queue to get a Rover SD1. But if they couldn't get one of those, they most definitely had a Daimler Sovereign parked out the back that was looking for a customer. The Sovereign was the posh version of the Jaguar XJ6, which had been regarded as the best saloon car in the world. Launched in 1968, it was the last model that the company's founder Sir William Lyons had been fully involved with. It embodied everything he thought the cars should be, and in the process established a standard of ride, comfort, quietness and road holding which led the world. It could take a corner quicker than the company's legendary E-Type, yet it was quieter and had a softer ride than a Rolls-Royce. To top it all, the styling was truly beautiful, and looked all crouching big cat as driver and passengers lowered themselves into what was essentially a sports saloon. Jaguar had invented a new breed of high-performance luxury missile that left even the larger offerings from Mercedes looking dull, efficient and typically German. Even more importantly for Jaguar, this one model replaced all the bank robber saloons that cluttered up their showrooms. So out went the Sweeney police chase staple that was the Mark 2 and the massive seventeen foot's worth 420G for when the criminals decided to stick the safe in the boot and take hostages too. Then there was the S-Type, which had a Mark 2 front end and the 420G's rear, and then the small 420, which had the bigger G's front and rear end. Confused? So were the buyers, who also had the choice of just the one Daimler-badged Jaguar, the Sovereign, really a 420, but also a Daimler-engined Jaguar which was finally known as the V8 250 (and in fact, fans, Inspector Morse's Jaguar Mark 2 was actually a Daimler, but with Jaguar trim). Then there was also the Daimler-engined Daimler, the Majestic Major, and a stretched limo version called the DR450.

In the newly rationalised world of British Leyland, culling all those models was a necessity, although if you liked real Daimlers, they had ceased to be, and simply became a badge to dress up and premium-price Jaguar saloons. There was, though, one stand-alone Daimler, the DS420, which was a Jaguar-engined limousine that became a favourite of Mayors and funeral directors. So if you have ever worn chains of local office or been to a funeral, chances are you've ridden in one. In 1968, though, what all this upheaval meant was that Jaguar were left with the world's greatest line-up of cars: the E-Type and the XJ6. What more would a family ever need?

For a while there, things looked pretty good for Jaguar. Everyone wanted the XJ6 and still lusted after the E-Type. Indeed the huge V12 engine that eventually went to live under the longest and most phallic bonnet ever designed also transferred over to the XJ6. This engine had originally been developed during Jaguar's motor sport hey day to directly take on the Italian Ferraris. Indeed Jaguar built the XJ13 racing car that they might have taken to Le Mans in the mid-1960s, but the merger with BMC soon stopped that exciting idea. Meanwhile, putting a racing car engine into a saloon wasn't that clever at a time of fuel crisis when it would manage only 12mpg on a good day. Just fewer than 600 were made, and it didn't help that the Jaguar factory was in the middle of the worst strike in its history. Jaguar quality was at an all-time low, and in the particularly fussy and demanding American market, the factory had to send teams of fitters to partially rebuild cars that had been delivered to showrooms in a state of disrepair.

The fact that every part of the British Leyland, and subsequently BL Ltd, built sub-standard products was not an issue. I'd like to think that Dad chose to give the company the benefit of the doubt based on the fact that our Mini Clubman and Triumph Dolomite hadn't broken down yet. Even if bits still dropped off. It wasn't as if Jaguar didn't want to make the XJ6 better. The one thing wrong with the original model was that the rear legroom was marginal for such a large car. So in 1973 they made it longer and generally tidied up the styling and, you would like to think, concentrated on building it better. Five years later though, Dad was in the market and alarm bells should have sounded when the local dodgy dealer found a spare Daimler Sovereign around the back. It was Squadron Blue, had a vinyl roof and white-wall tyres. No really it did – a pinstripe of white around the tyre so it looked like it belonged to a nightclub proprietor. Dad wasn't having any of that and said the tyres had to be reversed, and he wasn't going to pay for the black vinyl roof which was still just about fashionable. It had all the signs of a car that had been ordered by someone else who had failed to follow up the initial deposit with a full payment. Dad also got a discount, because he always did, but really he should have walked away and bought a Mercedes. Years later, Dad said to me, "I wished I'd bought a Mercedes."

Instead he borrowed some trade plates from the dealer and drove it to our house and said this is our new car. Me and Mum got in and it was a truly wonderful experience. It was a bright sunny day and it never broke down once in the half hour we drove around where we lived. All we had to do then was wait for the August 1, 1978 to come around for the latest registration. When it did, Dad parked it in our narrow drive. I clearly remember seeing the next door neighbours' youngest son run up to our gate and then start shouting, "It's a T, it's a T!" That was the sort of excitement that the new registration used to cause in those days. However, that was the last time any of us was truly excited by the Sovereign. After that it was all downhill. So now I have a choice of detailing all the woes, or spreading it through the rest of book. Actually I think I will get it over and done with now in a few paragraphs. This is the beginning of the end of my family's relationship with British cars.

Hold on though, I shouldn't really fast forward too far as there is still the small matter of me and my driving test before we can get stuck into the rest of 1978. Well, mid-Daimler daydream, a bloke in a cardigan and carrying a clipboard calls out my name and I have to follow him outside. I'm supposed to be reading some distant number plate, but really I'm looking at just how much air is left in my Mini's tyre. Luckily I can't tell and just get on with the job of getting in and going through the motions of the test. As instructed, I turn confidently out of the test centre car park, swinging left as a Triumph Spitfire turns right out of the opposite turning at full collision speed. The tester and his cardigan immediately swing around in the seat, which is easy as there are no belts, to see just how much of a near-miss there had been. Damn. I throw the Spitfire driver a nasty look in the rear-view mirror convinced that he's going to follow me for the rest of the test and put me off.

In the first minute, then, I've been attacked by a Triumph Spitfire and I'm convinced that the deflating rear tyre is making my Mini tilt to one side. I'm past caring as the tester takes me to the location for the hill start. Actually this isn't a hill, it's Mont Blanc. Really it's a service road in Woodford Green where nobody ever parked because it was so damned steep. All the blood in my body has relocated to my lower back, sometimes referred as my bottom. The Mini couldn't take it, in particular the overweight civil servant in the passenger seat. Meanwhile, the underweight nervous teenager was required to demonstrate super-human clutch control. For the nanosecond I took my foot off the brake the Mini momentarily surrendered to gravity before I caught it and powered up the mountain. He must have noticed that the handbrake didn't hold the Mini on the slope, so that's another cross in the unroadworthy box on top of the flat tyre. I wasn't feeling very confident at all, and mentally switched off.

I presume the reversing around the corner went without a hitch, as did the emergency stop, because although I can remember the rest of the test with terrifying clarity, those crucial bits are a blank. Luckily, I came to when a couple of pedestrians stepped into the road. I braked. Good move, as the Highway Code was still fresh in my head and I knew that they had right of way. Indeed, they stood in front of me for so long that any normal fully qualified driver would have driven around them by now, possibly gesturing rudely or simply shaking their head, in a "you pathetic pedestrian" sort of way. Indeed the pedestrians were so keen for the L-plated car and cardigan to proceed that they gestured in the traditional "after you" manner. I resisted the temptation, and with some frantic eye movements from me darting towards the opposite pavement, they finally got the hint and proceeded in the right direction.

After that everything went blank again until the cardigan said the word "congratulations", which was a nice surprise. Apparently I had passed my test and the man from the Ministry of Transport asked when I started my new job? Well, I was at sixth form college attempting to get some A-levels, so maybe he knew something I didn't. Then I remembered I had written a letter when applying for this test along the lines of please give me the earliest possible test date please as I need to drive in my new job. I blathered something about becoming a rep because that's how Dad had started his driving career more than 20 years before. So a big round of thanks to the clipboard and cardigan wearer who spotted someone who would at least pay attention to the Highway Code and not go out of their way to run someone over. It probably helped that I continually glanced into the rear-view for signs of that Kamikaze Spitfire.

Outside the test centre Dad and I looked at the Mini. The rear tyre couldn't have been flatter. We laughed and I asked him to drive. Quite rightly he refused and made me take it to the petrol station and over-inflate that tyre one last time before driving home. Passing my driving test now meant that I had rather more influence over what cars Dad bought, or so I thought anyway. However, it was too late for me to stop him signing on the dotted line for the Daimler. Not that I wanted to stop him anyway. It seemed such a fabulously glamorous car and surely it couldn't be that bad? After all they'd been building it for five years and the previous model five years before that, so surely they had the hang of it by now.

So where do I start? Well, Dad's first tug on the automatic gearbox had bristles catapulting all over the cabin as the brush at the base of the stick got a number one haircut. More alarmingly, a brake warning light suggested that bringing the Daimler to a halt would not be the formality Dad had hoped for. At least the failing fuel gauge indicated that the petrol would run out before the road did. However, the paint finish was truly awful and started to flake off in great big chunks right down to the metal. Not only that, there were periodic brake-fluid eruptions in the engine department, haunted petrol pumps and poltergeist electrics. So I won't bore you with all the coughs and sneezes suffered by the Daimler, but after a year it had got through a heater, several fuel pumps, a fuel tank and countless other sundries plus some localised resprays. It is worth pointing out that BL limited was aided and abetted by a servicing dealer staffed entirely by clowns. And like all clowns, they were not funny – just a little bit sinister as they drained petrol tanks dry, went on 100-mile test runs, applied spanner-shaped dents to the bodywork and pinched the floor mats.

Once conveniently out of warranty, the really big stuff started to go wrong. First it was the camshaft bearings, followed by an ominous rumble from below. The technical explanation from BL was: the number four big end bearing had turned in the cap and all the others were marked. Actual explanation: the engine was knackered. After a paltry 22,000 miles, the recommendation was a brand new engine. The failure was attributed to oil starvation, probably due to some blockage in the lubrication system. No one would take the rap. The three-ring circus at Jaguar wrote that there was no manufacturing fault despite the pile of evidence that this Sovereign was as mad and bad as George III and just as dangerous to drive. Suspicion also fell on Coco the Clown, who had replaced the camshaft bearings and probably mislaid his red nose in the cylinder head in the process.

Not a man to be messed about, Dad sent volleys of letters in all the relevant directions, while Jaguar and Leyland directors hid behind their desks, dodging the issues and playing dumb. It is a shame that this pantomime was not played out decades later and on another continent. That's because a disgruntled BMW buyer in America successfully sued for $5m because the bumper on his BMW was wonky. On that line of reasoning, Jaguar's then owner Ford owed my Dad a brand new Daimler plus the small matter of multi-million pound compensation. I wrote in Car magazine back in 1995 that, given the way we built, marketed and serviced cars in the 70s and 80s, our indigenous industry deserved to die, and I haven't changed my opinion. That's because governments should not dabble in business and clowns should stick to the circus. I went on that because the guilty Grimaldis were still at large, unpunished and arrogantly unapologetic, we'd go after them. Back then my Dad had a bit more time on his hands and was plotting our revenge. It would be as cold as a blown 4.2 XK (that's one which has ceased to work) and satisfyingly heavy. I added that we know where they live and one day they would wake up and find a 1978 Daimler Sovereign is about to be parked on their chests.

Sadly I can't carry out that threat as I no longer own the car or know its whereabouts. I'm not even sure who to blame either, or whether they are still alive. Certainly Michael Edwards had plenty to worry about in 1978 even before Dad took delivery of that dreadful car. Edwardes found himself running a company that was still getting it hugely wrong. While the engineers had been trying to replace the Mini with something more useful and grown up, Edwardes found that they had already splurged £300 million on what turned out to be an ugly and fairly useless prototype codenamed the ADO 88. When real car buyers were shown the prototype next to the current Ford Fiesta and Volkswagen Polo, virtually no one picked it as their favourite.

Not surprisingly it was partially abandoned, then rethought, and the launch date was put back a year to 1980, while replacing the Allegro and Marina became a matter of national importance. BL, despite being such a large concern, still didn't have the engineering expertise or facilities, so Edwardes was convinced that the company needed a partner. A junior one obviously. One serious consideration was Chrysler, who were in all sorts of trouble themselves. What stopped negotiation dead was the sudden and unexpected takeover by Peugeot. That didn't stop BL looking abroad and chatting to Fiat and Renault. Interestingly, they also spoke to BMW, who would ultimately take over what would be left of BL in 1994. Most significant of all though, they were prepared to look towards the far east. Honda stood in third place behind Toyota and Nissan in Japan, and built slightly fewer cars than BL at around 580,000. It was the end of 1978, and car building in Britain was about to change for ever.

My life had already changed by virtue of my getting a proper job – well, one in the City of London which, despite what I had told the nice man in the cardigan who had allowed me to drive on the Queen's Highway unaccompanied, did not involve any motorway mileage or repping of any description. Anyway, it meant I could at least start thinking about replacing my old Mini.

1978 was dominated by the arrival of Dad's Daimler, yet the most significant thing about that momentous event was actually the departure of the Audi. Dad had a long tradition of never actually selling, or at least advertising a car for sale. Mostly he gave them away. He absolutely hated people kicking the tyres on his car, making offers and generally being a pain in the backside. He didn't want or need the hassle. On occasions he accepted some token payments from me on a character-building basis to make sure that I understood the value of money and all that. But mostly he'd give them away to members of the family who needed them most. The Audi was a notable exception, and a disorderly queue was forming for that. So Dad got a decent offer and promise that there wouldn't be any moans afterwards. He'd sold a car which everyone wanted, and through no fault of his own bought another which no one in their right minds would ever want to have any sort of responsibility for. Least of all the company that had thrown it together in the first place.

Still in the garage: A Sovereign that was starting to become sickly, plus a more reliable Mini Clubman as back-up, while that 1963 Mini is poised to be replaced.

Births
1978 British Leyland becomes simply BL.
1978 Midas
1978 Talbot

Marriage
1978 Chrysler Europe to Peugeot

Deaths
1978 Trident
1978 Fairthorpe

Best Seller
1978 Ford Cortina 139,204

In the Car Park

Not much this chapter apart from the Daimler...

Experimental GTS on the left with loads of glass became the mould breaking Reliant GTE on the right.

14 MG Expires, the Mini goes Metro and Oriental Triumphs 1979–1981

In the garage: Daimler Sovereign getting worse by the day, however the Mini Clubman Automatic can be relied on and the Triumph 1500HL is back for a while and briefly there's a Triumph Spitfire belonging to my sister in the drive.

1979 continued much as it left off in our house, and that meant lots of letters to BL and Jaguar typed by Dad on his German electric typewriter. At least the Daimler worked long enough to get him to hospital. After feeling decidedly unwell one weekend he popped into the doctor's on Monday morning. They suggested a check-up at A&E would be in order. Rather than bothering me, or catching the bus, Dad drove himself to Whipps Cross Hospital and then sat patiently waiting to be seen. Luckily a switched-on doctor could see that all was not very well. "Get that man into intensive care now," she barked and saved Dad's life in the process.

It wasn't long before I was on a bus on my way to the hospital. Mum and my sister were at the other end of the country and when I saw Dad all wired up I thought I might be the last member of the family he'd ever see. All he was really concerned about was that I take his watch and wallet before someone else did. There was also the large matter of the Daimler in the hospital car park which needed to be taken home.

I drove the slightly longer way home because, for all its problems, when it worked the Daimler looked and drove beautifully, but I wasn't posing, I was worrying. If Dad died I would have had to sell it, and I really couldn't think of anyone who'd want to buy the Sovereign or who'd give anything approaching a reasonable price. Within months a new XJ6 would be launched. I knew that because I read all the car magazines and realised what it would do to the resale value. Obviously I was destined for a career in the motor trade, and also as a motoring hack.

Dad did get better, although it wasn't the last of his heart attacks, but he still wasn't well enough to go to the local launch of the Series 3 Jaguar XJ6, which for some reason the dealer thought he might want buy. So Dad gave the invite to me and one evening in October 79 I went to take a closer look. I didn't realise it at the time, but this was wonderful practice for being a motoring journalist. There was free food and drink, which I didn't touch, and one white XJ6 in the middle of the showroom. I did what any journo would do and made notes. I carefully sketched the subtle differences between Dad's old one and this new one. Driving impressions? Not a chance – you could just look and touch. I even tried to talk to the other customers who were a good 20 to 30 years older than me. They were polite enough, but I could see that they were thinking, "how the hell can he afford one of these?" I answered that question for them, with a pre-emptive "I'm here on behalf of my Dad". Now the subtext to that was, Jags are for old people like you. Right here Jaguar were storing up issues that would never properly be addressed for a generation as to why their cars never appealed to the under-40s. It also explained why, a few years later when given the choice, I went to work for a young thrusting continental brand, BMW, rather than the old farts at Jag.

Nationally everything was about to change. In 1979, as Mrs Thatcher became the new Prime Minister, trade union trouble-maker Derek "Red Robbo" Robinson would be ousted from power and robots would be taking over at BL. However, there wasn't a lot to get excited about as far as cars were concerned, although it was a change for industrial relations. The arrival Mrs T meant that there was no alternative but to get tough with the unions and radical with the business plan if British Leyland were to survive. Sir Keith Joseph was the new secretary of state for trade and industry, and he needed to be convinced that even more funding for the state-owned company would be well spent. Indeed, earlier that year, when BL had invited Mrs T to tea as the then leader of the opposition, she reportedly asked, "Well, Michael Edwardes, and why should we pour further funds into British Leyland?"

Mrs T would be elected months later with a mandate to decentralise, privatise and make businesses more efficient. On that basis, they should have shut BL within hours of coming to power. However, Sir Keith Joseph in particular wasn't stupid, and knew that putting so many people out of work would not be the smartest move if his party wanted to stay in power.

What with the Iranian oil crisis and a strong pound, the BL board had to get on with it, so convened at Ye Olde Bell Inn pub at Hurley in Berkshire and knocked out a plan. The gist of it was that 25,000 jobs would have to go, the Triumph factory at Canley would be shut as would the MG factory at Canley. Published in September 1979, it was put to the workforce, and 87 per cent of the 80 per cent who voted approved the plan. This led directly to BL being able to sack Derek Robinson, who, to give him his full title, was chairman of the Leyland Combine Trade Union Committee and senior conveyor at the Longbridge factory. He'd produced his own response to that report, snappily entitled The Edwardes Plan and Your Job. That was interpreted as gross misconduct, which was a sackable offence. In fact BL quantified his effect on the business over the previous two and half years, which amounted to 523 disputes resulting in the loss of 62,000 cars and 113,0000 engines, all worth over £200 million.

With Red Robbo out of the way it also became possible to get rid of many of the old restrictive working practices. So stupid rules that stopped workers being moved on to another job, or being paid a massive amount of money not to do something, were ended. That left the way clear in 1980 for Sir Keith Joseph to plough in £450 million and then another billion to keep the company going. So what did the company do? Well, Jaguar suddenly became concerned about quality and would get a new boss called John Egan in 1980, but all that did was give Dad another name to write to. Although things started to look up at Jaguar, the small sports cars, especially the ones that had MG badges on them, were reaching the end of the road.

British Leyland's official sports car had been the Triumph TR7, so it was almost inevitable when the company announced that MG production would finish. Apparently, the company was losing £900 on every MG sold in America. Sales had actually been good, but the strong pound had not helped matters in the export market. Even so, the MGB in particular had been in production since 1962 with hardly any changes, so how come they couldn't make any money out it? Especially when there were still plenty of buyers for a car that was so outdated? Lots of questions, but no answers as the timing could not have been worse. The announcement coincided with the company's fiftieth anniversary of production at Abingdon. There was a worldwide outcry as the MGB and Midget disappeared for what everyone thought would be forever. Obviously the MG owners' club and all its flat-capped members staged protests while others, a consortium led by the head of Aston Martin, attempted a rescue bid.

BL's response in October 1980 was to exploit the situation by making the last thousand MGBs limited editions. Imaginatively called LEs, they were fitted with front chin spoilers and the distinctive alloy wheels that had last been seen on the Triumph Stag. If you didn't like those leftovers then there was also the option of traditional wire wheels on the roadster version. This model was finished in bronze metallic paint with gold LE stripes running down each side. The interior was upholstered in orange and brown striped cloth trim, all for the not inconsiderable price of £6,445. A total of 420 Roadsters and 580 GTs were made before the closure of Abingdon. Probably the most depressing thing that happened is that most buyers regarded these last MGs as future investments and promptly parked them in heated garages. Finally BL were building cars that people wanted to buy, pay an inflated price for and then not use. Trouble is, this ultra clever marketing plan ran out of road once those 1,000 were sold.

MG had been tossed away and any residual worldwide goodwill went with it. There was much less of an outcry when the Triumph factory at Canley in Coventry stopped making cars. The year before, my sister had gone out and bought a Triumph Spitfire in white. She bought it because it was as pretty as it had ever been in 1961. Unlike the MG Midget, it had never been disfigured by big rubber bumpers; the chrome one had just been hoisted up a bit, and to be honest it looked even better. Plus, if she could persuade her brother to help lift off the hard top, my sister then had a convertible – the perfect environment to wear sunglasses and let her hair blow free. Not surprisingly, the following year she was remarried and the Spitfire was replaced by the beige Dolomite. But the old Dolly was now gone and the TR7 wasn't far behind and retired from the line-up in 1981. The sports car at BL was dead, and that could have made them a target for even more abuse.

As it was, the creation of Talbot in 1978 (see below) had not only saved BL from a merger that could have been disastrous, but it took the spotlight off BL for a while as the nation's joke car maker. It also helped that they were French owned. Actually, there was a surprisingly close connection between the two companies because the new head of Chrysler had previously been at BL. George Turnbull had been responsible for getting the Morris Marina into production, and then the Austin Allegro, and obviously he became very disillusioned with the whole organisation. He believed that breaking the company up and letting each marque get on with it without interference was the answer. He never got his way and resigned as the managing director of Austin Morris. What Turnbull did next was an astounding, brave and prescient: he went to South Korea.

There he helped Hyundai establish a car plant and get it running in two years, from scratch. The Hyundai Pony used second-hand technology from Mitsubishi, and it became incredibly successful and the first Korean car to be imported to Britain. At first hand he saw what could be achieved by a motivated workforce, a private company and a certain amount of carefully directed state funding. Staying abroad, Turnbull's next stop was Tehran. At the Iran National

Motor Company they assembled my Dad's old car. Yes, the Hillman Minx/Hunter was reworked and rebadged as the Paykan, which means "arrow" in Farsi, and was the original code name for this model. First assembled from kits of parts in 1967, it became an exclusively Iranian model after Chrysler UK discontinued it and sold sole manufacturing rights to Iran in 1979. In fact it stayed in production until 2005, and consistently sold in massive numbers and was far more successful than it had been in Britain. Turnbull had to move on though once the Ayatollahs arrived. As the Rootes Group was sold with the rest of Chrysler to Peugeot Talbot of France, it was time for Turnbull to come home.

The company previously known as Rootes and Chrysler was now renamed Talbot, and in 1979 Turnbull was put in charge, even though he favoured going with Chrysler-Talbot. These name changes just confused buyers, and Turnbull reckoned that, like his time at Standard-Triumph, this was a good way of introducing a new name before getting rid of the old one. Certainly everyone had forgotten how awful Standards were by the time the company became Triumph.

At Chrysler the rot set in as sales plummeted and products were revealed for what they were, very poor. We've already mentioned the Sunbeam, Alpine and Solara, but there was also the monumentally inappropriate Talbot Tagora that arrived a little while after. Here was the model that helped to snuff out the marque once and for all, which was a shame, as the initial design for Chrysler by Brits in Coventry was actually quite adventurous and striking. Trouble was, the American owners realised that this was their last chance, so they interfered and made it look like a big dumb American Chrysler, but a lot smaller of course. To us it still seemed like a large vehicle, and it was up against the Rover SD1, Ford Granada and the Germans. With a big and powerful V6 engine it was very quick, but inside it was dull and cheap while outside it looked square and stupid. Hardly anyone bought it.

There were far more credible and better-built cars around, usually in Germany, and no I'm not thinking BMW, Mercedes, or even Audi. Uncle Joe, the brother who was a chauffeur, had stopped turning up in old Humbers for the Port of London Authority, mainly because he now worked for News International and would soon be driving around Editors and Murdochs, and they had gave him a Granny. From 1977, the production was transferred from Dagenham to Cologne in Germany. The German Granada, or Mark 2 as it was better known, had a square-cut style that was fashionable at the time. But whereas the Talbot Tagora looked clumsy and out of proportion, Gerta the Granny was a very handsome affair. With Ghia trim, alloys and spot lamps (Ghia was an established Italian design house whose name Ford acquired) and a growly 2.8 V6 engine it was a proper working class saloon that geezers drove. In the later 70s you could see it doing tyre smoking stuff in seminal ITV shows like "The Sweeney" and also "Out", which had Tom Bell as a recently released felon getting his own back. So for war hero Uncle Joe, it was the perfect set of wheels for him to screech around in, and he rated the Granada as a reliable and no-nonsense vehicle that never let him down. I don't know if he'd have changed his mind had he known that Gerta was built in Germany. But that was the way that things were going. Everyone thought of Ford as a British company making cars east of London, when in fact they were pan-European and taking full advantage of the fact.

Nevertheless, working for Ford was still regarded as a career option, in my school at least. Back-tracking to the last chapter, my Commie careers teacher booked our year into several factory visits, on the basis that it was a highly unionised environment which made cars for the people. So we were off to Dagenham. As a car nut, going to a car factory was probably the most exciting thing to happen to me in 1975. I can remember clearly that bitterly cold but bright winter's day. Inside the factory it was warm, and I'd never seen so many Cortinas in my young life. The whole process fascinated me, but the behaviour of the "workers" was something of a surprise. These were supposed to be adults, but some of them were swinging from the machinery like monkeys, and even more alarmingly screeching like their close primate relatives. You could hear them clearly above the noise of the machinery, and apart from heckling scruffy, spotty, schoolboys, a lot of the comments were directed at the girls. To their credit, they just folded their arms and got on with the unpleasant task of walking around a grim, dark and noisy factory full of idiots. If this was what the workplace was really like, none of us was very impressed. More to the point, if these were the sort of people building our cars, is it any wonder that they often seemed indifferently assembled?

Ford made more cars, more successfully than anywhere else in the country, and within a few years, the Fiesta would be in full production, not just in Dagenham but in Europe too. By contrast, BL were still fiddling around with their small hatchbacks and still not exactly sure what they were doing. As we saw in the last chapter, Edwardes and his supervising board were horrified at what was intended to replace the Mini. It was cleverly packaged inside, but looked like a shed on the outside. So wholesale changes were made to the design so at least it stood a fighting chance against the Fiesta and Volkswagen Polo. A ballot of the workforce named the new small car Metro, narrowly in favour of Maestro.

The smartened up car offered as much interior space as many larger rivals, although the boot was small and the engines were revised versions of the Mini's original. Advanced Hydragas suspension meant a smoother ride, but there was plenty to criticise and plenty of areas where, apart from a rear door, it wasn't much different from the old Mini. Like the original, it had an uncomfortable seat position that would give you cramp after a few miles. Then the gears made an incredible racket, not least because there were just the four of them, rather than five. Even worse, there was no automatic version initially. But it was far from being a bad car compared with its contemporaries, and most important of all, it could not be allowed to fail. Indeed when the BL workers had to make the decision whether to support or effectively sack Red Robbo in 1978, on the other side of Birmingham Edwardes was waiting to address the Birmingham Chamber of Commerce. He had two speeches prepared.

One was a proper bombshell which explained how the company was closing as a direct result of union activity and worker inactivity. The other was a lot more positive with details of how the Metro was to be built in a state-of-the-art factory with loads of clever robots doing the assembly. As news of Robinson's defeat came through, Edwardes read the latter speech.

When the Metro was launched at the 1980 Motor Show to rapturous acclaim, the advertising was equally upbeat. "A British Car to Beat the World," it proclaimed hopefully. The TV ads went even further, and you could see the plucky little Metro repelling the foreign invasion. This was ironic considering the agreement that had recently been signed with Honda and the model that BL would launch next.

I remember all the positive coverage that the small car got at the time, and to me it looked like a lot of hatchbacks that were around then. Perfect for shopping, but really not my idea of a Mini, and there certainly wasn't a sporty one. Not like the one I had parked in Dad's garage that I was slowly taking apart. In 1979 I'd saved more than enough to buy the Mini I'd always promised myself – a Cooper. I told Dad and he said he knew a man who could help, which wasn't a surprise. Dad was at the height of is business powers and could do and get just about anything, so maybe I should have asked him for a Lotus Elan. Anyway, Dad now had a factory in Maidenhead which made the exhibition stands, and he knew a wheeler dealer bloke who did indeed come up with the goods. For £200 and a bottle of wine by way of an added thank you, I had bought myself an icon. It needed work, but then any 15-year-old Mini, let alone a Cooper that been driven at maximum speed at every possible opportunity, was lucky to still be running. Obviously if I had been really clever I would have asked the bloke to find me a Cooper S for £300, which would now be priceless.

So I had bought into the old BMC era while the current management seemed to have learned nothing from the previous decade or two. The arrival of the Metro had actually ushered in a very old-fashioned evil: badge engineering.

Whereas the Cooper name with it's Formula 1–winning associations actually meant something, dusting off a spare badge that just happened to be knocking about in the drawer seemed wrong. And applying one that had been a marque of road and sports car in its own right to an ordinary little shopper like the Metro seemed very wrong. At least the MG badge was back in play and ultimately it would lead to a partial resurrection. MG enthusiasts were fairly enraged, but then what did they really know? The MG Metro got the famous octagonal badge, firmed up suspension, weird finned alloy wheels and some extra power that pushed the top speed to a highly illegal but still modest 100mph. Oh yes, and it had red seat belts. In fact later versions went rather over the top in the MG logo department both inside and out. And as it became fashionable in the 1980s to stick a Turbo on an engine, the MG Metro Turbo was inevitable in 1983. It could just about cope with the extra oomph, and as conclusive proof that car enthusiasts know nothing, here was the best-selling MG saloon ever. The general public liked these slightly higher-speed hybrids, so badge engineering was back with a vengeance.

By comparison with all the disasters that had gone before – disasters such as the Allegro, Marina and Maxi – the Metro, or to give it it's full name, the Austin Mini Metro, was a success. After all, we saw one every night on the news as a shy nursery school teacher ran the paparazzi gauntlet. Lady Diana Spencer had a W-registered 1.0L, second from bottom of the Metro model range, with no head restraints and a stick-on coachline rather than a rubbing strip. Oh, and it was red. With that sort of exposure, how could it fail? Well, by BL's own benchmark, it did actually fail, and quite badly, too.

The root of the problem was the wildly over-optimistic predictions for sales. For a start the BL board never considered the effect of the competition from the established and really rather good superminis (such as the Ford Fiesta and Volkswagen Polo) which was always going to tempt buyers in a different direction. Indeed, the original sales estimates dated right back to Alec Issigonis's clever little prototype in the late 60s. In a world with virtually no tiny hatchbacks, projected sales figures of 350,000 were probably spot on, and may even have been modest. Ten years later, the world of the small shopping hatchback was a hard fought territory. Nevertheless some marketing suit wrote a report that they should sell at least 350,000, yet the Metro never even managed half that. The old Mini had managed an impressive 200,000 between 1975 and 1978, but production was cut back in expectation of its successor doing rather better. Interestingly, by 1982, worldwide sales of Minis amounted to 52,000, while the Metro was running at its peak of 174,000. This meant that BL had made no increase in small car sales, and then went on to lose out as both models became more dated and less popular as the 1980s wore on. Lucky for BL that they didn't can the old Mini as even market research indicated that the Metro would not completely replace it. BL dealers still wanted a second car that they could sell to the growing number of two-car families.

We were briefly a one-car family in 1980, not least because my Mini Cooper didn't have an MOT. But we soon caught up with all our neighbours who except for the rich Ron and his decade-old Skoda, had two or more cars. Dad didn't go for another Mini or try out the new Metro, but unbelievably we did get another Triumph Dolomite.

It was an automatic, so that in theory, Mum could renew her provisional licence and have a go at the driving test, although she never did. As an 1850HL, it was faster than the old model, but still not quite a Sprint, which may have been a good thing. Anyway, Dad needed a spare car because the Daimler was always in the garage being repaired.

We drove up to the garage at Gants Hill in Essex to collect it, as by this time the dealer in our local high street had shut – I would like to think out of shame after selling Dad such a pile of four-wheeled rubbish. Anyway, the Daimler made it the few miles down the Eastern Avenue. Dad paid and he asked me to drive it back. That was my first experience of driving a brand new car fresh out of the showroom, although in a few years time it would become a way of life for me. One thing I noticed was the smell of artificial lubricant. It was the dominant smell in the Mini Clubman, but the distinctive whiff of WD40 was for me the smell of a BL car from this era. When I drove brand new BMWs they just smelled of freshness, ambition and quite possibly accomplishment. British cars smelled of pure dog, as though they had recently seized up and taken half a spray can to get them going again.

Dad's decision to stick with BL would inevitably come back to haunt him a couple of years later, but before we get there, let's look at what BL had in store for the small-car buyer. Yet again Dad had bought a car that was past its best-before date and within a year of its expiry date, and BL clearly had a new car shortfall. The Dolly dated back to the 60s and the Allegro had never been as lovable as the 1100/1300, whose reputation and sales it never lived up to. Not only that, but there was also the Morris Marina, which continued to struggle, so an alternative saloon wasn't a bad idea. It was certainly better than keeping the old models on life support, as if calling the Morris Marina the Ital in 1980 would actually help. Certainly fitting rectangular headlamps, chunky bumpers, big rear light clusters and recessed door handles could not hide the fact that it was just a tarted-up Marina.

Well actually it was the Marina that had been touched by Italian genius, or rather that's what BL wanted you to think. Ital referred to Ital Design, which was run by legendary stylist Giorgetto Giugiaro, who had been responsible for the Volkswagen Golf and Lotus Esprit, to name just a couple of vehicles that you may not realise are your two favourite designs of the 1970s. Obviously Giorgetto didn't design the Ital – a British designer was given the unenviable and actually quite impossible task of making the Marina look a bit more contemporary. All Giorgetto's company did was productionise it – make sure that everything fitted together and worked. Quite why he agreed to allow his company's name to be used on such a car it is almost impossible to comprehend. I'm actually one of the people who paid £80 a decade ago for a comprehensive two volume in a slip case appreciation of every cough, sneeze, wheeze and vehicle that Giorgetto Giugiaro and Ital Design ever committed to a drawing board, built as a prototype, or thought about during a daydream. And you know what? There isn't even a mention or footnote for the Morris Ital.

Ital Design and its boss have forgotten all about the Ital, and so should we, although buyers sadly missed a fifth gear that would have made motorway progress a lot less frenetic. Giugiaro was reportedly tremendously embarrassed by the association and the advertisement that drew heavily on it with the headline, "Styled in Italy, Built in Britain." BL though would be rather more coy about their next co-operation.

In the meantime, Edwardes had secured funding for a car that would become the Maestro – at the same time as the Metro, although it was far from ready. Anyway there were gaps to be filled, both where the forthcoming Maestro would be, and also between the Metro and Maestro. Obviously funding a new model from scratch was always going to be a problem. Lucky then that Edwardes had signed a deal with Honda.

There was some mutual back-scratching involved as BL would help Honda to get a foothold in Europe. More importantly, Honda had a four-door version of their highly successful Civic that seemed ideal. It was called the Ballade, came with a smallish 1.4 engine and either a five-speed manual or three-speed Hondamatic gearbox, perfect for the mature buyers who loved their Dollies. BL reckoned it had sporting potential, i.e. they could make it go quicker and with the right specification it just might be acceptable to the traditional Triumph buyers.

From Boxing Day 1979, BL gave themselves until October 1981 to get the Ballade ready for the great British car buyer. At this point it was codenamed "Bounty" like the coconut-filled chocolate bar, or the ship they had the mutiny on. At least it was going to be built at BL's factory in Cowley, Oxford, and it was going to be tweaked for British tastes. So the suspension was firmed up a bit and twin carburettors were added to up the power. That was the extent of the engineering overhaul, otherwise the changes were cosmetic. A new front grille, bumpers and moving the mirrors from the wings to the doors. Inside, though, BL had to make room for larger-scale, overweight Britons. The seats were new (actually they were based on Ford Cortina frames) and the trim was very different with more acceptable trim colours, but surprisingly there wasn't any wood at all. That would be a tremendous disappointment to many Triumph buyers, although Honda were impressed enough to order an additional two thousand sets to make their own special edition Ballade for Japan.

The Ballade was a new model in Japan from September 1980, and BL started building them in April 1981, creating a stockpile of 6,000. "Totally Equipped to Triumph" ran the adverts, with no hint of the Japanese connection. Obviously that did not go unremarked in Her Majesty's press, and Edwardes even wrote a stiff letter to The Times defending the company's actions. This was badge engineering but with an international twist. At the time, though, plenty regarded it as a sell-out and a backdoor way of getting more Japanese cars into the country. For Triumph enthusiasts, it clearly wasn't a "proper" Triumph, so what was it really like?

Well, the Acclaim didn't get universal acclaim, but it did get a certain amount of respect. When it came to interior comfort, equipment, economy and performance, it was a good-value buy. Being a lightweight car, its small engine was quite responsive, which meant that it fulfilled Triumph's traditional sporty brief, even though there had been some very sluggish models in the past. Overall though, it was just a very small and not particularly spacious saloon which had a slightly more upmarket interior than a Ford Cortina or Vauxhall Cavalier. What the Acclaim became was the second most successful car to wear the Triumph badge, selling just over 133,000 in three years. It was beaten only by the old Herald that was around for 12 years in all sorts of different body styles. Probably the most important thing of all about the Acclaim is that it was undoubtedly the best-built and most reliable car to leave any BL factory ever.

So the Acclaim was the perfect car for someone who wanted to buy Japanese but carefully disguise it with a true Brit badge. A bit like eating some sushi carefully concealed beneath a layer of mash and pretending to be a shepherd's pie. Here was the socially acceptable way to drive Japanese and conclusive proof that our factories and workers could build decent cars. Not exciting, charismatic ones, but crucially cars that actually started in the morning. Although no one realised it at the time, this was the real turning point for the British car industry, and without it happening, all car production, not just BL, could have been wiped out in this country.

But in 1981, another attempt at building cars funded mostly by the taxpayer was not going entirely to plan. It would all end in drink, drugs and tears and cost millions of pounds, thousands of jobs and several reputations.

In the garage: That Daimler, and a new Triumph Dolomite 1850HL automatic, plus a 1964 Mini Cooper turns up just about clinging to an MOT.

Births
1979 Sunbeam-Lotus
1979 Talbot

Marriages
1980 Panther bought by a Korean businessman

Deaths
1980 MG
1980 Panther
1980 Vanden Plas

New Arrivals
1979 Suzuki

Best Sellers
1979 Ford Cortina 193,784
1980 Ford Cortina 190,281
1981 Ford Cortina 159,804

In the Car Park...

Top left is the Series 3 Jaguar XJ6, which looked smarter, but wasn't much more reliable than previous models. Next to that is the much more reliable shape of things to come, the Korean Cortina in the shape of the Hyundai Pony. Second row, German built Ford Granada and next to that a Chrysler Alpine. It later became the Talbot Alpine and third row left is the odd but spacious Talbot Tagora. Next to it is the Mini Metro, next row down on the right the high performance MG Metro Turbo. Rather slower and unforgivably ugly is the Morris Ital in 'pretty' estate format. Bottom row, spot the difference between the Honda Civic in Ballade saloon form and the all-new Triumph Acclaim.

15 Dodgy De Loreans and Muttering Maestros 1981–1983

In the garage: Daimler Sovereign and Triumph Dolomite 1850HL, neither are in the best of health. Even the Cooper is unroadworthy due to it being in pieces, before being hurriedly patched together and then driven away before '83 is out.

We're still in 1981, and when the Daimler works, it takes Dad to his Maidenhead factory making exhibition stands. He then travels around the UK, but mostly to Europe and the Middle East to make sure the units are installed properly. When he's not at the factory, someone else has to run it. He's a bloke with a moustache who is also a director, but doesn't have nearly as many shares in what is Dad's business. He does however need a company car. With rather less to spend than Dad had on his Daimler, this bloke goes out and does the only sensible thing. No, he doesn't buy a Ford Granada like everyone else. He turns up for work in a Toyota Crown.

As a decision based purely on how many gadgets you got for your money, it was a sensible one. Air conditioning, apart from the winding down the front windows, was usually restricted to limousines and newer office buildings. However, an air conditioned rear shelf drinks cooler was pure science fiction to me. Such kitchen sink specifications would become the norm, and within the decade, the Toyota Crown would effectively become Lexus. Just in case you wondered, Lexus actually stands for Luxury Export United States, which gives you a hint of which market Toyota were aiming for. Consequently the dynamic and cosmetic sides of the, Crown were soggy and gaudy. Like American cars of the period, it had the softest suspension and bounced around corners. Stylewise, well there wasn't any. It was extremely square on the outside and chintzy on the inside, with seats that looked like and felt like your mum's sofa and rather too much plastic chrome. So the Crown looked rubbish parked next to my Dad's Daimler, but then again it never broke down.

Given BL's success with the Acclaim, it is a wonder they didn't simply go to Japan and take their pick of the models and rebadge them as Brits. The Toyota Crown would certainly have worked as the Triumph Crown. With such an approach at least the government might have got our money back. Instead they were trying to build an ethical sports car in Northern Ireland.

There are several things wrong with that last sentence. Firstly, no one ever understood exactly what an "ethical sports car" actually was. Secondly Northern Ireland was never known for its motor industry. Ship-building certainly, as they did knock the Titanic together, but never cars. The De Lorean, though, was a road going Titanic, and when the company that built it sank, all hands went down with it. The De Lorean story is a modern-day tragedy, and there isn't enough room here to go into huge detail. It is worth recapping, though, simply because it provides further proof that governments are stupid, gullible and shouldn't be involved in the car business. De Lorean dominated the news, and even before it failed was the last car any sane person in Britain would ever buy. Obviously that wasn't the point, because the ESCs – sorry, ethical sports cars, as De Lorean described them, without any explanation – were meant to be for export only. That only made the whole situation more ridiculous. You didn't need to know anything about cars to see that this was the wrong car, being built in the wrong place at the wrong time. Everything about De Lorean, the man and the car, was just wrong.

We'd never heard of him over here, but he was a legendary figure in the American motor industry, and De Lorean wasn't about to argue with anyone about his reputation as a car engineer and businessman. However, from what anyone can gather, his one clever idea was dropping a largish engine into a smallish car to create the Pontiac GTO. However, with an ego the size of a planet and his surgically-enhanced features, he was all about style rather than substance, and it hardly surprising that his vanity dictated that he should want to stick his name on the front of a car. So he formed DMC (De Lorean Motor Company) in 1974 with the help of Bank of America business loans and gullible celebrities, including TV interviewer Johnny Carson.

So De Lorean wasn't stupid enough to use his own money, and he also started a investment program in which the car dealerships were made shareholders in the company. Best of all though, he targeted desperate government organisations keen to subsidise any company that might bring hope and jobs to a deprived region. Cleverly, Des O'Malley, the Republic of Ireland's Industry

Minister, decided against building cars in his backyard. Switching to the warmer climes of Puerto Rico thousands of miles away, De Lorean got a call to return to the windswept island. This time the call came from north of the Irish border, and it came with the promise of much more money. NIDA (Northern Ireland Development Agency) made an offer of £80 million that De Lorean could not refuse.

If there was an upside to the project it was that it actually brought the divided community together, even if the Protestants and Catholics entered the buildings by separate doors. That was due to architectural practicality rather than deliberate religious divide, as it was located between the two communities in Dunmurry, a suburb of Belfast. Building work began in October 1978 and the plant was finished in just 16 months. However, they didn't start building ethical sports cars yet, as it was far from ready. De Lorean had been faffing around for years and didn't make things easier by deciding to fit attention-seeking gull-wing doors which would be hinged in the roof and lifted up rather than simply pulled open. He also thought stainless steel panels over a plastic structure would be a good idea. In theory, working with plastic would be easier for an unskilled workforce and cheaper to make.

Giorgetto Giugiaro was asked to design the body, and as a result it didn't look unlike the Lotus Esprit which had recently been introduced, and that's quite an important thing to remember as this story progresses. Oh yes, and there were engine issues as well, because it had to be in the rear and initially needlessly complicated. That's because De Lorean chose a Citroën engine that was uneconomical with rotors rather than pistons and a risqué name that was only really funny in Britain, Wankel. However, he eventually settled on a V6 engine that had been built jointly by Peugeot, Renault and Volvo, none of whom were famous for making high-performance cars or engines at the time.

The early De Lorean prototypes, and there were only two, were shockingly bad, something that the Government could have found out for themselves. It wouldn't have been difficult to get their own car company (BL) to go and have a closer look. Anyway, in the summer of 1978, De Lorean did let Lotus near it, and engineering genius Colin Chapman was horrified at what he saw. Mind you, he calmed down when commissioned to rework this lash-up into something driveable within 18 months. Interestingly, De Lorean had already called in at Porsche, who would rather have four years and a sackload of cash. At this point the financial waters got a little murky. The Lotus money didn't exactly come directly from Mr De Lorean. General Products Development Services Inc, registered in Panama, wrote the cheques. Meanwhile Lotus got on with the grim business of turning the De Lorean into a proper car.

Never mind that that it drove so badly, those gullwing doors didn't help rigidity and computer analysis revealed that at just 26 mph if the De Lorean was hit from behind the engine would end up on the driver's and passenger's laps. Or rather what was left of their laps. Effectively, Lotus took the sensible short cut and based the De Lorean on their Esprit. However, it still retained an engine, and a Renault engine at that, which was at the rear (rather than nicely balanced in the middle like the Esprit) and those great big stupid doors. Just to delay matters further, De Lorean decided that this shape, which been around for five years, had to be freshened up, so got the Italians to restyle it. That must have annoyed Lotus, who had to reengineer most of the design, so it is a wonder that the De Lorean ever got finished. It is also a shame that it did, because the results were not impressive. Not that, they ever allowed a British motoring journalist anywhere near one during its brief production run.

The American press did get their hands on De Loreans though, and to their credit, weren't taken in. From the stainless steel finish which picked up oily fingermarks to the slightly wayward handling caused by having the engine in the wrong place, all was carefully noted. Even the Americans spotted how slow it was. Plenty of weight had been saved, but it wasn't enough to overcome the inadequate and underpowered French-Swedish engine. Road & Track, America's leading magazine, managed a mere 109 mph top speed and acceleration that meant getting to 60 mph took a leisurely 10.5 seconds. A contemporary Volkswagen Golf GTI hatchback would have left the De Lorean trailing, and even more importantly it would not have crashed on the first corner and then trapped it's driver with its broken gull-wing doors.

Lotus had done a sensational job under the circumstances by making something so badly conceived just about drivable. For a start it was only averagely well built by people who, in many cases, had never had a job before. The workers did their very best, but were also let down by the engineering and lack of development which led to Quality Assurance Centers being set up in California, Delaware and Michigan to fix the most obvious faults. They had to sort out the fit of the body panels and install higher output alternators which could cope with the car's electrical shortfalls. They also needed to fiddle endlessly with the gullwing doors so they at least lifted like gulls wings rather than flapping like a waterlogged duck. Indeed a certain Doctor Sheldon Weinstein who ordered one unseen always carried an umbrella to deal with the water leaks and a hammer in case he was ever trapped inside in an accident.

The De Lorean didn't last very long. Official production began in January 1981 and the first ones left for the States in June 1981, at which point 40 cars per day were built. That rate doubled to 80 per day in November, but by this time De Lorean meant trouble as stocks of unsold cars piled up in both Belfast and North America. The receivers (the aptly named Cork Gully) were appointed in February 1982, and the company limped on until October. It was at that point that John De Lorean was arrested and charged with conspiring to smuggle $24 million worth of cocaine into the US. The key element of evidence for the prosecution was a videotape showing De Lorean discussing the drugs deal with undercover FBI agents. However, De Lorean's attorney successfully demonstrated to the court that he was coerced into participation in the deal by the agents who initially approached him as legitimate investors. He was acquitted of all charges, but his reputation was forever tarnished. After his trial and subsequent acquittal, De Lorean quipped, "Would you buy a used car from me?" Well it is amazing that anyone actually bought a brand new one in the first place.

Not only was the De Lorean a bad car, it was an expensive one too. At $25,000 it cost more than a Porsche 944 and not much less than a top-of-the-range Porsche 911. Just how many De Loreans got made is a matter for dispute, but somewhere between 8,000 and 9,200 would be about right. This figure is as accurate as the level of accounting they used. That's why many millions of pounds of British government aid (estimated at least £10m) never reached Lotus. Colin Chapman took the secret of his share to the grave when he died in December 1982. If he had stood trial and been found guilty of fraud, he would have been looking at a 10-year stretch. Indeed John De Lorean was indicted, but chose to stay in the USA, from where he could avoid extradition to Great Britain. It's lucky then that someone made a Hollywood film with his crappy sports car as one of the main props, or no one would ever have heard of it again. The same lucky fate never befell the Austin Maestro.

Before we get all excited about the Maestro the design and engineering departments at BL's Longbridge office had been busily doing something that no one really cared about – turning the Austin Princess into a hatchback seven years too late. Oddly enough, the original plan, simply to cut a hole in the back for an extra door, was changed. Somewhere money was found to allow the designers to re-skin the model with a lot of new body panels. In fact the only surviving panels from the original Princess were the front doors, but it was hard to spot the difference between the four-door Princess and the five-door Ambassador as it was now known. Making it not just a demotion but a possible sex change too. The ultimate irony is that the Ambassador only stayed in production for another two years when it was then replaced by the slightly upmarket Austin Montego, which was not a hatchback. Clearly BL didn't know what they were doing offering cars with limited buyer appeal. One buyer they had lost forever was Dad, who made a long overdue return to the Volkswagen Group.

One important factor in Dad's decision was the Triumph Dolly's spectacular failure just as its warranty expired. Dad had to go to Scotland on business, and storming up the A1 was easy enough, but he thought that doing it in the Daimler was just asking for trouble. Better to take the newer and more reliable car then. A few miles outside of Edinburgh though, the Dolly became hesitant. It lost power before coming to an unscheduled halt. The RAC came out and said that Dad hasn't put enough transmission fluid in it. Suitably topped up, the Dolly started and ran for several miles before Dad reached Edinburgh. He then monitored the growing pool of fluid beneath the gearbox that had turned into a lake by the time he had to come home.

On the return journey Dad bought a bottle of fluid as a precaution. Inevitably the Dolly played up, spluttered and hesitated before the magic fluid was added. At the next garage Dad bought every bottle of fluid they had and put them in the boot. To this day I still have more than enough automatic transmission fluid in my garage. Every half hour or so he had to stop and top up. Driving from Edinburgh to London is long enough, but with repeated pitstops it was unbearable. A gearbox rebuild was the only cure, although this wasn't the last time it happened. Dad wrote to BL without getting any satisfactory response. So having paid for repairs, he didn't dare give it away but preferred to park it in the garage and forget about it. Years later I did coax Dolly out of retirement, and apart from some dodgy handling in the ice, it behaved itself. Until, that is, I went on a long journey to Berkshire and it exploded in a haze of transmission fluid.

So Dad needed another small reserve car while he continued to wrestle with the Daimler's unreliability issues. Almost without hesitation we pitched up at the local Volkswagen dealer and ordered a Volkswagen Golf four-door Automatic in black. Very slightly it reminded me of the Hillman Minx, because the interior was quite dark and plastic. The plastic, though, was of a heavier duty and was clearly premium quality. It didn't have the wood and chrome bits like the Dolly, but then it didn't have a leaky gearbox either, or the skittish behaviour on ice, or the severely dating styling that marked it out as a car for the recently retired. The Golf looked purposeful, sharp, practical and was every bit the sort of package that BL should have had on sale. Instead they were still working on the Austin Maestro, although it did share one important feature with the Golf: it had the same gearbox.

Michael Edwardes left BL in 1982 before the Maestro arrived, probably feeling quite pleased with what he'd achieved. With fresh products in the showroom and in the pipeline and workers spending more time building cars than gathered around a lighted brazier waving placards and forming unofficial picket lines, it was almost job done. Trouble was, the new products weren't much to get really excited about. The Maestro had been conceived at a difficult time for the company, and it showed. To many, the car ended up looking like nothing less than a bigger and, if it is possible, an even uglier Allegro. As a distraction, the car business was renamed yet again, this time as Austin Rover. The man who took over from Edwardes was Harold Musgrove, who had joined Austin as an apprentice in 1945, and the Maestro arrived on his watch in 1983.

That was unfortunate because the Maestro had been developed during particularly cash strapped times, when almost a toss of the coin decided that the smaller Metro should be given priority and launched ahead of the bigger car. Consequently the styling had almost been frozen in time in the mid-70s and then finally approved in 1979. So what might have looked OK back then ended up being rather dated in the 80s. Indeed, just as the Maestro arrived, the square-cut old Golf was replaced, by a softer and friendlier Mark 2 model. Indeed Austin

Rover's new chief stylist at the time, a chap called Roy Axe who had worked at Rootes, wasn't impressed. But it was too late to stop production. And anyway, Austin Rover as we must now remember to call them, were desperate to replace the two-years-dead Maxi and the more recently deceased Allegro. However it used engines that had been fitted to both of those models, with simple suspension (simpler than the Allegro had) and that Golf gearbox.

Apparently Austin Rover resorted to using VW parts because they had "forgotten" how to engineer the basics. At least it was spacious, practical and likely to be reliable, and it talked to you. No really it did talk, and her name was Nicolette. It says a lot about the Maestro that its voice synthesizer system was the most memorable thing about the car. The voice belonged to New Zealand-born actress Nicolette McKenzie, who appeared in numerous roles including TV's General Hospital, Van Der Valk and Churchill's People. It was not an industry first though, because although Nicolette could be programmed to speak fifteen languages, including French, indeed the Renault 11 had introduced the feature a couple of months before.

In an era long before satellite navigation systems, many drivers were irritated by a woman telling them what to do through the driver's side radio speaker. Not surprisingly, along with the distracting and colourful electronic dashboard, the feature was dropped a year later. Eventually the Maestro became accepted as a loyal workhorse, but in the early days build-quality wasn't brilliant. An electronic carburettor seem to operate fairly selfishly, and that led to poor idling, starting and acceleration and generally less than satisfactory operation. Not only that, the robot-bonded windscreens leaked, and alarmingly the bumpers did not take 5mph impacts, but that didn't matter as the paint had already flaked off them before any collision. Also, those brittle plastic bumpers didn't like any extremes of temperature, which is a bit of a problem in the British climate. To distract you from those minor shortfalls, you could buy a super-posh Vanden Plas version which had Nicolette McKenzie as standard, and some fancy badges and trim. And seeing how everyone loved the MG Metro, the MG Maestro was inevitable, but it was rushed into production and suffered badly from all those issues previously mentioned. No wonder then that the Maestro made no inroads whatsoever into Ford's heartland.

Ford's Escort, what the Maestro was really up against, became the best selling car in the world in 1981, and there was nothing that anyone else could do about it after that. In the UK it went to number one of course, while oddly enough, the mighty Ford hit a little local difficulty in the jelly-mould shape of the Ford Sierra. Here was proof that the British car-buying public could be a fickle bunch and not especially certain about what they really wanted: a squareish Maestro, or a softer Sierra. You might wonder what all the fuss was about, but at the time it was a major worry for Ford, and anyone who worked in the car industry, which included me. A Ford Sierra as a part-exchange was a cause for concern, as it was almost deemed unsaleable in the very early days.

Obviously following on from the Ford Cortina was never going to be easy, especially as it had been the best-selling car in Britain until discontinued in 1981. Although all Ford had done was plonk a new body on top of the old Cortina, it was the design that caused all the controversy. The rear hatchback was a useful addition, but the aerodynamic angle was not something that many people got as they nicknamed it "the sales rep's spaceship". Some suggested that, never mind the scary styling, it was the lack of a saloon model which concerned buyers. Meanwhile, this gave Ford's real rivals – Vauxhall, not Austin Rover – time to take advantage of the situation.

The new Vauxhall Cavalier was launched a year ahead of the Sierra in 1981, and wasn't remotely blobby. Indeed the Cavalier was sharp and modern and, most importantly, available from day one with a boot and a hatch. Unlike the Sierra, it was front-wheel-drive, which was now generally accepted as the best way to package a car, freeing up extra room inside. All that pioneering work by BMC and BL had finally paid off, but for the American-owned company and not the Brits. Vauxhall also had an answer to the Escort in the shape of the Astra. Designed in Germany, but at least it was still made in Britain, whereas increasing numbers of Ford cars were being assembled in Europe. Clearly the battle lines for the British car industry had been drawn. It was now Vauxhall vs Ford as the Ford Escort was the top seller followed by the Vauxhall Cavalier and then the Sierra despite it's problems in third. However, Austin Rover were fading fast as the imports were becoming, well, much more important.

Although this book isn't about me, it's about my Dad and the way he bought and ran cars over a 50-year period, what I did next was very significant. I went to work at a BMW dealership in the west end of London in 1983. Before that happened, though, I had to go and do something really dreadful: dismantle my first car.

Having been passed on to Uncle Charles and Auntie Flo, who had now retired to Norfolk, the plucky little Mini had replaced an Austin Allegro that was 10 years younger and several thousand times worse when it came to reliability, comfort and general all-round decent carness. However, after a few years by the coast, the rust bug had bitten hard. Like Japanese cars of the time, the mechanics were perfect, but the body was shot full of holes. Welding it up yet again wasn't worth it as the floor already resembled a patchwork quilt of metal squares. The least I could do was take all the bits off it that still worked. After all, they would come in handy as I continued with protracted task of making my old Mini Cooper roadworthy again. Plenty of parts were interchangeable because the decision to make an Austin or Morris Mini into a Cooper or Cooper S was taken fairly late on in the production process. Just as taking them apart was a hands-on job, so was building them. You can't beat the exclusivity and feel-good factor of owning a hand-built car like, say, a Morgan. And I think that's what tempted Dad to dip back into the new car market, and the fact that he didn't have to pay VAT.

Still in the garage: That Daimler and Triumph, but at last there's some reliability in the drive courtesy of a Volkswagen Golf CL Automatic.

Births
1981 BL renamed Austin Rover Group
1981 De Lorean
1982 MG badge
1982 Westfield

Deaths
1981 Sunbeam-Lotus
1982 De Lorean
1982 Princess
1983 Davrian

New arrivals
1982 Hyundai

Best Sellers
1981 Ford Cortina 159,804
1982 Ford Escort 166,942
1983 Ford Escort 174,190

In the Car Park

There's a Toyota Crown at the top, then below it on the left Top left is a De Lorean, only slightly based on the Lotus Esprit on the right. Next row is the Volkswagen Golf GTI which virtually wiped out the old sports car and Austin Rover's response with the MG Maestro. Next row are the basic but successful Fords, Escort on the left and Cortina on the right. Bottom has the Sierra on the left which was only a rebodied Sierra, but many could not abide its jelly mould styling. Thank goodness for the reassuringly square Vauxhall Astra.

16 Rondas and Monty Ego while Bluebirds are spotted in Sunderland 1984–1986

In the garage: Both Daimler and Triumph go into dry storage whilst the Golf Automatic takes on the daily grind. Meanwhile there's a spare commercial vehicle on its way.

I didn't know quite what to make of Dad's latest purchase.

On the basis that he needed a commercial vehicle for business, we went to the other local BL dealer that only offered the prestigious Land Rover and Jaguar brands, but crucially had not supplied the disappointing Dolly and Daimler. It fitted the usual pattern of Dad ordering a vehicle that was at the very end of its production run, so was just about to be replaced. Of course, this had its advantages as he could ask for and get a half decent discount. Dad also quite liked the fact that being a business buyer he could claim the VAT back, so he felt as though he was getting one over on the tax man.

Long before there was any controversy over 4x4s in urban environments and Chelsea tractors, Dad parked a great big sod-off, off-roader on our drive. Actually this Land Rover wasn't that big. It was a Series 3 that could be traced all the way back to Chapter 2 and the 1947 part of this book. So unlike the current generation of gargantuan school-run lorries, it was only a couple of feet longer than an old Mini. Indeed the only thing truly big about it was that it was quite tall. Otherwise it was a handy size, but even in 1984 when dad threw me the keys and I got out of a brand new BMW 3 series to drive it, I couldn't believe how old-fashioned it all was. It crashed over urban potholes, was incredibly noisy and didn't even have wind up windows. They slid backwards and forwards just like a Mini, and the upright driving position with a massive bus-like steering wheel was also remarkably similar to the tiny car. Both also seemed to have been around forever, and they remained two of the models that BL could rely on.

Hand-built, characterful and still selling in comfortingly consistent numbers. As for their latest products, well there wasn't one which would ever tempt dad to sign on the dotted line, so what were they?

As a vital part of their regeneration, the next Austin Rover model to be launched in 1984 was the Montego. Effectively this was the replacement for the shortlived Ambassador and not much missed Morris Ital. Although the intention had been to use the middle bit of the Maestro, that didn't work out, so it only shared the front doors with the hatchback. Roy Axe, the new stylist who had so hated the Maestro, but didn't have the time to change it, managed to overhaul the Montego a bit, and it showed. Although it was a Maestro with the boot and almost as boring, it looked much tidier if not that adventurous. Given Ford's experience with their overly adventurous Sierra, that was a good thing. What worked a lot better, though, was the estate version, which looked almost handsome. Indeed there was a seven-seat option which put it in the same class as Mercedes E Class and Volvo estates, something that Ford's Sierra and Vauxhall's Cavalier never offered. Here was an example of Austin Rover getting just about everything right.

The Montego wasn't half bad as a medium-sized saloon car aimed at the fleet market which came in a variety of models to tempt a variety of buyers. There were slightly exciting MG versions, the leather and bits of wood Vanden Plas and the slightly mad MG Turbo. It came along at the same time as the Maestro version, and the performance stats were very impressive as both cars were given the instant accolades as the fastest production MGs ever. To be honest, MGs had never been that quick, but getting to 60mph in just over 7 seconds and managing to reach a dizzy 126mph was a match for most contemporary hot hatches. The Montego turned out to be the very last new model to bear the name Austin, it having replaced the last model to bear the Morris badge, the awful Ital. And while we are on the subject of "last ofs", the very last model to bear the name Triumph was being discontinued as the Acclaim went into retirement. Luckily, the best car that BMC, BLMC, BL and Austin Rover had ever built was not disappearing forever. It was replaced by a brand new Honda Ballade, but with a Rover badge on it.

The great British car-buying public said hello to the Ronda. Well, they didn't, but that is what it should have been called. With the lowest ever claims against its warranty, Austin Rover regarded the outgoing Triumph Acclaim as an unqualified success. The name, though, was regarded as a problem, especially in Europe, where management reckoned that Triumph was forever associated with cheap sports cars. So with the car business now renamed Austin Rover and a determination to move their models upmarket, Rover was deemed the appropriate moniker. Once again, they took what was a Honda Civic saloon and Roverised it, hence the nickname "Ronda". However, there was more of a Roverisation process than there had been with the Acclaim, especially inside. Indeed after many years of abusing the old coach builders' name of Vanden Plas on dodgy Allegros and also Mangy Maestros, it started to seem a little more appropriate when applied to the Rover 200.

Clearly copying BMW's success by giving numerical values to each range of cars and the relevant engine size (316, 320, 323 etc) was the way to go. So the Honda Ballade became the Rover 200 series, with the 1.3 engined model being the 213 and the 1.6, well you were way ahead of me there, was the 216. Here was the clearest indication yet that Austin Rover had every intention of becoming a sort of British BMW. And actually it worked as Austin Rover surveyed the general public about how much they thought the 200 was worth and heard the answer £10,000 rather than the £7,000 which was actually being charged. No wonder sales of the Maestro suffered as the 200 was seen as the more upmarket car, rather than being spacious, good value and nicer to drive. So here was Austin Rover's future, building high-quality cars that had been adapted for the British and European market. However, it was no BMW, and I knew because I sold them and Dad asked to buy one.

Having decided that the Daimler and Dolly were a joke double act of the most unfunny proportions, Dad resolved never to drive them again and, more to the point, not even give them to a deserving member of the family. My sister had moved on to the Golf GL by then, and Uncle Charles had the Mini Clubman. Daimler and Dolly were dry stored while he used the Land Rover and asked me for a BMW. Dad was after a 318i, which was really nice, but I didn't think was particularly good value. Everything was an extra on a BMW back then, including the radio. If you wanted alloy wheels or a sunroof then that was second mortgage territory for the buyer, and even more money for the dealer's floor tiles and potted plants. My recommendation was that for slightly less, a brand new Volkswagen GTI was the answer. That's the one I would have bought anyway, with it's eager engine, stripes, badges and alloys. Even better, there was an onboard computer that didn't talk at you. A careful prod on the column stalk brought all the information you needed. Outside temperature, oil temperature, average speed and mpg and how long the journey took. It was a gimmick, but one that worked and was actually useful. Nothing looked more purposeful or was quicker and more fun to drive than a Golf GTI, especially when compared to a BMW 318i. Dad thought I could do with the commission, but I reckoned he should go for the better car. Dad drove home in the Golf.

So if Austin Rover were going in the right direction with their smaller cars like the 200, what about their division which made the proper full-sized luxury saloons? Well Jaguar was floated on the stock exchange, which in English means that it was sold off. It was at precisely this moment that Dad's correspondence with the company stopped. They now argued that the rubbishness of their earlier models no longer had anything to do with what was now a private company. It was mooted that the government should maintain a shareholding of up to 25% to avoid a foreign company like Ford taking control. Maggie Thatcher didn't want to do that, but she did come up with a "golden share" idea which meant there was no chance of a takeover bid for a set period, which was until 1990.

For all of the Conservative government's claims not to want to be involved in the day-to-day running of Austin Rover, actually they were quite proactive. But then they were trying to look after and make the most of taxpayers money. Indeed they were actively trying to find a solution, which meant selling the whole company off. Austin Rover still needed money from the government, and in 1985 managed to get a further £1.5 billion. Although Dad had contributed to that sum, instead of a supportive Rover 200 series purchase, he responded with another visit to the Volkswagen dealer to get a spare GTI, this time with five practical doors rather than three. Reason enough then for the government to start sounding out potential suitors for the more attractive parts of Austin Rover. Indeed, a year later, in 1986, it was revealed by the deputy leader of the Labour Party, Roy Hattersley, that as part of a sell-off plan, General Motors were lined up to buy Leyland Trucks and Land Rover. That would have made them part of Vauxhall's Bedford brand.

However, it wasn't the trucks that got everyone all heated and emotional; it was the Land Rover element that led to questions in Parliament about selling the country's automotive crown jewels. That led to a thousand Land Rover owners on-roading their way to Downing Street. Meanwhile, unknown to anyone, the government was holding talks with Ford about taking Austin Rover off their hands. However, the pressure from within the government itself about keeping Land Rover British worked, although like Jaguar, the future for the whole company, according to the owners, was still to be in private hands, but obviously the hands had to be the right nationality.

With this in mind, the government appointed Canadian lawyer Graham Day as the new chairman in May 1986. He came from three years of running the nationalised British Shipbuilders. He wanted to drive the company upmarket, and openly stated that he wanted it to be like a British version of BMW. Within the year, Day had changed the company's name yet again, to the Rover Group, leaving the company with just two main marques, Rover and MG. Day then went on a disposal spree when it came to corporate assets which could be spun off privately. As a result, the Unipart spares business was sold to its management while the same thing happened to Leyland Buses and then Leyland Trucks. Finally, the vans business, Freight Rover, merged with Dutch Daf Trucks.

Without Jaguar, Austin Rover only had the Rover SD1 to rely on for premium-priced sales which, was a problem as the model no longer had much of a reputation. It's a good job then that there was a plan, which was to build a Honda Ballade, but a lot bigger. This was Project XX and it was a lot more of a joint venture with Honda than the Rover 200 had ever been. Instead of planning a Rover-modified Honda, both the companies sat down and designed two models together. One would become the Rover 800 and the other the Honda Legend. However, it seemed obvious early on that the model probably had a lot more Japanese that Brummie input. First of all the styling was certainly clean like the smaller 200, and equally Honda-ish, which really meant that it was just a little bit dull and bland. Not only that, the dimensions were decidedly Oriental, being slightly more narrow than a European executive and with less interior space than many rivals. Also, the complex Honda suspension meant that it couldn't be tuned for comfort. So although there was co-operation between the two companies, it wasn't entirely successful, especially as the two seemingly identical cars did not share the majority of their parts. Never mind though, because this was the first genuinely all-new model produced by the reborn Rover Group. It was also available with either Japanese or British engines, a 2.0-litre Brit and a 2.7-litre V6 Jap. Here was the car that everyone said was going to save the company, and just as importantly, it was going to spearhead the company's return to the profitable American market.

Now I've looked at statistics until my eyes glazed over and I lost the will to eat biscuits ever again, and I don't want to bore you rigid with them, but these figures are so mind-boggling that I want to share them with you. Because by the mid-1980s, it looked as though Austin Rover had forgotten to export anything at all. Overall exports had halved from 40 per cent of production in 1978 down to 20 per cent by 1984. I could now trawl around various cheerful European destinations with sales breakdowns that show how poorly Austin Rovers travelled. There were exceptions, though, as there was a massive blip in France where sales had increased four-fold to 27,518, and Germany, where they had levelled out at 9,330 in 1984. But everywhere else was a disaster. Worst of all, from a buoyant 75,291 in 1976, BL cars in American managed to export just the one in 1984. Yes really, one. That's how bad it had become. Certainly it was possible to point to the lack of Jaguar and suggest that the closure of production lines in Belgium didn't help. But in the big nasty old world, it was no different in 1985 from 1945 when car companies had to either export or die. So what were Jaguar doing about it all?

Well, a few months after the 800 came another potential saviour of the newly independent Jaguar: their all-new XJ6. Now this wasn't something that they had cooked up in 1984 and launched a few years later. In fact the original design stretched way back into the British Leyland era. In 1972, project XJ40, as enthusiasts still refer to this model, was first commissioned. Now it was always going to look like the original XJ which had been so successful, but such a long gestation period was never going to be a good thing. The number of styling proposals from the UK and more particularly from Italy piled up. One thing was certain, though: the familiar shape would be squared off, as was fashionable in the 70s. Rumours also abounded that the under-bonnet area was designed in such a way that only Jaguar engines would fit. In the highly political and competitive climate where the various BL marques fought among themselves, it was important for them to preserve their engineering independence, and the last thing they wanted was a Rover V8 under there. However, the actual explanation is a lot simpler, as BL management simply believed the senior Jaguar engineer who claimed that no other engines would fit under the bonnet. It was sheer laziness rather than a conspiracy, as no one bothered to check whether that was true.

Incredibly, the XJ40 was not approved until the arrival of Jaguar's new boss in 1980, and scheduled for a 1984 launch, which of course never happened. Another six years of development which should have meant Mercedes and BMW levels of over-engineering and quality. It didn't, but the sheer anticipation and the fact that it looked like a Jaguar meant that it was even crowned Car of the Year for 1987. Up against the bland Rover 800 the Jaguar badge was always a big help, but then it was always competing in a different price bracket. Except that right at the bottom of the XJ40 range, if you didn't mind sitting on cloth seats, changing gears manually through the smallest 2.9 engine, then you paid less than someone with a top-of-the-range Rover 800. So which do you think buyers chose – a sexy Jag or dog of a Rover?

In America the XJ40 did boost sales and save the company, even though build-quality was not brilliant and there were enough issues to suggest that they hadn't come that far since they had thrown together Dad's Daimler. The digital dashboard was something of a novelty (it could fail expensively too) and the overall sophistication and electronic complexity created a lot of reliability issues. Without boring you, the Americans soon found that, apart from the dashboard going into an electronic sulk, the exterior door handles would seize and break. Something called a crankshaft position sensor would fail to sense anything so the engine wouldn't start. The batteries were not up to the job and in certain situations would not be able to turn the engine and when parked would just go flat anyway. The front wheel bearings were weak and would fail after exploring a few pot holes, while the clever self-levelling suspension would forget to do any self-levelling and cost a fortune to fix. Despite all this and more, especially the fact that the shape had begun to date badly and that sensible people bought BMW 7 series or a Mercedes S Class, the Jaguar was a success. After years of decline, export sales were up. However, we shouldn't worry about Jaguar when it was the state-owned Rover Group who really needed to make it in the States.

First of all Rover had a problem because the SD1 had done so badly in America with the usual shoddy quality issues that it was decided to drop the name Rover altogether and call the car and brand Sterling. Surely no one would notice? Now creating a new brand was a costly though potentially clever thing to do. Honda were doing the same in 1986 with the Acura, which marketed high-quality luxury saloons and exotic sports cars with a new badge (which looked like a retro space rocket). Sterling had to rely on a single model, the Rover 800, and a badge with a cross and winged Lion on it. That didn't help build-quality for what is one of the most fussy car markets in the world.

The Sterling actually sold quite well initially, with around 15,000 finding buyers, but the part time electrics, fragile trim and poor paint quality soon hit customer confidence. Indeed, The Sterling Plus Motor Club was created as a marketing exercise, but actually ended up providing accommodation for drivers stranded in the middle of somewhere next to their broken-down Sterling. In later years, massive discounts amounting to $6,000 were employed in a desperate effort to shift the cars. So while the Acura brand and the Legend in particular topped the JD Power reliability survey, the Sterling was at the other end propping it up. After proving that they could build great cars (Acclaim and Rover 200), albeit Japanese-engineered ones, Rover had reverted to type and delivered shoddy products to the most important and lucrative car market in the world. Bad move.

However, other manufacturers had noticed what was going on in Britain, so it was no real surprise that Nissan and the Government signed an agreement to build a car plant at the former Sunderland Airfield in February 1984. This wasn't as bonkers as building an ethical sports car in Northern Ireland, not least because the vehicle involved was an ultra-reliable, properly engineered Nissan. Plus, in the North East there were plenty of skilled manufacturing workers. Prime Minister Margaret Thatcher officially opened the plant alongside Nissan president Yutaka Kume in September 1986, although Bluebirds had started to roll out back in July. These were assembled from Japanese-supplied parts and full manufacture did not occur for another two years. All around the country, minicab drivers breathed a sigh of relief as they could now buy a spacious, practical and very ugly company vehicle.

Clearly car manufacturing was changing forever in Britain, with industrial relations now under some sort of sane control and workers proving that they could build reliable cars that the public wanted to buy. One remarkable turnaround had been Talbot, whose former Leyland man George Turnbull had cleverly steered this seeming basket case to profitability before his contract was up in 1984. Talbot even took the opportunity to dust down some old Rootes model names for the last few years. They created the Talbot Minx and Rapier to take over from the Alpine and Solara, and had a few more extras like a door mirror you could adjust from inside the cabin, but their days were numbered.

In 1985 the Horizon, which had been around since 1977, was replaced by the Peugeot 309, whilst the car plant at Ryton in Coventry was refitted to make, well, Peugeots. Cars, even French ones, were still being built in Britain, but significantly the days of engineering and designing them seemed to be over. This was confirmed when Peugeot sold Jaguar their former Whitley design centre that had been part of Chryslers set up.

In 1986, Dad also decided to offshore all his car purchases. We did for a while in 85/86 seriously consider buying abroad and personally importing any further vehicles that we may need. These were the first stirrings of rip-off Britain when the Consumer's Association first suggested that the prices on our island were unreasonably high. We actually got as far as contacting a Volkswagen dealer in Belgium and shouting at him in English. Actually his English was brilliant, but we were still a bit hesitant at paying a large deposit into a foreign bank account. There were also UK brokers getting involved, and they seemed even more suspect to deal with. So rather than risk buying a model that wasn't exactly UK specification and possibly getting the wrong colour, we decided against it. Obviously buying a car was still less than straightforward and needed to be properly explained. So I went off and wrote a book called Dealing with Car Dealers and became a motoring journalist.

Dad went and got himself another Golf, this time a GL automatic, and had conclusively severed his relationship with the British car industry. Even though it was going to do all it possibly could to tempt him back.

In the garage: Volkswagen Golf GTi while the Land Rover Series 3 isn't even on the drive because it actually would not fit inside. Oh yes and there's a Mark 2 Golf GL automatic as replacement for the Mark 1.

Births
1984 Jaguar float as a private company
1986 Austin Rover renamed Rover Group PLC

Marriages
1986 Lotus to General Motors

Deaths
1984 Morris
1984 Triumph
1985 Arkley
1986 Talbot

New Arrivals
1986 SEAT
Best Sellers – 1985 Country of origin in brackets.

Ford Escort   157,269 (GB)
Vauxhall Cavalier   134,335 (GB)
Ford Fiesta   124,143 (GB)
Austin/MG Metro   118,817 (GB)
Ford Sierra   101,642 (D)
Vauxhall Astra   76,553 (GB)
Austin/MG Montego   73,955 (GB)
Ford Orion   65,363 (GB)
Vauxhall Nova   61,358 (SP)
Austin/MG Maestro   57,527 (GB)

Best Sellers by Year
1984 Ford Escort 157,340
1985 Ford Escort 157,269
1986 Ford Escort 156,895

In the Car Park

Right at the top is a BMW 3-series a premium priced range of sporty saloons that found customers easily and kept them happy. Below that is the less than premium Austin Montego a range of safe saloons and estate cars. Next to it is the Rover 216, closely related to a Honda Ballade. Directly below the Montego is the Rover 800 a version of the Honda Legend next to it. At the bottom is the Jaguar XJ40 designed to save the company. Finally the Nissan Bluebird brought jobs to the North East.

17 Rover Flogged, Mini saved, Dad Buys more Golfs 1987-1989

In the garage: There's a replacement Golf GTi with five doors, and the Land Rover is still around too.

Probably the best news to come out of 1987 for anyone who liked Minis, was that it would stay in production. Market research conducted before Graham Day's arrival at Rover revealed that many potential customers thought the Mini had been discontinued. However, reports of its demise had been hugely exaggerated and Rover were keen to get buyers back into their showrooms. This was especially as the research revealed that people didn't just like the Mini, they absolutely loved and adored it. Already the "Minis have feelings too" TV advert had been running at Christmas. So as well as getting the supposedly downmarket Austin badge taken off Metros, Maestros and Montegos, they went on a special-edition offensive. Without the money to revamp the engineering or upgrade it, they took the cheap option of tarting up models with silly names and cosmetic additions. It worked absolutely brilliantly in raising the Mini's profile, not just in the UK, but also in vital export markets such as France and Japan. The Mini was back in business until at least 1991, according to Rover management. However, in the massive scheme of things, this really wasn't terribly important.

The truth is that all car companies need ferocious amounts of money to stay in business and build new models. Mrs Thatcher and her government never understood this until, that is, Graham Day submitted his corporate plan for the following year which had a £1 billion price tag attached in order to get it through the next five years.

Meanwhile British companies were being swallowed up and in some cases spat out again. Tiddler motor manufacturer Panther cars had been best known for building the frankly bizarre. Most were pastiches of legendary classics like the J72, which was essentially a pre-war Jaguar sports car (the SS100) but with modern Jaguar running gear. The Deville was an updated Bugatti that no one had really asked for, while the Rio was a humble Triumph Dolly Sprint with a Rolls-Royce-style radiator. They all cost a fortune of course, but for about five minutes in 1987 it looked as though their Solo prototype would be the most exciting sports car to come out of Britain for a generation. Unpronounceable South Korean conglomerate SsangYong bought the company, and very rapidly pronounced that the Solo was unfeasible.

At the other end of the scale, Ford and their bank vault full of money decided to buy up poverty-stricken, small but glamorous British motor manufacturers. First there was Aston Martin. The closest Dad and I had ever come to one was in 1978 when I went with him on a job and we took the Mini Clubman. An Aston V8 parked next to us, and a bloke who looked not unlike Peter Wyngarde (droopy 70s tache and biggish hair – yes, they still dressed that way in post-punk years) stepped out. Dad offered a swap and it was enough to make Wyngarde stop and quip back that he would like to swap petrol bills. Anyway, the history of Aston Martin is fabulously complicated and involves lots of very rich men and their wallets which were rapidly emptied by the glamorous sports car company. Their most famous owner was Sir David Brown, who made his fortune making honest, muddy, industrial tractors. His DB initials live on to this day in the model names, DB7 and DB9. An apocryphal story perfectly illustrates the realities of running a specialist British car company when a friend asked DB for an Aston at cost price. "In that case, you need to pay me £2,000 more." A 75 per cent stake cost Ford rather more than that in 1987.

Ford then bought AC Cars, or rather a controlling interest. AC could trace its roots back to 1902 when a butcher and an engineer got together to make cars. However, it was their three-wheeled delivery vehicles which proved more commercially viable. American racing car builder Carroll Shelby's decision to install a massive Ford V8 engine into the beautiful AC Ace sports car in 1962 created an instant icon. By 1990 though, the whole deal, which involved building a quite handsome all-new Ace, was unscrambled leaving everyone wondering what the point was.

Maybe Ford were copying their big rivals General Motors, who the previous year had bought another prestigious British sports car company, Lotus. Although they could afford to lose a small and even a very large fortune without feeling the effects, GM didn't realise what a rough ride they were in for. Build-quality, though, had never been at the forefront of the company's thinking. Founder Colin Chapman regarded the manufacturer's one-year warranty as an approximation of the model's lifespan. Dad got closest to a Lotus through a very clever engineer and designer he worked with called Richard Vinyl, who bought a Lotus Elan kit. Being an engineer, he wasn't easily fooled and found countless gaps in the instructions (all reported to an indifferent Lotus) which culminated in the day he fitted the electric windows. Richard watched as they rose majestically upwards out of the doors and then balance precariously for a second before toppling over and smashing on the ground. Sadly Dad was never going to buy a Lotus, but then General Motors probably shouldn't have done either as it was little more than a plastic-bodied money pit.

That's probably how the government were feeling at the time as they were being asked to pump more taxpayers money into Rover while the prospects for a flotation seemed more distant than ever. Meanwhile, one of Britain's few credible international companies, British Aerospace, were in a mood to get bigger. They wanted to generate more cash on a regular basis rather than rely on long-term defence contracts. Clearly they knew little about how the car industry operated and how much cash it needed just to stay operational. However, in 1987 the new chairman, Professor Roland Smith, had dropped a hint to Rover chairman Graham Day that he'd be interested in picking up Land Rover. The government liked the sound of this because there was some interest from Ford and also Volkswagen, whereas British Aerospace were, as their name indicated, British.

With a little bit of persuasion, though, British Aerospace were convinced to take the whole lot for what has subsequently been regarded as a giveaway price: £150 million.

That was March 1, 1988, and the British car industry – well, the largest single manufacturer anyway – was back in British hands. On the face of it, Rover looked in good health and had reasonable prospects. Scratch the surface, though, and most of the products looked tired and needed to be updated or replaced altogether. The Maestro and Montego in particular were limping along as Ford Escorts and Sierras and Vauxhall Astras and Cavaliers dominated the marketplace. However, there was a new variation on the Rover 800 theme too: the Fastback. Well, that sounded a lot better than hatchback, which is of course what it really was. "Fastback" is a term that had fallen out of use and had described a coupe with sloping rear screens, which is of course exactly what the Fastback had. As ever, Rover had high hopes for this model, and the TV adverts featured a couple of Germans being understatedly excited about a Fastback. Firstly in an atmospheric underground car park, then later on the autobahn, before arriving at their destination, the weird and iconic art gallery in Stuttgart, designed by James Stirling. The punchline was "Britischer Architekt", but the subtext was this: the Rover 800 is so brilliant those discerning Germans who know a good car when they build/drive/own one, will buy an 800 fastback. Rover should have been careful what they wished for.

The reality was that the 800, after the ongoing Sterling disaster in America, only really sold in significant numbers in its home market to patriotic company directors who ran carpet warehouses and regional sales managers who probably weren't hitting their targets. Otherwise they would be driving a BMW 5 series. In the executive car market the competition was getting fierce and the standards were getting high and image was absolutely crucial. In the company car park, what you drove said everything about what you wanted others to know. For instance, a Saab 9000 was a large safe hatchback which was not a conventional choice. Saab meant middle class, Swedish good minimalist taste, so it is likely that a senior University Lecturer, or maybe a dentist drove one and paid their own, or company money for it. A Ford Granada was the quintessential fleet car, being big on value and equipment, chosen by the company for those who had reached a certain level. The Rover 800 oddly fell between both in that it would be a company default buy, but there were also the buy-British loyalists (who no longer included Dad) spending their own hard-earned. Of course what everyone really wanted was a BMW or Mercedes.

If you had a BMW you may just have run your own successful company or you were doing really well. Director level stuff. The same with Mercedes, although you may also have been an accountant with an eye on the bottom line, because a Merc and also a BMW was always going to be worth more than a discounted Ford Granada, odd Saab, or very average Rover 800 after a few years.

Image really was absolutely everything, and Rover were starting to discover just how tarnished their brand had become. Rovers were now as peculiar as Morris Dancing. Yes, they weren't even British anymore, just weirdly English. Not only that, the Maestro and Montego had been Austins and now they weren't even that. Not posh enough to be real Rovers, they may have been made by Rover, but they were just slightly embarrassing and only kept in production because they shared lots of parts with each other and there was a low level, but fairly constant demand which kept the Cowley factory busy.

And then there was the 200 reaching the end of its life as arguably the most Rovery Rover of all, being reliable, smart and nicely finished – qualities that Rovers of old enjoyed as of right. It may have been low on innovation, but it ticked the most important boxes for buyers. Rover, though, hadn't really contributed that much to the 200's development, and when they did more on the 800, it didn't exactly go according to anyone's plans. Ending up with an executive car as average as the 800 which didn't share nearly enough parts with its Legend cousin taught Honda and Rover that they ought to get along a lot better. Indeed for Honda, it was vital that instead of the sometimes oddly bland vehicles they offered, which didn't travel well in Europe, they needed something more appealing. With that in mind, Rover engineers took charge of the interior and suspension. Back in Japan, Honda did everything else. However, Honda were interested in the way that Rover designed cars from the inside out, rather than outside in. That explained why Japanese cars didn't break down, whereas ours did, but at least you sat in some degree of comfort and serenity in a British car waiting for the AA. Both the resulting Rover and Honda would share some 80 per cent of parts and, quite significantly, almost 100 per cent of the styling.

Badge engineering had returned yet again, but in a good way. The differences would be fairly minor items, including grilles, headlights, front wings and the tailgate. Actually, one important difference would be under the bonnet, as Rover's new range of advanced alloy engines would be used. These had caused all sorts of conflict with Mrs Thatcher's government as Rover kept asking for more money to keep development going. Rover, though, did not have the money available to build a gearbox, so bought one from Peugeot. Here was proof that the car industry was becoming increasingly global. Interestingly, Honda were so obsessed by their own engineering excellence that they insisted on making some unique models for their own market that would never come to Europe and that shared almost no parts at all with the Rover 200 and had four-wheel-drive systems and new suspensions. But then Honda could afford to do that.

Finally Rover were learning to premium-price these models, and would avoid competing with Ford Escorts and Vauxhall Astras with basic specification. Whereas the Honda's 200 was called the Concerto in a typically bizarre Oriental way because it sounded OK in Japanese, Rover stuck to the same naming system as before. The 214 had a Rover engine and the 216 came with a Honda engine. However, it was the Honda-engined Concerto that everyone got to know first, because it was launched a full 18 months before the Rover. It was fairly obvious then who was running the show.

By the time the Rover 200 was ready for the UK in October 1989, I had been working for Car magazine for a few years, writing a column about used cars called Pre-Owned. I didn't have much to do with new cars at all, but they asked me to help with some driving and taking some cars up to an RAF airfield at Bruntingthorpe and then to various locations around the country for pictures. They said it would be good experience, which it was, even though the line-up of models didn't seem very much more exciting than what you might ram a trolley into at the supermarket. Vauxhall Astra, Fiat Tipo, Ford Escort and Renault 19 all had engines that were 1.4 in size or thereabouts and aimed at the small family hatchback buyer. This was probably the most closely fought and crucial market for all the manufacturers, and one which the Escort had dominated for the last decade. Oh yes, and nestling amongst that lot was the new Rover 214.

The new 200 was not yet on sale, and what I noticed first was the two-tone paint scheme which was predominately metallic red over grey paintwork from the door rubbing strip down. Inside there was a bit of wood, but it seemed to be so much more solid and comfortable than previous Rovers. The styling was like a scaled down 800, but it seemed a lot neater and next to the other cars was so much smarter. Over three days I drove all the cars, and the Rover in particular was reassuringly solid and comfortable. The best bit was being told off by a high-performance driving instructor in a BMW for performing a "dangerous manoeuvre" on the airfield. Well I didn't cause a crash, only sniggers at the self-importance of the anoraked man who didn't even realise I was driving the all-new Rover.

I was never allowed to take the Rover home over those few days, but found the Escort and Astra boring, the Tipo the most fun to drive, while the Renault 19 I was lumbered with lost its gear linkage when I tried to engage reverse in a car park. I had to walk to a station and take a train home. So here was the best new Rover for a generation, or at least since everyone found out that the SD1 looked great, but was actually held together with flour paste. Indeed the 200 won loads of awards for all sorts of reasons, but just missed out on the Car of the Year to the Citroën XM, which deserved it as much as the SD1, being large, complex and occasionally troublesome. After those thrilling few days I excitedly told Dad all about the new Rover and how very nice it was and that quite possibly he ought to take a closer look at one.

Obviously he responded in the only way he knew how, by going out and ordering another Volkswagen Golf GL automatic.

In the garage: Volkswagen Golf GTI, a Volkswagen Golf GL automatic and the Land Rover.

Births
1988 Jensen
1988 Middlebridge

Death
1988 Austin

New Arrivals
1989 Proton

Best Sellers

1987 Ford Escort 178,001
1988 Ford Escort 172,706
1989 Ford Escort 181,218

In the Car Park...

Top row is full of Panthers, their J72 Jaguar copy is their most famous, the Rio
a rebodied Dolly Sprint their most infamous and finally the Solo that sank the
company. Row 2 with the classic AC Cobra on the right, Ace in the middle and
a Lotus Elan on the end. Third row has an Aston Martin V8 for some excitement
offset by the Vauxhall Cavalier's dullness. Bottom row Rover 800 fastback and
the new Rover 200.

18 Supercarspeculators, the Cooper reborn and a car called Trevor 1990–1992

In the garage: Volkswagen Golf GTi, Volkswagen Golf GL automatic, while Land Rover goes into retirement.

The problem I have now is that the Volkswagen Golf GL which was registered in 1990 turned out to be the last car Dad bought. For the next 15 years that was all he ever needed. It wasn't as if we didn't discuss new cars, or the possibility of something rather more contemporary, but effectively Dad had decided that he had better things to do than hang around Volkswagen showrooms any more. He even found a local VW specialist in a tiny one-ramp, two-brother-operated garage who looked after the GL with a level of care and attention to detail that you might have thought had long since been abandoned by British engineers.

So maybe I should end the book right here. Certainly it would be on an upbeat note, as the Rover 200 won prizes and customers with a build-quality that was more than a match for the Concerto in Japan. So look away now if you don't want to be depressed by the inevitable downward spiral to the industry's demise.

But hey, we've all come this far, so we might as well finish. I think you will want to know what happened next to the British-owned companies and manufacturing of cars as a whole in England. I also think the next few chapters are really rather good at linking up the loose ends and unravelling some needlessly complicated purchases and sales that led to car manufacturing becoming a lot less British.

In fact in the late 80s and early 90s it was hard for me to get away from British Leyland's finer products. I actually bought some of the worst examples of BL bodgery, but in the interests of research and of keeping a mate mobile. Obviously I wasn't much of a mate if I was inflicting these old sheds on him. But these were only short-term flings because my mate Steve was only visiting the country before going back abroad to work.

I bought British because rubbish BL cars were all you could get for a few hundred quid back then. Fords and Vauxhalls could be too pricey, Fiats and Renaults too untrustworthy, while Japanese cars were just far too ugly and rusty. Austins and Morrises, though, were easy to find, unloved and cheap. That's why I bought an Austin Allegro unseen and undriven that belonged to a car trade delivery driver's wife. Actually it was such a favourable deal, on my part obviously, that he pulled out at the last minute.

So in a blinding hurry I bought an Austin Princess by mistake. It was a large wedge-shaped lump of blue cheese that reeked of failure. The brown velour interior was actually fairly immaculate and comfortable. The more I drove it, though, the less happy I became when it met an upward incline. At that point, the engine would cut out because the petrol pump was only working part-time. So after driving from west London to deepest south in the early morning rush hour, I decided that I couldn't fob this Princess on to someone I actually liked. Consequently I drove back, avoiding all inclines, which took at least double the travel time.

The thing is, though, I didn't make it all the way home. A few miles short of safety I coasted into a service road just off the A40 with absolutely nothing working. I left the dead Princess where she stopped and walked home. Then I got a cheery phone call offering me that Allegro. The seller had changed his mind. Collecting it in North London, I made the journey south yet again, feeling hot, sweaty, stupid and out of pocket, officially owning two rubbish cars. The Allegro didn't mind hills and it was a later model without the weird "quartic" steering wheel, just a soiled furry cover which was almost as bad. The Allegro, though, was still well over a decade old and it looked and felt terminally tired. It was also incontinent.

When I'd left the keys with Steve's mum, it hadn't seemed so bad, but over the next few days, petrol seeped out of the rusty tank and eventually it was drained and removed. That left Steve's mum with quite a few gallons of fuel that she didn't have a clue what to do with. When it got dark, she crept outside and tipped it over the grass verge in a watering can. The next morning the milkman flicked his smouldering fag stub out of his cab with predictably inflammatory results. And what happened to the Princess? Well, eventually I phoned Billy the carbreaker and described what it was and he said, "is it that bright blue one parked off the A40?" You just couldn't miss it. Billy turned up with cash and a promise that the Princess would be smashed royally to bits, not in a crusher, but in a banger race. There wasn't much demand for old wedge-shaped Princesses any more or the bits that could be prised off them. So down the banger racing stadium it was.

And then there was the Morris Ital that I bought deliberately because I was paid to. Carweek magazine issued a challenge to three hacks to buy a heap for £250. I was the one who didn't buy an old Volvo, or Mercedes because they looked cool. I bought the Ital – okay, then Marina with Italian pretensions – because it had five new tyres and an MOT. Whilst the others fell apart, didn't work and ate money, I gave the Ital to my mate Steve who was back in the country permanently, for a bit. In fact it went on working until Carweek Magazine stopped working. Although Steve was still using it, the Ital now technically belonged to Carweek's publishing company, so he had to hand it back to the Editor of a defunct magazine who was not exactly overjoyed at calling in the company's marginal assets. He took the keys as if they had traces of the black death on them. As it was still running, there is every reason to believe that the multi-billion-pound publishing empire managed to get back the £245 I had paid for it.

In the cold, harsh light of the early 1990s, these were all truly terrible cars. They looked ugly and stupid when it didn't have to be that way at all. The Ital was a model development rather too far, the Allegro was a badly-built dumpy frump that was never as lovable as the 1100/1300. The Princess was blighted by a daft name, but was far better to look at and drive than any Cortina. In essence, though, the 200 effectively replaced all of those very ugly ducklings and became middle England's new favourite smallish car. Everything was looking good, except that the juicy deal to buy Rover came back to haunt British Aerospace, courtesy of the European Union. Clearly there was a bit more to it than simply paying £150 million. That's because all the previous debts built up while it was nationalised were written off and British Aerospace were given £800 million to help run the company.

It always was a curious deal too, and the whole purpose had obviously been to get Rover off the government's books. Ford, though, were a bit cheesed off at being rebuffed and got together with the EU to estimate that the true value of the company was really £800 million and anyway, it was really, really unfair because this was a closed sale. So British Aerospace had to repay £48 million of illegal sweeteners. Never mind, though, because Honda bought a 20 per cent stake in Rover with a reciprocal holding by Rover in a newly-formed company called Honda UK Manufacturing. That should give you some idea of what was going to happen in the near future. Rover, though, wasn't due to be sold, as British Aerospace had promised not to sell it for five years. Meanwhile, they wanted to concentrate on making some money, and that meant bringing back a very old favourite.

The Mini Cooper did not die in 1971 when they got fed up with paying John Cooper a fiver per car for the privilege of using his name. Cooper simply retreated to his Leyland-franchised garage and cooked up his own versions for eager customers. Not only that but he would sign your bonnet or the interior trim if he was in the office that day. Cooper also turned his attention to the Metro, and the version he produced would have been more acceptable than the "hot" MG version, but BL would not cover it with their warranty. Cooper, though, had a good thing going in Japan, a country that worshipped the Mini in general and the Cooper version in particular. He sold tuning kits direct, and that was good business for the former World Championship-winning constructor.

1989 had been the little car's 30th anniversary and Rover reckoned that the Japanese conversions could work on home soil. A John Cooper Conversion Kit was now on the options list. Next stop was the full resurrection of the Cooper model, and with that, John Cooper was back in the fold. The small fast car would never go away, and the residual worldwide love for the model would last well into the next century when the Mini Cooper became something else altogether; namely a smallish BMW.

As the Mini Cooper seemingly came back from the dead, the Metro, which had long since dropped the Mini prefix, got some long overdue resuscitation. Rather than leaving it unloved and lonely outside of the Rover family like the Maestro and Montego, the Metro was welcomed in. Rover needed a small prestigious car to complete their line up, so they made the Metro much better. They did this by getting inventor Alex Moulton, who had developed highly-advanced suspension systems in the past, to do so again. He had a W-registered Metro as his runabout, to which he'd fitted his Hydragas system. It was interconnected, there was gas, and it resulted in a very smooth and fuss-free ride. With the evidence right before them courtesy of a typically British and resourceful engineer, they could hardly refuse. However, Moulton had failed to get this particular system accepted for the original Metro in 1980 – it was still Hydragas, but not interconnected. So better 10 years late than never. Indeed, Moulton had invited Car magazine in to drive his modified Metro, and they marvelled at the suspension. But the key dinner guest was former BL boss Sir Michael Edwardes. He was just as impressed and phoned the current Rover boss, Graham Day, to tell him how good the suspension was.

So the new 1990 Metro was upgraded, but looked largely identical to the old one, and that also meant that it was smaller than the competition like the Ford Fiesta and Fiat Uno. Nevertheless, backed by a big advertising campaign, it proved something of hit. Also this year, those who preferred a traditional boot to a practical hatch had their prayers answered in the shape of the 400, definitely something for the older, more retiring driver. Clearly Rover had started to get things right, whereas Ford's new Escort, a rival to the 200 and 400, was universally slated as being very bad to look at, drive and generally own. To their credit, Ford rolled up their sleeves, opened their wallet and tried to put the car right.

1990 was also memorable because the business of building cars was brought right into our home by the BBC. Well, building cars the ancient cart without the horse way rather than stamping them out in industrial quantities. Yes, Morgan were on the box with offering sports cars that people had to queue up to buy. The programme was called Troubleshooter, and it was fronted by the thoroughly affable Sir John Harvey-Jones, the former chairman of ICI. After observing the way they did business in a wide-eyed and quite incredulous manner, he brushed his slightly wild hair out of his eyes for a moment and made a few recommendations. First off he suggested a doubling of production which would reduce the waiting list, then running at six years. Meanwhile raising prices would boost profits while streamlining the car-building process. Sir J-H-J was well intentioned and was only trying to help, but Morgan did the sensible thing and continued as they had done for the previous 80 years.

When it came to killing off small British sports car companies, that was something which Ford did quite easily as they cancelled the proposed Ace sports car and put the company they had bought two years previously into liquidation. Doing rather better, though, was TVR, which was a typically British maker of sports cars, which meant that it was usually on the verge of bankruptcy. Based in Blackpool, a town more famous for sticks of rock and a tower, TVR could trace its roots back to 1947 when Trevor Wilkinson decided to make the most of his first name. With his Trevcar Motors garage established in the town, he went on to found TVR, constructed from parts of his first name (TreVoR, in case you wondered) to build sports cars. By the middle 50s the steel chassis with a plastic body on top was their preferred method of construction, utilising melted-down plastic buckets and spades from the sea front and girders pinched from the tower. Well they didn't, but the cars were crude, brutish and established an enthusiastic following for their uncompromising behaviour. Between regular collapses, it was TVR dealer Arthur Lilley and his son Martin who brought calm and money to the company in 1965. They also revived the TVR concept of relying on a first name for automotive inspiration, in this case Martin Lilley's girlfriend's name, which resulted in the all-new TVR Tasmin. It looked a bit like a Lotus with similar quintessential 70s straight-edged bodywork. However, it took another change of ownership to really make changes and establish them as one of the most successful and uncompromising British sports car companies of the 1990s.

This happened when TVR owner and businessman Martin Wheeler took over in 1981. As well as pumping even more testosterone into the company's designs and engines he did something about the model names. Instead of Christian names he initiated a programme of naming the new cars after terrifying mythical beasts (although the first one was actually named after a Welsh postmaster... not really). So at the 1990 British Motor Show TVR unveiled a sensational prototype called the Griffith. It looked gorgeous and the public agreed as 350 firm orders were placed during the show. So for the rest of the 90s, the small company went on making cars with scary names (Chimera, Cerbera etc) and even scarier handling. It was a clever combination of massive engines and swoopy bodies with minimal safety devices. It was a brilliantly successful combination.

1991 was interesting because the Rover 800 got a major makeover which made it a bit better, but mostly it will be remembered because they stuck a comedy chrome grille on the front. The other important thing about 1991 is that a bloke called John Towers was promoted to the role of group managing director. We will hear more about him later. Probably the most disturbing thing to happen that year was the fact that the Rolls-Royce car division was ever so discreetly put up for sale.

The truth was that they just didn't have enough money to update an engine that dated back to 1959 and a body structure which first appeared in 1965. It was expensive to run a car company even if that company made seriously expensive cars. There was also the small matter of a recession, which meant that demand for their cars, which had rather more substantial chrome grilles than Rover 800s, was somewhat down. Meanwhile, the Bentley brand, the most upmarket incarnation of badge engineering, was still a big hit with those who could afford one. The sporting heritage, the fact that the grilles were rather more subtle, had lost the lady and were painted the same colour as the car, obviously helped, as did the often more powerful engines. Bentleys were cool. That's why Rolls-Royce commissioned the Continental R coupe, which was the first Bentley to have a distinct body from the Rollers since the 1950s.

The Car of the Year award was won that year by the new Volkswagen Golf, but there was nothing wrong with Dad's one. And actually his Mark 2 Golf was much better than the newer one with it's blobby styling and underwhelming performance. Reassuringly, the Germans were finally getting it wrong. Volkswagen, BMW and Mercedes had all decided that they had been over-engineering their cars and that this was something their buyers didn't deserve anymore. So they decided to let quality drop and profits go up. But the gain was very short-term. The Japanese would never allow themselves to get caught out like that, and 1992 would be their year in the UK.

Already Nissan's factory in Sunderland was Britain's most efficient car plant, and probably the best in Europe. The Micra was crowned Car of the Year, the first Japanese vehicle to win that prize. Honda started building engines for Rover cars in their new Swindon factory, and fully-built Accords would soon follow. Without anyone really noticing, Toyota established a factory at Burnaston in Derbyshire and churned out the Carina E, a sort of Japanese Ford Sierra. The presence of these factories had the effect of boosting local parts suppliers and bringing their lean production techniques (components delivered as they were needed and not piled up by the assembly lines) to the country and that increased productivity and quality. Globally though, Honda, Nissan and Toyota all reported losses, which was unheard of, but 1992 saw the recession in full effect. And anyway, those companies could take it. And they were building for the future.

Recession, though, was never good news for Britain's small and vulnerable specialist sports car makers like Ginetta. Following the familiar pattern of making pretty plastic bodies and selling kits to enthusiasts, the company went bankrupt. Don't worry though, because Ginetta always bounced back with new owners, or their designs were leased or copied by someone else who thought that they could make it work properly.

Another sports car maker also known for the prettiness of their plastic bodies and their willingness to sell kits with marginal instructions to enthusiasts were Lotus. However, instead of ceasing operations altogether, they just cancelled their sports car, the Elan. Unlike their 1960s version, which was small, with cheeky pop-up headlamps and driven by Emma Peel in the Avengers, this one looked like a squashed Frog. It was also incredibly wide at 6 foot 2 inches, which was more than a Rolls-Royce, Range Rover and Mercedes S Class, to name just three contemporary road hogs that you would think were bigger. Under the bonnet was a Japanese Isuzu engine that had been given the Lotus treatment. Now Isuzu were part of General Motors that also owned Lotus, which explains both the installation and the realities of making cars in the 90s. That engine drove the front wheels like an ordinary car, which may have been the final straw for Lotus purists, but they could not argue with the performance or handling, which was every inch a proper sports car. Sadly, not many agreed and although it had been on sale since 1990, just 3,857 found homes. Apparently it was difficult and expensive to build and very expensive to buy. The Elan was supposed to be a small, nippy little roadster that was cheap to own and run. Unfortunately, one company had got there already: Mazda.

Their MX-5 in 1989 was small and curvaceous, and came with pop-up head-lamps. The influence of the original Lotus Elan was undeniable. Clearly Lotus had forgotten how to make a simple sports car, whilst the Japanese (and incidentally this was an American-owned company) had copied all the right elements of the Elan, except one. Build-quality was a universe away from Colin Chapman's idea that customers ought to do the final development work and feel lucky that he allowed them a year's warranty. Rover saw what was happening and thought they could go back to the future and revive one of the old company's greatest hits.

Indeed, Rover really were going to make a sports car to rival the MX-5, but it wasn't ready yet, so the decision was made to remind the public that MG was a name to be associated with proper hairy-chested cars rather than go-faster Metros, Maestros and Montegos with garish paint jobs. The budget was tight – just £5m, which at the time wouldn't even pay for a new tail-light design on a mass production car. But Rover engineers excelled at improvising, so they ended up using the majority of parts from stock. And so the MGB RV8 was born. It was a good old MGB from the 1960s, with a bit of 1990s bodykit bolted on. Unveiled in 1992, the RV8 actually failed to grab the British public's imagination despite a V8 engine and an image that was a more civilised TVR for the flat-cap wearing generation. British buyers didn't want it and wouldn't pay a price that was more than double that of the much more fun and easier and cheaper to live with MX-5. The Japanese did though, and at least 75 per cent of the 2,000 built ended up there as a bizarre Brit curio.

So a result of sorts for Rover, whereas the Elan experience cost General Motors a fortune. Not only that, Ford weren't doing much better with their colonial Brit car companies either. Jaguar in particular was swallowing a lot of money because their production facilities were described by senior Ford bosses as being in worse state than in Eastern Block car factories. To add to those costs, Jaguar had also decided to enter the supercar market. For a while in the late 80s early 90s, low-volume, ultra-high-performance cars costing large fortunes were big business. Ferrari had led the way with something called the F40, which was basically a road-legal racing car that could crack the psychological 200 mph barrier. There was also the Porsche 959, which was the most technically advanced car on sale at the time. Jaguar certainly had the credibility to carry it off with recent wins at the famous Le Mans 24 hours and World Sports Car Championships. In many ways the XJ220 (220 referred to the projected top speed of 220mph) didn't emerge on to the market as originally envisaged. It had an engine that was half the proposed size, and closely related to one that been fitted to an Austin Metro 6R4 rally car. That wasn't a bad thing as it was more powerful than the proposed V12, it just wasn't very sexy, and indeed it didn't sound as sexy as a supercar should. Four-wheel drive had been dumped and doors didn't open upwards scissor-style as had been proposed. The rear-view mirrors came from an old Citroën and the wheels resembled after-market plastic trims you could buy in a pound shop. It also looked a bit clumsy and bloated, especially in silver, although the shape was dictated by the need to keep the engine cool and the aerodynamics involved using air to keep it glued to the ground instead of taking off. Dark colours were a lot more Darth Vader evil, but those who had placed a £50,000 deposit weren't amused.

Jaguar had promised to make an appropriately modest 220 of these, and gave a further assurance that they would not exceed 350, although they eventually made 281. Trouble was, the price went up from £361,000 to £403,000 despite the specification changes. And there was another problem. Tom Walkinshaw, who had been contracted to build it, was also offering on the side a more exclusive, faster and better looking car based directly on the race-winning XJ-15 that he had already developed for Jaguar.

The fundamental problem was the rise of the greedy speculator who had seen that it was possible with the Ferrari in particular to take advantage of stupidly rich people who wanted to jump the queue, or avoid it altogether. In the avaricious late 80s and early 90s, this actually worked, until the recession started to bite and supercars fell out of fashion. Now they wanted their £50,000 deposit back so that they could fight the effects of negative equity on their penthouse apartments. There were court cases and the law found in favour of Jaguar.

Clearly getting the supercar thing right was tricky, but one British company managed it in spectacular fashion, with a little help from BMW – who else? There is a book's worth of stories associated with the design, development and racing success of the McLaren F1, but all we really need to remember here is that it was a meeting of the right people at the right time and the clearest design brief since the Mini.

Formula 1 designer Gordon Murray got the idea in 1988 while waiting to fly back from Italy when he sketched a fairly unique three-seater layout. With the driver dead centre (like a Formula 1 car) which would make the car easier to drive around twisty roads. Low weight and powerful engine were the key ingredients, and most important of all there were no big car company budget constraints and only the best materials would do.

The core ingredient was a huge V12 engine engineered from scratch by BMW's motor sport division. Weight watching, though, was the key, and they had a target weight of just 1,000 kg (2,205 lbs). Every component was specifically designed to be as light as possible. Using racing technology, the body was made from light but incredibly strong carbon fibre. And when it came to using the very best materials, nothing less than gold leaf was used to line the engine bay to reflect the heat. With the driver/pilot sitting in the middle (on a seat that was fitted to their body shape) and two co-pilots positioned either side, they could not only enjoy the bespoke Kenwood stereo that weighed almost nothing, but also a 231 mph top speed. Best of all, it looked beautiful and purposeful like a supercar should.

However, this supercar went a lot further than most. Rather than simply being parked under a dust sheet in a heated garage, this one went racing. In 1995 the F1 GTR motor sport version won the Le Mans race at its first attempt, finishing first, third, fourth, fifth and thirteenth.

Here was proof if anyone needed it that Britain could make the best of the very best. It obviously helped that there was no interference from government, company accountants or customer focus groups asking for cupholders. Here was a true no-compromise car, which was worth every penny of the £634,500 that was asked. But even when 100 had been built, there were doubts as to whether McLaren had been able to make a profit. Apparently that had not been the intention, but maybe it should have been.

British companies obviously got on well with BMW, and news that they were co-operating with Rolls-Royce had to be viewed in a positive light, but you had to wonder just what was in it for them.

In the garage: Golf GTI is now in the garage, replaced full-time by the automatic GL while the Land Rover goes into dry storage.

Rebirth:
1990 Vanden Plas badge
1991 Marcos

Marriage
1990 Jaguar to Ford

Death
1990 Middlebridge
1990 Panther
1991 MG Badge

New Arrivals
1990 Lexus
1991 Kia

Best Sellers
1990 Ford Fiesta 151,475
1991 Ford Fiesta 117,181
1992 Ford Escort 121,140

In the Car Park

Top left is the Rover 400, then Mini Cooper and Toyota Carina E.
Second row from left the razor edged TVR Tasmin with softer but just as aggressive Griffith next to it. Hand built Continental R and equally hand finished
Ginetta on the next row. Ultra wide Lotus Elan just fits on row four with the
Mazda MX-5 a clever copy of the original, but far more reliable. MGB returns
as an R V8 on row five next to the Ferrari F40 that started the whole supercar
speculation situation. Bottom row the Jaguar XJ220 never lived up to expectations, while the McLaren F1 exceeded what anyone thought a supercar could be.

19 Rover gets New Parents and Crown Jewels Flogged 1993–1999

In the garage: Volkswagen Golf GL Automatic.

As the middle 1990s got going, things started happening to the British car industry at a more accelerated rate, just as Dad, never a slow or indecisive driver, continued to go places at an accelerated rate, in his Golf of course.

Meanwhile, anyone attempting to buy a decent British-built car wasn't finding the going any easier. So the fact that Ford introduced it's most important car in the shape of the Mondeo, while over at Vauxhall they had a new shopper hatchback called the Corsa and a new executive saloon, the Omega, didn't matter. That's because none of those models were made in Britain.

Of course Rover delivered real car-shaped excitement with the MG RV8, which was now in production despite a high level of national indifference. Oddly, it was the replacement for the old Montego which got Britons rather more excited. The Rover 600 was a Roverised Honda Accord. Technically it was all Honda, but stylistically the shape was all Rover, including the stick-on grille at the front which was now a fixed Rover design element. If anyone had been in any doubt, it was now very clear who was the senior and junior partner in this automotive relationship. The interior, previously a British area of expertise, was now completely Honda, but the overall package was just what Rover needed. Classy, reliable and stylish. They also felt confident enough to charge more money, taking it away from the Mondeo crowd and putting it closer to a BMW 3 Series.

Now the 600 was a very good car, but if you were an ambitious executive, a business owner, or knew a bit about cars, you'd still rather go for a pure BMW rather than a diluted Rover. It might sound unfair considering that it was very well built and, unlike previous generations of BL products, reliable, but the 600 still had limited appeal. Limited to older people who wanted to buy British and company car buyers with a limited model choice. By contrast, it was possible to combine a whole heap of corporate parts and still come up with a winner at the pricier end of the market.

Remember that Ford bought Aston Martin and Jaguar a while back? Well in 1993 they showed a prototype that absolutely everyone fell in love with. It was called the DB7, and shortly before the original DB's death, David Brown, who ran the company during its glory years, gave his permission to use his instantly-recognisable initials. Even better, Ford indicated that this gorgeous looking car would be relatively affordable. Instead of hefty six figure asking prices it was decided to take on premium-priced Porsches and Mercedes.

Ford had taken a close look at what Jaguar were working on and found Project XX, which was a new coupe proposal to replace the ancient XJS which had been around for 20 years. Jaguar were told to go away and start again, while Aston took it all on. That included a Jaguar engine and running gear which they tweaked appropriately, and a whole heap of Ford group parts such as rear lights from a Mazda 323F and some switches inside the otherwise lovely interior that could also be found on a Ford Fiesta. It wasn't even built in Aston's factory, but sub-contracted out to a company called TWR, which had built the Jaguar XJ220. None of that mattered to Aston Martin buyers though, because it was so damned beautiful, and when it came out two years later it became the company's best-ever seller. We have Ian Callum to thank for that shape – further proof that Britain hadn't lost the ability to design cars.

Sadly, General Motors weren't running their British sports car company Lotus as successfully. Production slumped to just 688 cars in 1993, and the firm was put up for sale. Lotus was bought for £30 million by a company who, for simplicity's sake, we could just call Bugatti. But it wasn't that simple. The buyers were ACBN Holdings SA of Luxembourg, a company controlled by Italian businessman Romano Artioli, who also owned Bugatti Automobili SpA. It wouldn't last, but there was takeover fever in the automotive industry. And while few paid much attention to a small rural Norfolk car builder being sold to some Italians, or Luxemburgers, 1994's transfer from British Aerospace to BMW for £800 million attracted rather more attention.

After trying for so many years to be perceived as a Brit BMW, it had actually happened, and Rover were now a subsidiary of the company they had tried to copy. It was inevitable that Rover would be sold. First of all British Aerospace had only agreed to own Rover for five years and the sell-by date was now active. Incredibly, British Aerospace had made no other promises to the government about continuing to make and develop new cars or do anything other than own Rover. Indeed, British Aerospace had only one thing going for them when they took over Rover, and that was the presence of the word British in their name. For the government, they were the only acceptable bidders, which was why the deal was made so sweet. However, it quickly became clear to British

Aerospace that Rover would never make enough profit for them, while eating up over £200 million a year in running costs. So the new owners changed their policy overnight and rather than diversifying they decided to concentrate on making planes and armaments. Yes, the clue to what they did best was in their own name, and thank goodness British Aerospace realised that eventually.

By 1994 though, no company with British in their title was keen to get into the car business, and short-term UK-based investors were not that enthusiastic either as they were aware of the pitfalls and the amount of money that had to be poured in before there was any return. The government were not that fussy about who bought Rover next provided they weren't seen as being responsible for mass unemployment or the further slow death of manufacturing industry in this country. Before we bang on about BMW, obviously there was one company which wasn't at all happy about this development. Honda, which had pretty much been behind Rover's revival, were cut out of the deal. Although British Aerospace had offered the Japanese the whole company, the Japanese were not interested. Why would they be? After all, Rover had helped them suss out the European market and what British buyers wanted from their cars. So apart from a larger holding in Rover, owning the whole show was pointless, especially as they were successfully manufacturing cars in Britain already. All they had to do was unravel the cross-holdings and forget the two companies had ever been together. It was a quickie divorce, but the kids, Rover 800, 200, 400 and 600 would have to learn to get along with their new step-dad.

The deal to buy Rover was concluded incredibly quickly, in just 10 days. So what did the suave and sophisticated BMW see in stuffy old Rover? Briefly, BMW wanted to get much bigger and thought that they couldn't do so simply by diluting their strong brand by making far more Bimmers. Rover was a readymade volume brand that would slot below their models. There was also some world class expertise at Rover, especially when it came to four-wheel drive. Bagging Land Rover was very good business indeed, and obviously the BMW engineers could learn a lot. Also, BMWs were all rear-wheel drive, whereas Rover, BL and BMC before them had been making front-wheel drive since 1959. Oh yes, and at a stroke, or rather £800 million, BMW had removed their largest single largest competitor in the UK car market.

At this point the Rover/BMW story could get very complicated, with precise details of the financial deal and who said what to whom. We won't go there, and will just get on with telling the story of what's left of the British car industry on a roughly year-by-year basis. BMW boss Bernd Pischetsrieder, whom we met at the beginning of the book, made all the right reassuring noises that there was nothing to worry about. Indeed, John Towers was kept on and promoted from managing director to chief executive, so there was a British face at the head of the company. Meanwhile Japanese corporate culture soon disappeared so workers and management no longer looked like Tweedledum and Tweedledee in their matching overalls.

Not only did Rover management get their suits back but BMW bosses also endorsed the MG and Rover models in the pipeline, probably because they couldn't do much about them. Then there were exciting things that Anglophile Pischetsrieder wanted to do with the dormant Austin Healey, Triumph and Riley badges. 1995 would be a busy year for Ronda-BMWs. However, there was still the matter of two Rover orphans.

Apparently Pischetsrieder was somewhat surprised to learn that both the Maestro and Montego were still being made, so before 1994 was over, both models were discontinued, the last batch of Montego saloons going to the Ministry of Defence while private buyers hurried to snap up the practical Countryman estates. For the Maestro, things were rather less final as there was a latent demand for a basic and practical hatchback in developing countries. That meant Maestro bodyshells and parts kits ended up in Bulgaria, Macedonia, Jordan, Syria Uruguay and Argentina for local assembly. And that won't be the last we hear about the gruesome twosome. Also there was another survivor of the British Leyland era that refused to go away: the Metro.

Roverised in 1990, by January 1995 it was updated again, and this time given the honour of a series designation. The world said hello to the Rover 100, but apart from smoother styling, it was really just the old Metro. The idea was for it to last until the all-new Mini could be launched at the end of the decade. At the moment though, this would be the most embarrassing car that BMW built, being outdated, noisy and not very safe. But no one realised just how dodgy it was. Luckily, there was an alternative launched in 1995, and it was all Rover's own work.

Completed on a tight budget, the 200 was a nicely styled, well-engineered car that confused everyone. That's because it was priced way out of it's small car bracket and went head on with the Golf, which it was never going to beat for image or practicality. Charging more simply because it was a Rover still didn't work. No one believed it was a replacement for the Metro, because that was still around, so it got bracketed with Golfs and Escorts, and as it wasn't as big as those inside, why pay more for less? Consequently the 200 was another car for the hardcore Buy Brit loyalists (which no longer included Dad), who bought it simply because it was a Rover.

When it came to the 400 that was also launched in 1995, there was no mistaking that this was a Honda with a Rover grille on the front. Indeed a royalty was paid to the Japanese for every 400 made, as in the case of the 600. At least there were some very good Rover engines, but sales were very modest for both the saloon and hatch version. Premium pricing didn't help, and there were strength-of-the-pound issues when it came to exports and rival imports. But who cared about boring saloons and hatches when MG was back?

The MGF was as British as you could get, which was great news for the enthusiasts, even though the hood was engineered by the Italian company Pinin Farina. Yes, this was the first all-British car that wasn't Honda related since the old Montego. Whereas the MGRV8 was supposed to resurrect the brand, it was actually a laughable and unnecessary throwback. It is a miracle then that the MGF not only managed to restore some lustre to the Octagon badge, but even made it sparkle. Lack of funds meant that they had to use the engine from the Rover 200, but the stroke of genius was to put it behind the driver; effectively creating a pocket-sized Ferrari. The exterior was soap-bar soft, but at least it wasn't given a tacky MG retro treatment. As usual, the brilliant Rover engineers had created something quite remarkable on a tiny budget. Not only that, it handled both tidily and safely. So with the Mazda MX-5 dominating the small sports car market, it now had a credible, good-value rival. That made it perfect for the American market, meaning that MG could get their territory back. Er, no chance.

The last thing BMW needed was a rival for its own Z3 convertible. That would be the one that appeared briefly in GoldenEye with James Bond at the wheel, when he'd have looked an awful lot cooler in a MGF. Maybe.

Already questions were being asked about whether BMW really was a force for good. On the surface everything looked fine, and there was a decent income for Rover and lots of new car projects under way. In 1996 though, a BBC film crew arrived at just the right time to capture the bizarre union that was "When Rover met BMW". Turtle-necked and pasty-faced John Towers resigned, his place taken by perma-tanned and pencil-moustached Wolfgang Reitzle, who could not have been more German. He was followed by a chap called Walter Hasselkus, who was much more of an Anglophile than Reitzle. But the most depressing thing of all is that they all sat around debating the Britishness of Rover.

It was decided to make Rover distinct from BMW by emphasising the comfort, clubbiness and cosiness of the cars. Well, that's how the Germans saw Rovers, and that unfortunately left out the word innovative. This thinking would lead directly to the single most important car that BMW would make with Rover. Indeed it would be the only car that BMW made with Rover.

Meanwhile, Lotus would now be making cars for someone else. A Malaysian multinational, DRB HICOM, took a majority shareholding in the Lotus Group of Companies. That meant Lotus would now be helping to make Proton cars (from Malaysia) go around corners faster. At least they brought much needed investment with them, but here was further evidence that the British motor industry was unlikely to be British-owned ever again.

The next major vehicle to be launched under the BMW ownership banner in 1997 had been started way back when the Rover name still had Austin in front of it. Back then, Land Rover 4x4 and Rover car engineers were thrown together to make what was then codenamed "Lifestyle". You only had to look around the roads of late 80s Britain and apart from Dad's growing collection of Mark 2 Golfs there was a massive outbreak of Suzuki Vitaras. These were small 4x4s with Rhino logos all over them, and they were the first indication that people who didn't actually need four-wheel drive could convince themselves that they really did. As insurance premiums for hot hatches went up, car buyers looked elsewhere for their thrills. Those who wanted to indicate that they had interesting, busy, fun-packed lives and could go wherever they wanted, including the tricky incline at Tesco's car park, went for small 4x4s.

Dad's Land Rover Series III was just as small, and far more useful off-road, but dating from the Jurassic era made it far too Farmer Giles. What the car-buying public wanted was frivolous chrome, big fat tyres that actually didn't help off-road, and lairy paint schemes. So that explains why loads of Suzukis got sold, and Rover wanted some of that business. After all, Land Rover was *the* off-road brand. So why not make a much tougher car which could do some clever all-terrain tricks?

Under British Aerospace, when money was tight, development was pretty slow, but when BMW arrived they loved what they saw and backed it unreservedly with real cash. The baby Land Rover managed without a big, heavy separate chassis, but being a Land Rover meant that it still left far-eastern rivals scrabbling in the mud. The Freelander looked tough and stylish, and was a very big sales success. Even though some very old problems came back to haunt it, like poor build-quality and inherent unreliability. The Land Rover brand, though, was a strong one, and people kept on buying them. BMW were also paying very close attention to the technology, which could well come in handy at a later date when they entered this profitable 4x4 market. Not only that but their brand was so unbelievably strong, what did they really need Land Rover for now?

BMW seemed to have the whole market covered. BMWs were the prestige sporty cars, Rovers had the middle market and smaller hatches, Land Rovers had 4x4s sewn up, while work was going on to replace the Mini right at the bottom. Hold on... the Mini? Was that still going? In many ways, the original Mini, which had been designed by Bernd Pischetsrieder's distant relative, would have been the vehicle that they were both most proud of and also most embarrassed about. The Mini was still built in the same plant, at Longbridge, in the same way, by hand, as it had been since 1959. BMW couldn't do much about how the Mini was built, but they could tart it up a bit and fit things that had so far passed it by, like an airbag. So having not been updated since 1969, when it finally got wind up windows, one of the most significant things about the reborn Mini was the total absence of Rover badges.

Pischetsrieder believed that the Mini was a completely separate brand. He had begun the process of moving Mini away from Rover, and also ensuring that Mini would outlast the car that was designed to replace it, the Rover 100, previously known as the Metro. Sales had slumped, but what really killed it was a bunch of Europeans (The European New Car Assessment Programme) who revealed very disappointing crash test results that seemed to suggest certain death if it collided with anything more substantial than a mosquito.

No tears were shed when the 100 went because you could be hip and groovy in a new, old Mini. From 1996, buyers could choose between a plain Mini or a Mini Cooper with stripes on the bonnet. Oh yes, and BMW put the prices up. Clearly BMW were never going to make the same mistake as BMC, and they had big plans for their smallest brand. They also realised that, just as their own brand couldn't be stretched downward, hence the Mini, there was a limit as to just how far it could be tugged upwards. Their top-of-the-range 7 series was a technical marvel, but it was no Rolls-Royce, or Bentley for that matter. Never mind, because BMW had a habit of getting exactly what they wanted, and if they fancied owning the crown jewels of the British Motor industry it wasn't going to be a problem.

Just how BMW came to acquire Rolls-Royce is a very complex little tale. Depressingly, it involves the heads of the Germany's industrial giants carving up the spoils of their victory like a couple of bickering Wermacht Generals. Of course none of this would have happened if the owners of Rolls-Royce and Bentley cars, owners Vickers, hadn't decided to sell. Yet again it was a question of money and market share. As clever as the companies had been at updating their old cars, time, the Germans, and even the Japanese were catching up. Toyota's Lexus brand had made huge headway in America, and although it wasn't a direct rival to a Rolls-Royce, their large saloons were more spacious, better equipped, quieter and far better screwed together. All it lacked was the right badge. Image was everything, and although Rolls-Royce and Bentley had that, they didn't have the money to back it up and make the best cars in the world again. That explained why Rolls-Royce got into bed with BMW in the first place, which ultimately led to installing BMW engines and other technology into their cars. Badge-engineered BMW 7 series anyone? But what BMW really wanted was the badge.

So when in 1998 Vickers put the car businesses up for sale, BMW seemed the most likely destination, even though Volkswagen were interested enough to make an offer. Indeed, their offer of £430m was comfortably more than BMW's £340m. Incredibly, it wasn't as cut-and-dried as that because there was more than one Rolls-Royce. As well as the car company there was another one which makes aircraft engines and had plc at the end of its name.

Rolls-Royce plc decided to license vital trademarks (the Rolls-Royce name and logo) not to VW but to BMW, with whom it had been working closely. It also had a lot to do with Pischetsrieder's powers of persuasion. Possession of these trademarks dated from the time when the jet engine side of the company had gone broke and the cars and engine divisions were split. So VW had bought the rights to the "Spirit of Ecstasy" flying lady mascot and the shape of the radiator grille, but not the rights to the Rolls-Royce name in order to build the cars. In turn, BMW lacked rights to the grille and mascot. However, BMW took out the option on the trademarks, licensing the name and logo for just £40m. That left VW with Bentley, which wasn't exactly the booby prize in all this, as it had been the more popular, sporting and cooler badge of the two.

Obviously Volkswagen claimed that they had really only wanted Bentley, but that was a face-saving claim as the value of their buy had been effectively halved, and anyway they had to sort out with their German friends just how to unravel the mess. So for the period from 1998 to 2002, BMW would continue to supply engines for the cars (Rolls-Royce Silver Seraphs with V12 engines), and would allow use of the names. However, this would cease on January 1, 2003. From that date, only BMW would be able to name cars "Rolls-Royce", and VW's former Rolls-Royce/Bentley division would only build cars called "Bentley". Rolls-Royce's convertible, the Corniche, ceased production in 2002. This historic carve-up was reached in a private golf club at Neuen-an-der-Donau in Bavaria, southern Germany, and Britain's most prestigious car makers were no longer national assets. Back in Britain, though, Rover were adding the finishing touches to their own baby Bentley.

The Rover 75 was just that – a curious mixture of ancient and modern which had enough chrome ornamentation and soft edges to indicate that this was distantly related to a car that cost 10 times the price. It was superbly designed by the British and Richard Woolley in particular, with a good deal of engineering input from BMW. Inside it really was a lot more over-the-top, with almost Edwardian instrumentation and timber panelwork. The 75 was supposed to be the car that would prove Rover was a living, breathing car company that could make vehicles which people actually wanted to buy. A cut above a Ford Mondeo and Vauxhall Vectra, it was aimed squarely at the British middle-class private car buyers and company car users who wanted something posher. The last thing this launch needed was any negativity.

Apart from the Rolls-Royce coup, 1998 was turning into a difficult year for the exiled BMW executives in England. Rover was now sucking money out of Germany at a furious rate and questions were being asked and jokes being made. The English Patient gag was certainly doing the rounds in Germany as Rover's losses reached a substantial £642m. BMW, despite its size, was still a private company and answerable to the major shareholders, the Quandt family, who had backed them since the bleak 1950s. To them, the situation looked even bleaker, especially as the pound was so strong and the British government were resisting requests for subsidies. Wolfgang Reitzle was installed as chief executive of Rover to try to control the company. So obviously launching the 75 was going to be a positive thing, right? Especially as it was the home motor show and everything.

The launch at the 1998 Birmingham Motor Show was scheduled to start at 4.00pm precisely, The world's press patiently waited until 4.30pm, convinced that something special was going to happen. Everyone was expecting to hear Pischetsrieder say some suitably upbeat things about Rover in general and to make some complimentary asides in impeccable English about the 75 in particular. Instead he went into one. The gist of it was that Rover was in deep crisis and they, BMW, needed money from the Government to sort it out and update the Longbridge factory. The subtext was: pay up or we're off. Not the cleverest thing for the boss of a global car company to do, run down and demoralise a subsidiary while ignoring their super fabulous new car.

Despite the unhelpful start, the 75 did go down very well with press and public. Not everyone liked the retro styling, while the actual size of the car, which was dictated by BMW, meant it was a bit small inside. The 75, though, did have the job of replacing two cars – the 600 and 800 – but cleverly, BMW had also ensured that it did not compete directly with their 3 and 5 series. Certainly the 75 seemed to do better than the Jaguar S-Type, which was unveiled at the same show. It, too, was unashamedly retro, but the styling wasn't as happy, with a front end that resembled the facial surprise of a four-eyed pig that had been poked in the bottom with a stick. Many car hacks preferred the Rover to the piggy Jaguar, which seemed rather clumsy. The big difference was that the Jaguar was made in England with the full support of its owner, Ford, while BMW's backing for the 75 seemed less than enthusiastic.

1999 was a bad year for the management of BMW, who were involved in lots of unseemly squabbling and scheming. There was Reitzle, who reckoned that Rover was dead and that BMW should clear off with the best bits, and Pischetsrieder, who thought that Rover had a future and had detailed plans to prove it. This spat came to a head in BMW's Munich boardroom rather than one in Birmingham. Pischetsrieder's plan for Rover was rejected as too costly, so he resigned. Reitzle was next in line for the top job, but the majority of the board said no, and he resigned too.

So as two old management models departed from Rover and BMW forever, in came two more: the Rover 25 and 45. These oldsters, previously badged as the 200 and 400, were given a makeover with Rover 75-like fronts, better Rover 75 seats and other little styling touches. The cars looked better, but more crucially, the prices were realigned (that means lowered). These models were now better value, and the buying public looked at the 25 against a Vauxhall Corsa rather than a Golf.

Rather worryingly, this overhaul on the cheap hinted at things to come. The future for Rover had never been more uncertain, yet some models just wouldn't go away.

Still in the garage: Volkswagen Golf GL Automatic.

Re-birth
1993 MG
1999 Jensen Motors

Marriages
1994 Rover to BMW
1998 Bentley to Volkswagen
1998 Rolls-Royce to BMW

Death
1996 AC. Bought by Pride Automotive.

New Arrivals
1997 Perodua

Best Sellers – 1995 Country of origin in brackets.

Escort	137,760 (GB)
Fiesta	129,574 (GB)
Mondeo	118,040 (D)
Astra	100,709 (GB)
Cavalier	73,978 (GB)
Corsa	72,502 (SP)
Rover 200	68,141 (GB)
Peugeot 306	56,112 (F)
Renault Clio	52,576 (F)
Rover 100	52,392 (GB)

Best Sellers by Year
1993 Ford Escort 122,022
1994 Ford Escort 144,089
1995 Ford Escort 137,760
1996 Ford Fiesta 139,552
1997 Ford Fiesta 119,471
1998 Ford Fiesta 116,110
1999 Ford Focus 103,228

In the Car Park

Top is the Rover 600 and next to it is the Rover 100 although really it's a made over Metro. Next row on the left is the MGF partly based on the Metro whilst BMW got in on the roadster act with their Z3. A Ford Mondeo is next down and beside it a Vauxhall Vectra below that is the strangely popular and family friendly Suzuki Vitara next to a Bentley Turbo R. Bottom left were company fleet buyers favourites. These were the cars that the new Rover 75 had to beat. Next to it are the men from BMW who made sure it was built, left is Bernd Pischetsrieder and on the right Wolfgang Reitzle.

20 The Phoenix Four/Five Farago and the Great Chinese Takeaway 2000–2005

In the garage: Volkswagen Golf GL Automatic.

Do I have to write this last bit? Sadly I do. But even at this late stage there is time for a wry smile at two old Austins that refused to go to the scrapyard in the sky.

In 1998 the production tools used to make the Maestro ended up with a company called Etsong, who were based in China. They churned out at least 2,000 examples of the hatchback and van, which were known as the QE6400 and QE6440 respectively (presumably because that sounded better than Maestro). Another Chinese manufacturer, First Auto Works, apparently acquired the production rights some time later for both the Maestro and Montego. Obviously they had time on their hands and created a monster: the front end was Montego, then it was all Maestro from the cabin backwards. Sadly, it wasn't called the Maestego, or Montestro, but the rather more obscure FAW Lubao QE6400. Austins in China, eh? Who'd have thought that would happen? About as likely as the Maestro making a comeback in the UK.

Remember those Maestro kits that were sent to needy, sparsely-motorised countries around the world? Well, not all of them were assembled and some 600 were left over. Luckily, a company called Trans European Trading bought the remaining kits, which included vans. These were then bolted together on the premises of a small service station in Ledbury, Herefordshire. Like the original Maestro, there wasn't much in the way of equipment, which was a huge part of its appeal and one reason for its low price of £4,995. The last of these phoenix Maestros was registered in 2001, a year after the Phoenix Consortium took over Rover and renamed it MG Rover.

Yes, a lot happened at this time, and there is a book's worth of anecdote, speculation and confusion, so maybe the easiest way to approach to this is to stick to the facts as they happened in 2000 and compress the story into a few months of diary dates.

15 March Newspapers and magazines start to report that venture capitalists Alchemy Partners have been in contact with BMW about buying Rover. The next day, BMW agrees to break up Rover, selling Land Rover to Ford.

17 March Alchemy's managing partner Jon Moulton details his plans for Rover and how sports cars will be produced under the MG badge.

23 March Industry minister Stephen Byers meets BMW's management in Munich, and Alchemy name Chris Woodwark, a former chief executive of Rolls-Royce Motors, as chief executive of their proposed MG Car Company.

28 March BMW's annual results show big losses at Rover, which cost the firm £2.85bn in the six years since they bought the British car maker. That's not far off what BL/Austin Rover/Rover Group cost the government when they ran it.

29 March BMW reveals that unsuccessful efforts have been made to sell Rover to Ford, General Motors, Volkswagen and Toyota.

6 April The Phoenix consortium, headed by former Rover executive John Towers, meets with BMW. The other members of the consortium are Nick Stephenson, John Edwards and Peter Beale.

17 April Meanwhile, Alchemy announces its plans for Rover, including using Longbridge to build a family of MG sports cars.

27 April BMW says the Phoenix bid lacks proper finance, and the next day, Alchemy says negotiations with BMW have ended. All this free publicity leads to a boost in heavy-discount-assisted sales. April turns out to be Rover's best month ever, with 22,000 cars going to patriotic homes.

8 May Phoenix gets £200m in finance from US regional bank First Union. The next day, BMW says it will sell Rover to Phoenix for a symbolic £10. Phoenix says it will shift production of the Rover 75 from Cowley to Longbridge and launch an estate version. Phoenix also retains production of the full Rover range, including the brands MG, Morris, Wolseley and Austin, and the old Mini.

On prime-time television news, John Towers drove into Longbridge in a Rover 75 to rapturous applause and was hailed as the saviour of thousands of jobs. Phoenix had triumphed over evil Alchemy, who wanted to sack everyone and just build a few MG sports cars a year. The Phoenix four were John Towers (former Rover employee) chairman; Nick Stephenson (engineer) deputy chairman; Peter Beale (accountant and former car dealer) vice-chairman; John Edwards (dealer principal in charge of 20 dealers) director. Each of them put up £60,000 of risk capital against the sale.

Hurrah! Britain's biggest car maker had come back home, helped by an American bank loan and also £500m that BMW had coughed up to help cover the cost of redundancies and restructuring, repayable in 2049. However, BMW didn't walk away empty handed as they kept the new MINI, to be produced at the factory at Cowley, and retained rights to the Rover, Triumph and Riley names. Oh yes, and Rover had to lease the Rover part of their name from BMW. Not only that, but BMW had already agreed to sell Land Rover to Ford for £1.8 billion, a billion more than they had paid for Rover in the first place.

So having learned all they needed to about off-road technology in order to make their new X5 model work, they then forbade Rover from developing any four-wheel-drive car in order to avoid any confusion with Land Rover. Never mind, at least Rover, or rather MG Rover as it was now called, kept the Mini, except it was the wrong one, they should have had the one with capital letters: MINI.

Yes, this was now a tale of two Minis, because the one that MG Rover had the rights to produce never made it out of the year 2000. After 42 years, the struggle to keep it Euro legal for emissions purposes was being lost, and anyway, it had never been a cheap car to produce. So as Rover waved goodbye to their most characterful and loveable car, BMW were preparing to launch their retro update of the old classic with no guarantee that it was the right way to go. The thing is, BMW rarely made mistakes, and even purchasing Rover would turn out brilliantly for them in the end. Apart from selling Land Rover for a profit, the uppercase MINI would become a massive success, as BMW rightly guessed that it was the slightly familiar shape and the way it drove that were the two most important factors. Oh yes, and charging a premium price for it, something that had only been done in later years when BMW owned the brand.

So BMW brought out a small hatchback in 2001 with a boot that could barely hold a packet of crisps, laughably inadequate rear seats, slightly wonky old Mini through a distorted mirror styling and less than Mini-like proportions. Indeed the overall measurements and position of the wheels was virtually identical to the original Range Rover. Also, hardly anything came as standard, and customers had to pay extra for equipment packages with condiment and ingredient-based names such as Salt, Pepper and Chilli. Now if this had been BL 20 years previously they would have been laughed at, not least because the new MINI even had a few high-profile recalls just like the bad old days. BMW, though, had cleverly created a separate, funky little brand, which sold the coolest smallish cars you could buy. And because everyone knew that BMW were behind MINI, they knew that any problems would be short-term and completely sorted out.

Yet back in 1996, Rover engineers had been proposing a clever take on the original Mini that Issigonis would have been proud of. These "Spiritual" concept cars were shown at international motor shows with loads of room inside, putting the engine in the middle of the car and tons of headroom, but clearly they were wrong. BMW were right to go retro, but it wasn't as if MG Rover could respond with a new small car of their own. For a start, they had lost the Mini brand they had created, and all they could ever afford to do from now on was change their existing models on the cheap. However, their first go at sprucing up the range looked quite good.

The "Zed" cars weren't just tarted-up Rovers with fancy badges; they drove very differently. The suspension was re-engineered and the engines were re-tuned, while there were clever bodykits designed by Peter Stevens, the man who had made the McLaren F1 look so good. The 25 was the ZR, 45 the ZS, and 75 the ZT, with the ZT-T as the estate tourer version. They didn't just look good, they drove very well indeed. By contrast, a BMW performance saloon was a very subtle affair, with just a different alloy wheel design, or lower suspension, whereas the "Zeds" were rather more "in yer face". The fact was that MG Rover had to try harder, and they desperately needed to get noticed. There was no escaping the fact that they were automotive minnows and that this was a treading-water exercise. The new "Zeds", and the addition of a Union Flag on the boot lids of all MG Rovers, were a distraction from reality. And the reality was that MG Rover needed a partner. Without an automotive chum to share the cost of making new models, MG Rover would keep on struggling.

However, the ever resourceful engineers had managed to come up with a good looking replacement for the now quite ancient 45 that was to form the basis of a whole range of mid sized models. They spoke to Tom Walkinshaw Racing (TWR) who had built the Aston DB7, Jaguar XJ 220 supercar and some Volvos, to put the proposal into production. Meanwhile, MG Rover were talking to Tata, an India-based car maker about selling their smallest car in the UK with a Rover badge on it. That seemed a sensible thing to do with both the Mini and Metro out of the picture. But MG Rover themselves were behaving a bit like a bloke in full-on mid-life crisis when for some reason they went to Italy and bought a sports car company for £10m.

The Qvale Mangusta was a furiously ugly car with far too much fiddly detail, but the clever angle was that it was fully developed and was approved for importation to America. All MG Rover had to do was to make it pretty, and half an hour with a sledgehammer could have fixed that.

Strangely, there were all sorts of distant connections with MG Rover. The car had started life as a Maserati, then a De Tomaso, who had bought the Innocenti brand from British Leyland in the 70s. De Tomaso's owner Kjell Qvale had previously imported MGs into America back in 1947 (small world, isn't it?). So here was a car with a complicated gestation that was restyled by designer Peter Stevens in just three months and named the X80. Not everyone liked the look of it when it was shown as a prototype at the Frankfurt Motor Show in 2001, so Peter Stevens went back to the drawing board and would return the following year with something that looked as mad and bad as anything TVR were offering at the time. And at this point, you wonder what on earth MG Rover thought they were doing wasting time trying to build a supercar.

Well, it gets worse, because also in 2001 MG Rover went to Le Mans with sports car maker Lola (where one of the Phoenix Four, Nick Stephenson, had worked). So here was more middle-aged bloke behaviour, which involved not just buying a fast car but booking track days to show off. This time they were showing chest hair through racing overalls, which is double cool if you are over 50. So when they should have been concentrating on getting new road cars made, they had gone racing, and obviously the cars involved did well initially before breaking down and failing to finish. If ever there was a metaphor for MG Rover, that was it.

Not concentrating on the really important issues meant that, when disasters happened, MG Rover couldn't cope. So in 2003, just when they thought that things couldn't get worse, TWR, the company getting that all-important new car into production, went into liquidation. MG Rover were more desperate then ever to find a partner. Honda, Hyundai, Fiat, Matra in France and Proton – all of them turned down the chance to work with MG Rover. One firm, China Brilliance, did leap at the opportunity. But as fast as they hooked up, they bailed out again, and it was all BMW's fault. An existing partnership agreement between the Chinese and Germans expressly forbade any outside co-operations.

That may have spelled the end for MG Rover as a car manufacturer, but already the credibility of the management team was seriously in question as details of their pension arrangements emerged in November 2003. The Phoenix Four (not so poor), plus Kevin Howe, MG Rover's chief executive, had set up a £13 million trust fund that mainly benefited themselves and their families. It was started in 2002, the year that MG Rover made a pre-tax loss of £77 million. The trust helped to increase the total pay to Phoenix's directors by more than 300 per cent to £15.1 million, according to the full company accounts for 2002. It gets murkier, and depending on who you believe, the amounts vary. There was also the small matter of Studely Castle, a stately pile that they'd bought as a conference centre on behalf of MG Rover. Meanwhile the Longbridge plant was sold off for housing development and then leased back. So all the company needed was a great new car to focus everyone's attention on what a great job they were doing. Sadly the CityRover wasn't it.

That's because the CityRover wasn't a real Rover, or MG Rover, but a Tata Indica. Here was one company not too embarrassed to hook up with Britain's biggest homegrown and home-owned car maker. MG Rover would slightly redesign the front and rear and reset the suspension and the Indians would build it for next to nothing and then MG Rover would sell it for rather more. In principle, this is what all the clever people in the car business were up to, building in a cheap place and adding value. MG Rover dealers were unusually excited as it would bring back small car buyers to their quiet showrooms. In the end, though, the showrooms stayed fairly quiet as MG Rover seemed to have lost heart and there was not much of a fanfare when the car was launched, almost apologetically. Dealers were surprised at just how expensive it was considering the fairly average quality, especially inside. As a budget car from India, it was quite spacious and honest, but with a Rover badge (and a Union flag on the boot) and some seriously high prices, it was up against small cars that were really rather good. Consequently hardly anyone bought it.

At the time I was talking to Dad about a long overdue replacement for the Golf, and the CityRover never came up once. The Toyota Yaris did though, frequently.

Another MG Rover not discussed by Dad and I in 2003 was the Streetwise. There are at least three possible reactions to this model. For some it was a Rover 25 or even 200 too far. Others may view it as an utterly inspired throwback to the era of the Talbot Ranchero which was styled to look like a hardcase Range Rover but wasn't as it had no four-wheel-drive system at all. And then there were those convinced it was a joke. In reality it was all three. A clever way of keeping the press and public paying attention to what they were up to, it also proved that Rover were running out of money and models to practice on.

Whereas other companies like Renault produced the Scenic RX4, which was a genuine four-wheel drive with chunky urban warrior styling, the Streetwise just had the styling. But at least it was honest. The problem was that MG Rover no longer had the image to carry the joke off, despite the old gag that people would buy a rotten sausage (use your imagination) with a BMW, Porsche or Mercedes badge on it. These brands were that strong it almost didn't matter what badge they had. So a Rover 25 with raised suspension, roof bars and added plastic to the front, sides and rear, however cleverly done, was just regarded as silly.

The very last MG Rover from 2003 not to be mentioned by me or Dad as a substitute for the Golf was the XPower SV. This is what the X80 sports car had become, and it was a shock. MG Rover had clearly gone down the TVR route – actually, the designer Peter Stevens had not only gone down that route but caught the connecting bus and gone several stops further on. It had scoops and slats and wings and creases and bulges and grilles and everything. It did render onlookers speechless, which is what a supercar should do. The trouble is MG weren't known for supercars, only good-value roadsters that blokes in tweed flat caps bought. Building the car in Italy, then shipping it back to the UK for painting and finishing, seemed to work in principle, but in practice sales only just managed double figures. People would rather buy a Porsche 911 for similar money, or a proper mad Brit like a TVR or Noble. Oh yes, and it didn't help that the ones lent to the press broke down a bit too often.

So a revised XPower SV in 2004 seemed really pointless. As pointless as taking a 75 estate car to the American salt flats in Bonneville and making it break the speed limit at 225mph. Clearly MG Rover were still in the publicity stunt business rather than the car making one. What they did do, though, was update the whole 25 to 75 range and on very limited resources. Changing the parts that simply unbolted was a quick visual fix, with new headlamps, grilles, bootlids and model inscriptions. And in yet another moment of madness the company gave the world a car it didn't need, but actually rather admired. Here was the return of the V8 Rover that had been such a charismatic and important part of their 1960s and 70s line-up. However, it didn't have the same V8 that Rover had so cleverly re-engineered and reinvented for the British market and which went on to power just about every important sports car from Morgans to TVRs and off-roading Land and Range Rovers. Nope, under the bonnet was a Ford V8.

That was as British as you were going to get, especially as, if you wanted a British-owned bonkers sports car, there was now even fewer options. In July 2004 teenaged Russian banker (well he looked like a teenager and had a rich dad) Nikolai Smolenski paid a reputed £15m for TVR. Maybe MG Rover should have offered 20p more and saved themselves the bother of building the XPower.

The XPower adventure was as misguided as stretching the Rover 75 to give it much more room in the back so that Lord Mayors might buy it. But here was an excuse to use the long-forgotten Vanden Plas badge for the long-wheelbase car, to use a technical term. Because no one knew what Vanden Plas really stood for, the name was dropped in favour of the easier-to-comprehend 75 Limousine.

However, the 75 was under attack as engineering cutbacks were only noticed by the particularly attentive. So wood dashboards were replaced by genuine plastic ones and door mirrors from the lower ranges were being screwed onto the 75 in the interests of cost saving. That might have been a minor gripe, but cutting corners with the suspension, meant that the 75 now literally cut corners.

Clearly MG Rover needed help, cash and customers more than ever, and China had all of those things in abundance. What follows is a confusing, embarrassing clash of cultures and companies as they all scrabbled to pick over the remains of MG Rover.

Starting in June 2004, MG Rover boasted that they were talking to Shanghai Automotive Industry Corporation (SAIC) about working together, which would lead to cars being made in China as well as Longbridge. Not only that, there was an agreement to sell SAIC the rights to make this car, as well as the Rover-designed engines, for just £67m. There is hearsay about drunken MG Rover executives and just-pretending-to-be-inebriated SAIC executives signing such a favourable deal. This resulted in the best-value Chinese takeaway in history. £67 million was certainly cheap, and it looked like a short-term way of bringing in money for MG Rover, but that was just half of the deal. The most important part was continuing to build MG Rovers at Longbridge. Apparently MG Rover had been trying to get a £100 million bridging loan from the government prior to a full Chinese takeover. There was a Rover 22, or rather Catch 22, as SAIC would not sign until it could be proved that MG Rover were solvent, and the government would not loan the money until the agreement with SAIC was signed.

Suppliers, anxious about whether their bills would be paid, stopped providing components to the Longbridge factory. When production was stopped on April 7, and MG Rover was declared bankrupt, this was the day that the British car industry effectively died. Along with it went 6,000 jobs and a century of car building at Longbridge.

In the months leading up to the British company's collapse, there had been frantic shuttling of Rover executives as well as Trade and Industry department civil servants trying to stitch something together. This continued after SAIC had left with what they had paid for. Worst of all, there was something very unseemly about the British government desperately trying to entice Chinese corporations to buy their several uncarefully owned, used car company, which was also a category A write-off. This was only slightly less nauseating than seeing trade and industry secretary Patricia Hewitt tearfully saying how sorry she was about it all.

As an object lesson in how to deal with the Chinese, take Volkswagen. They had spotted the opportunities in China two decades before when in 1984 they established Shanghai Volkswagen, and it gave them a massive 70 per cent of their market by the early 1990s.

Once the administrators, PricewaterhouseCoopers (PwC) were dealing with the mess, SAIC announced it would be building its own 75s and using British engineering firm Ricardo to shift production to China. Oddly that didn't happen either, as yet another Chinese company called Nanjing Automobile Corporation (a car maker since 1947) emerged out of nowhere (from a pack of 200 other keen bidders) and bought MG Rover's assets for a sum not unadjacent to £60m. Initially they talked about restarting production at Longbridge and creating 2,000 jobs.

In a situation reminiscent of the Rolls-Royce/Bentley "have we, haven't we, got the right badge?" type of mix up, SAIC and NAC bickered. Ultimately, SAIC went off and started work on their version of the Rover 75, although it could never be called that as BMW owned the rights to the name, even though both Montego and Maestro were readily available of course. NAC did, have the rights to use MG, and would remake the MG TF and also the 75 ZT. As depressing and demeaning as it was to see two Chinese companies pick over the remnants of a once great British industry, attention inevitably turned to the less-than-fabulous Phoenix four – or was it five?

Dad just shook his head at all the nonsense. To someone who conducted himself with the utmost propriety in business, their conduct was totally perplexing. He believed that honesty, caring about your most important asset – the employees – and never borrowing more than you could pay back were the minimal requirements for just being in business. Sadly, he never got the chance to run a PLC, unlike that shower John Towers, Nick Stephenson, Peter Beale, John Edwards and managing director Kevin Howe. I can't suggest that they did anything illegal because it unlikely that they did. However, there was a parliamentary committee set up to investigate the collapse, and answer all the many questions that members of the public and workforce would have. At the time of writing though (spring 2008), after spending more than £10m, the committee has yet to publish a report.

Morally though, whether they should have drawn such huge salaries of almost £1m a year and set up a £12.9m pension fund while the company consistently made massive losses is certainly open to question. There was also a £10m windfall shared between them as the result of a loan note they issued to the company, and a further £1m each when MG Rover's car leasing arm, MGR Capital, was wound up. Many, certainly in the Birmingham area, believe that the estimated £40m they amassed should be paid back, especially as those out-of-work workers left Longbridge with just £2,800 each.

Still in the garage: Volkswagen Golf GL Automatic.

Re-Birth
2002 Marcos

Death
2001 Marcos
2002 Jensen
2005 MG Rover

On Holiday
2005 AC production transferred to Malta

In Retirement
2001 Reliant stops car production and simply import vehicles.

Marriage
2005 Ginetta to LNT Automotive

New Arrivals
2004 Ferrari GB
2005 Maserati GB
2005 Chevrolet

Best Sellers – 2005. Country of origin in brackets.
Ford Focus 145,010 (D/Sp)
Vauxhall Astra 108,461 (GB)
Vauxhall Corsa 89,463 (Sp)
Renault Megane 87,093 (F)
Ford Fiesta 83,803 (D)
Volkswagen Golf 67,749 (D)
Peugeot 206 67,450 (GB)
Ford Mondeo 57,589 (D/B)
Renault Clio 56,538 (F)
BMW 3 series 44,844 (D)

Best Sellers by Year
2000 Ford Focus 114,512
2001 Ford Focus 137,074
2002 Ford Focus 151,209
2003 Ford Focus 131,684
2004 Ford Focus 141,021
2005 Ford Focus 145,010

In the Car Park

Top left the all-new uppercase MINI here in Cooper S form. BMW's offroader the X5 and below the MG ZT range of souped up Rover 75s. Next is the Qvale Mangusta, and on the right the MG Rover X80 and below that on the left the XPower SV it turned into. World's fastest estate car is on the right then bottom left the MG Lola at Le Mans. Next to it the Streetwise, urban on roader, otherwise just a Rover 25 with bits glued on see next page below on the right.

City Rover top left is really a Tata Indica, Rover 400 below it and a Toyota Yaris. Left to right John Edwards, Peter Beale, Nick Stephenson, Kevin Howe and bottom John Towers.

21 A Nation of Lilliput Car Builders
   September 2005

The garage is now empty...but is it? You could actually park an Autogyro or Gyroplane in one you know. The rotary blade comes off and it really isn't that big. Especially as it only needs minimal take off and landing space, so an urban side road would do with no need for a proper run way.

Exactly six months to the day after MG Rover ceased to be, so did Dad. You don't need to know the details, but my sister and I had spent a lot of time in hospital wards. When there was no hope of recovery then obviously we wanted to be there at the end. On the evening of September 7, 2005, the nurses said there was no change and that we should go home. Wrong decision.

Two hours later, at 11.30pm, we were driving back to the hospital. On a deserted dual carriageway I drove like an idiot – at 49, 39 and 29mph, so as not to set the cameras off (how different from the sometimes unrestricted, often unregulated roads that Dad drove in the early 1950s). Another wrong decision. By the time we arrived at the hospital, it was too late.

So did Dad have anything to do with the downfall of the British motor industry? After all, buying an Audi in 1974 can't have helped, and that huge succession of Volkswagen Golfs must have knocked our balance of payments for six. Now I have heard it argued by some that the Austin Maestro was a much better car than the Golf, being cheaper, better to drive and more spacious. They may have a point. As for Dad, by the time the Maestro came out he'd been well and truly lost to the Buy British cause, after two spectacular failures. It wasn't just the manufacturers and their shoddy products – it was also the dealer networks. They could be indifferent, offhand and incapable of fixing some of the simplest mechanical problems.

Now a car company thrives or dies on one thing alone: its products, the cars. So if you parked a contemporary Maestro and Golf next to each other, the difference in material and build-quality was blindly obvious. You could see that the Golf's seat trim would be around for the long haul. It wouldn't rust nearly as furiously, and the proof is that today, numerous 1980s Golfs have a tenacious grip on a full MOT whereas the Maestro is practically extinct, except as the FAW Lubao QE6400 in China, of course. Significantly, none of Dad's Golfs expired or needed anything more substantial than a battery, tyre or exhaust. When his 15-year-old Golf was sold, it was immaculate. Yet apart from models cherished by maniac owners, I've never seen one Maestro that didn't look as though it had a bad case of automotive mange that wouldn't be improved by a visit to the crusher. In fact I rarely see a Maestro, but spot dozens of Mark 2 Golfs every day.

Dad didn't care about how it drove, and like millions of other buyers, just wanted a reliable, practical car which also looked smart. It really was as simple as that. Because when it comes to theories about why the British car industry imploded, there are millions of them, blaming just about everyone including British car buyers like my Dad, exchange rates, the workers, the owners, Her Majesty's motoring press and the government.

Before I get into the blame game, motoring pundits who always like to see the fuel tank as mostly half full are always very keen to point out that Britain has never been better at building cars. They will gesture at all sorts of diagrams and flow charts to indicate a resolutely upward trend. So although in 1972 Britain made a record 1.9 million cars and then inevitably fell to under million by the early 1980s, as recently as 1999 the output was back up to 1.8 million.

What needs to be remembered is that, back in 1972, there were loads of men and women on the production line whereas now robots easily outnumber the real people. Otherwise the fact that Britain has been making more a million cars is certainly encouraging, proof that there never was a problem with the British worker. With the proper tools and facilities, they can build cars that people actually want to buy. Unlike 1972, though, these cars are now made for someone else. The sad fact is that the British car industry isn't British-owned any more, and that really matters.

As vehicle production has declined from 1999 on, the huge danger is that these foreign owners will simply transfer car production to lower-wage economies. So however efficient the British factories are and no matter how brilliant the quality is, it becomes harder for them to build new models and win new contracts.

So it is unlikely that Honda, Nissan or Toyota are going to invest much more in Britain when their money goes so much further in Eastern Europe. Gradually from the 70s on, Ford transferred more of their production to Europe, leaving only the Transit van in Southampton and diesel engines in Dagenham. Who's to say that the same thing may not happen to their quintessentially British car marques, such as Jaguar and Land Rover? If BMW and Mercedes can build models in America and export them back to Europe without any discernable loss in credibility or image, then both Jaguar and Land Rover are vulnerable.

Higher up the price scale, a major element of certain marques has been the craftsmanship that goes into Aston Martins, Bentleys and Rolls-Royces. But even these cannot be regarded as guaranteed to be manufactured in Britain forever. The Rolls-Royce "factory", impressive as it undoubtedly is, certainly isn't a factory. Actually it's little more than a glorified assembly plant. That's because all the big important parts, including the body and engine, are delivered from Germany. Significantly, half the British workforce toil away in the leather and woodworking shops, adding the craftsmanship element to the build. Yes that's what British Rolls-Royce workers have been reduced to, nailing and stitching on the frippery and finishing touches rather than properly engineering a car from scratch and then building it. British interior decorators moving in after the German builders have done all the hard work. Then again, Britain does have a unique cottage industry of Lilliputian car builders.

Now if Dad and I weren't discussing the Toyota Yaris in 2005 and had decided to go for a British-owned manufacturer, the choice would have been extremely limited. After MG Rover's disappearance, absolutely no one was offering a hatch-back to suit a pensioner. There was, though, a pensioner offering their virtually unchanged 1920s product line in the ancient shape of Morgan. At least you could never accuse Morgan of taking advantage of the fashion for retro designs as that was all they have ever done. Even so, when they tried something a little bit different in the upper sports car league, they had to rely on the generosity of Herr BMW. They liked the company, so much that they were happy to let Morgan buy their brilliant V8 engine which was installed into the weird Aero, the world's first cross-eyed car (the headlamps looked a bit odd). That might have put Dad off a bit, as well as the fact there wasn't anywhere to put much shopping.

Then there were the cars without any doors at all, which were even less suitable. Caterham can trace their cars, which are effectively Morgans with racing attitude, back to the late 1950s when Colin Chapman designed the most beautifully simple road and race car ever, the Lotus Seven. It was such a brilliant design that it remains in production by Caterham, and has been much copied, not least by Westfield, who Caterham had to sue to make them change their designs. Now I might have been able to help Dad into the Caterham, or even a Westfield, but I don't think he would ever have managed to climb out again. At least we could have bought it as a kit from Caterham and built it together, which would have been nice.

By comparison with the Ariel Atom, though, the Caterham was positively luxurious. Here was a car that was not only missing doors, but also the windscreen and the entire body. In fact the driver's own body is the bodywork, surrounded by what looks like scaffolding. Putting the minimal into minimalist motoring, it is the most innovative design since the Caterham and proof that Great British ingenuity is still alive and well. The company name had an interesting history and dated back to 1874, when James Starley designed and manufactured a bicycle with a large 48-inch front spoked wheel and a smaller rear wheel. Starley called this the Ariel, but most onlookers pointed and said "penny farthing". From bikes to motorbikes, and even some car-like contraptions, the company never really made it far into the 1970s. It was only in the 90s that the Ariel name was revived by designer Simon Saunders. The Atom was launched in 2000, the same year as MG Rover, and was powered by a Rover engine. His company outlived MG Rover, and almost inevitably, the Atom went on to use a Honda engine.

So choosing a Morgan, Caterham or Ariel Atom would have been patriotic but stupid, but then so would the only other two companies offering cars with more conventional doorage. Noble was a one-man company in the mould of Lotus. Lee Noble designed and built (partially in South Africa) a car that competed head-on with Porsche and earned universal praise as an utterly focused performance projectile.

Noble was obviously out of contention too, which just left Bristol. Like the Noble, it only had two doors, but at least they were big ones, opening up into a decent-sized area with comfy seats in both front and back. There was also plenty of room for the shopping in its massive boot. Even better, it was hand-built by proper craftsmen in Bristol. Sounds perfect. But all that practicality came at a price: about £130K.

We last met Bristol in an earlier chapter taking advantage of the availability of recently liberated BMW designs, right down to the kidney grille at the front. As an aircraft manufacturer, applying the same rigour to the construction and design of cars meant that what we got was an utterly unique vehicle. In the 1950s it had the Bentley's ability to travel great distances with four on board, as well as their luggage, in refined comfort. The difference was, and still is, that the Bristol is much more exclusive than the Bentley. And in recent years the company have made good use of the legendary fighter aircraft they once built by reviving their names. The Bristol Blenheim 3 is a car for the discerning gent, who reckons Bentleys and Rollers are vulgar.

Designed without compromise or the input of superfluous stylists, in more recent years Bristols could never be described as easy on the eye, apart from the 200mph supercar, badged as the Fighter. To many, the Blenheim is just uncompromisingly ugly, although I like to think that it is actually thuggishly handsome. Under the bonnet, the BMW-based engine has long since been replaced by a large American V8 from Chrysler. The same basic design seems to have survived since the 1940s through sheer bloody mindedness rather than seeking to please anyone except its loyal and, it has to be said, loaded customers. I rather like that, and it explains why, along with the equally stubborn Morgan, Bristol is all that's really left of the wholly-British car industry.

The secret of their success – and that success amounts to sales that at best can be measured in hundreds rather than millions – is that they don't just know their customers personally, they also keep it simple, like Caterham and Ariel, or exactly the same, like Morgan and Bristol. Being utterly unique is also what makes cars that hold a British passport, special. That is why they will never be a threat to any other global manufacturer, but will still be a joy to own. But in an increasingly over-regulated world, survival is as difficult as ever.

So if buying truly British in 2005 was hard enough for the ordinary car buyer, simply buying British-built was a huge problem for civil servants. They couldn't help but shop abroad for public service vehicles. Coppers who had been happy enough with Rovers for generations, but could be forgiven for loathing their Allegro Panda cars, almost exclusively bought foreign. By 2005 you were more likely to be stopped by a Rozzer in a Volvo, a BMW, or whatever models had been given to them for evaluation. Panda cars mostly seemed to be Vauxhall Astras, but there was a growing number of Skodas, too. Get knocked over, though, and you will be riding in the back of a Mercedes. Yes, the commercial vehicle sector had long since migrated overseas.

Now there is a prevailing view that the car industry is a notoriously difficult one in which to thrive or even just survive. That is true as the amount of money involved in remaining in business is phenomenal. Also the high-volume nature of vehicle production means that, in recent years, there have often been more cars than customers. Even so, the basics of building cars is universal because, at the very least, they need to be reliable and practical – like Golfs used to be. Once you've cracked that one then you can go on to sexy and double your money with a car that people don't actually need, but really, really want. For instance, Volkswagen using their Audi brand to make the TT, which underneath the pretty bodywork was essentially a Golf.

That's all Britain needed to do – build a Golf – and the Austin/Morris 1100/1300 was probably the closest we ever came. It wasn't priced right, of course, but a hatchback model in the 70s would have helped, instead of the Allegro. It's not as though Brits aren't clever when it comes to engineering and design. High-tech wonders like the McLaren F1 could only have originated in Britain, despite the fine profession of engineering having been undermined for generations as being a dirty and undignified job, unlike an accountant or solicitor. Nevertheless, Britain has managed to create some of the finest motoring minds and excel in the richest, most ruthless and competitive car business of all, Formula One. The best designers, teams and engineers are all UK-based.

On a slightly diversionary note, Dad was right there when motor racing turned a tight corner into a double chicane to become the biggest sporting business on the planet.

The Race of Champions pitched all sorts of different classes of racing cars from around the world in a 312-mile, 118-lap race at the Brands Hatch Grand Prix circuit on August Bank holiday 1972. This year, though, it was called the Rothmans £50,000, which indicated the amount of prize money on offer as well as the sponsor. It was a substantial sum, and was comfortably £20K more than was on offer at most Formula One races. And Dad was building all the promotional areas and organising all of the Rothmans signage.

It was a bonkers but truly inspired idea to bring so many different types of racing cars and drivers together, which inevitably led to all sorts of squabbling over prize money and the fact that some cars would need to refuel while others would have bigger fuel tanks. All that politicking didn't matter much to Dad, who had loads of practical things to worry about. But he still found time to take me and Mum to one of the practice days when I would have seen James Hunt, Emerson Fittipaldi, Jody Schectkter and other present and future world champs in action. It was the noisiest day of my life so far, and it was truly wonderful.

Back home on bank holiday race day, I watched Emerson win the race in a Lotus 72, leading from start to finish. I didn't realise at the time that it was the wrong result. Dad found out much sooner that the wrong fag packet had crossed the line first. It wasn't just a Lotus 72, but a John Player Special Lotus 72, with distinctive black and gold paintwork. That livery made a huge impression on this 12-year-old, just as the previous red and white Gold Leaf tobacco livery had when I was 9. Long-term, though, it never led to my ever taking a drag on a fag.

"Danny, this is a bloody disaster – take all this and dump it." Rothmans marketing people were having tobacco-induced seizures and gave Dad sundry promotional items to destroy, so that they were never reminded again of what had been a pretty poor bank holiday Monday for them. Lotus were the winners that day, but longer term it wouldn't work out so well. So the only conclusion it's possible to make is that Lotus in particular and the British car industry in general were never very good at marketing.

Take Ferrari, builder of predominantly red supercars, founded by a single-minded engineer called Enzo who went on to dominate Formula One. Then compare that to Lotus, builder of any colour the customer, or cigarette sponsor wanted, sports and supercars, founded by a single-minded engineer called Colin who went on to dominate Formula One. The difference is that Ferrari is a global brand that sells thousands of highly profitable supercars every year, whilst Lotus doesn't. Lotus are well regarded and respected for their engineering skill and small sports cars that handle and perform exactly as their founder intended. Lotus also hasn't managed to transform it's subtle yellow and green logo into something as ubiquitous as Ferrari's prancing dobbin. While you can find that old nag stuck on as many unrelated products as the Playboy bunny, the Lotus one still has some integrity. While an old Ferrari breaking down is all part of its period charm, a Lotus that probably hasn't been looked after and overheats, is rubbish.

Yes, there has been a lot of prejudice and bias over the years that condemned British Leyland cars when Fiat (interestingly Ferrari's owner/benefactor) were building models that were far grimmer and equally unreliable. British Leyland were easy targets for having ugly, badly-built cars, but it wasn't the press – certainly not the motoring sections – that took advantage. In fact the specialist car magazines were always cheering for the home team, and continued to do so, even when they are now British-built but not British-owned cars. So maybe national newspapers had the occasional unfair pop, but really they had absolutely nothing to do with the demise of the British car industry. No, by far the biggest culprit in the downfall was politics.

Harold Wilson was behind the fateful decision to push all the car manufacturers together in one big, unhappy family. It was the government who ended up putting the BL into the British Leyland Motor Corporation when they decided to run the company on behalf of the country. Mrs T couldn't wait to get rid of Austin Rover, and it took nearly 10 years to do it, but unfortunately to the most inappropriate owner. And finally, Tony Blair's government had a simple choice – Phoenix or Alchemy – and they went with the mythical creature, which turned out to be a group of individuals who managed to transform a living, breathing British car company into a Chinese one. And politics had everything to do with the way that the unions operated as they tried to create some socialist workers' paradise, or tried to re-recreate Cuba in Coventry. Now that was never going to work, was it?

The fact that car buyers like Dad got fed up with being taken for granted and opted to buy abroad had absolutely nothing to do with the disappearance of a once mighty industry. Just as the Japanese motorcycle invasion that swept away an un-nationalised but arrogant industry, the same effectively happened to a nationalised one.

The British car industry wasn't so much arrogant as ill-equipped to deal with the threat. Hampered by the unions and internal mismanagement, and being answerable to civil servants, was not a recipe for success. Whereas foreign governments had been cleverly protective of their car industries, the British ones simply interfered and relocated parts of it to inappropriate areas of the country. It is no accident that Volkswagen, the company that the British Army once ran, was immune from takeover, however many shares any other company bought. Just as it is unthinkable that Mercedes or BMW would fall into foreign-owned hands, they have been guided, protected and subsidised by the regional governments where the factories are based. It also helped that they made cars that people wanted to buy and were run seemingly by the staff of a major teaching hospital, hence the proliferation of Doctors of Engineering at every significant level.

Sadly, the conclusion has to be that the British car industry actually deserved to die. The truth is that it wasn't that good in the first place, except for inspirational automotive icons like the Mini, Jaguar E-Type and Land Rover. Yet the British companies were no worse than the indigenous industries in France or Italy, which had their share of hits and misses, and also union unrest that at some stages was frankly far more terrifying and violent than a few Brummies standing around a roaring brazier (that's a small, self-contained bonfire in a metal basket, or oil drum rather than a car called a Brazier by the way?)

The difference was that, in most European countries, there seemed to be far more evidence of a national will that their industries should survive. And when the state took a stake, as with Renault in France, their government made it work. Britain's car buyers had all given up on Austin Rovers because they expected better, hence the Volkswagen Golf sales boom initiated by Mr Reginald Dennis Ruppert. However, even Dad knew that four wheels wasn't the answer when it came to matters of personal transportation.

Using the Royal Mail forwarding service is essential after a loved-one dies. It's a sad, often annoying and occasionally surprising experience. The sad bits are the Christmas cards and letters to which you have to reply and explain the worst. Mostly, though, it is quite therapeutic as you discover that others thought as much of your parents as you did. The annoying bit is the sheer volume of junk that comes through the post, belated invitations to take out life insurance, join wine clubs, political parties and buy exercise machines. The really unexpected package, though, was a buff A4 one addressed to Dad.

The most surprising thing initially was the date stamp: 1995. Here was proof that the last major nationalised institution since the demise of BL – the Post Office – was up its old tricks again. I would have thought they might have shredded such incriminating evidence of their ineptitude rather than forwarding it to me, but then again Austin Rover should have crushed every Morris Ital before it left the factory. So what had Postman Pat denied Dad ever reading in his lifetime? Well I never saw it coming, or even hovering, but it was a brochure for a Gyroplane.*

For the price of a 1995 Volkswagen Golf – £13,500 plus VAT, according to the Gyroplane price list – Dad could have taken to the air in the brilliantly named Skyraider. It was made by a company called Sycamore Aviation, based in Lancashire, which meant that Dad would have been buying British again. The car industry may have been run into the ground, but the aviation business offered the prospect of flying high over the speed cameras, the congestion and the heads of the small-minded petty bureaucrats who make modern life and motoring such a depressing experience. As always, Dad had the right idea, and right now I'm relieved to say, he really is above it all.

---

*Not that Gyroplanes routinely hover, but they can manage it in a strong headwind. Just in case you wondered, they have one less wheel than a car, plus a tiny rear-mounted engine and propeller, with one or two seats and a large rotary blade overhead which relies on air flowing upwards to make it turn.

In the Car Park and battling for Britain in 2005 are Bristol, Aerial, Caterham, Noble Westfield and Morgan. Well done chaps. Please keep up the good work.

Picture captions. I don't think you need them for these distinctively Brit motors.

Lightning Source UK Ltd.
Milton Keynes UK
01 December 2009

146952UK00001B/15/P